Multi-Asset Investing

Founded in 1807, John Wiley & Sons is the oldest independent publishing company in the United States. With offices in North America, Europe, Australia and Asia, Wiley is globally committed to developing and marketing print and electronic products and services for our customers' professional and personal knowledge and understanding.

The Wiley Finance series contains books written specifically for finance and investment professionals as well as sophisticated individual investors and their financial advisors. Book topics range from portfolio management to e-commerce, risk management, financial engineering, valuation and financial instrument analysis, as well as much more.

For a list of available titles, visit our Web site at www.WileyFinance.com.

Multi-Asset Investing

A Practitioner's Framework

PRANAY GUPTA

SVEN SKALLSJÖ

BING LI

Library of Congress Cataloging-in-Publication Data

Names: Gupta, Pranay, 1966- author. | Skallsj?o, Sven R., 1969- author. | Li, Bing, 1963- author.
Title: Multi-asset investing : a practitioner's framework / Pranay Gupta, Sven R. Skallsjo, Bing Li.
Description: Chichester, West Sussex, United Kingdom : John Wiley & Sons Ltd., 2016. | Includes bibliographical references and index.
Identifiers: LCCN 2015050873 | ISBN 9781119241522 (hardback) | Subjects: LCSH: Portfolio management. | Asset allocation. | Investments. | BISAC: BUSINESS & ECONOMICS / Finance.
Classification: LCC HG4529.5 .G87 2016 | DDC 332.6–dc23 LC record available at http://lccn.loc.gov/2015050873
A catalogue record for this book is available from the British Library.

ISBN 978-1-119-24152-2 (hbk)   ISBN 978-1-119-24159-1 (ebk)
ISBN 978-1-119-24157-7 (ebk)   ISBN 978-1-119-24161-4 (ebk)

Cover Design: Wiley
Cover Image: © Allocationmetrics Limited

Set in 10/13 Photina MT Std by Aptara, New Delhi, India
Printed in Great Britain by TJ International Ltd, Padstow, Cornwall, UK

"I don't pretend we have all the answers,
but the questions are certainly worth thinking about."

— *Arthur C. Clarke*

For Aanya and Jennifer

May you have the
wisdom to not stop questioning,
the creativity to innovate,
and the courage to express your power,
and fulfill your potential.

Contents

Preface

I was asked once in an interview, "Why do you want to become an investment manager?" My reply was that it is the only business where anything and everything that happens in any corner of the world can impact the decisions that you will make that day. This is even more true today.

The problem of course is that we all perceive these events differently, have different processes to assimilate the information, and have different views on how they will impact economies and asset prices. This diversity of views, on the one hand, is what creates a financial market, and on the other creates numerous debates on the "correct" solution to any investment problem. The dimensions of these views are numerous: academia versus practitioner, fundamental versus systematic, bottom-up versus top-down, rigorous versus conceptual, utopian versus practical, return-oriented versus risk-oriented or global versus local. With each side having defined the lens they will use for their perspective, there is seldom much debate on creating a framework which can accommodate everyone and which may well turn out to be the most investment optimal solution for the asset owner. This text is an attempt in this direction.

Multi-asset investing as a term has been used to mean many things as it is probably one of the broadest investment problems for any portfolio, which covers all geographies, all asset classes, all sectors and almost all financial market instruments. An attempt to analyze this investment problem often leads us down paths which can be very subjective in nature and thus open to criticism for lack of evidence or proof. At other times we end up creating an extensive theoretical quantitative framework, which may not be practical to implement. All these viewpoints are valid and we believe that each sub-issue within the scope of multi-asset investing lends itself to a solution, which may be biased in one of these directions.

Beginning with an overview of how multi-asset investing functions today, we detail the areas where we believe the incumbent framework needs improvement to create a more robust investment solution. Addressing these specific areas one at a time in each chapter, we aim to describe the methods that we have come to believe in, as a function of our experience in managing global multi-asset portfolios. Often these methods are very fundamental in nature, and at other times quite quantitative; however, at all times we have aimed to describe processes which are implementable in practice, and have proved useful in managing portfolios. The intention of the book is to ask the question, "If you could redesign the multi-asset investment process today, starting with a clean sheet of paper, what would that process look like?"

Concurrent with the multi-asset investment problem, we also examine the business of multi-asset investing. The diversity of current multi-asset products today affords us a rich landscape to ask how we would structure a multi-asset business today, as well as how we would tackle the associated issues such as manager compensation and multi-asset investing for individual investors.

Finally, we close with a guest chapter from Willis Towers Watson Investment Services on how they are helping their asset owner clients to think about these issues.

Pranay Gupta

Sven Skallsjö

Bing Li

About the Authors

Pranay Gupta, **Sven Skallsjö** and **Bing Li** have worked together for the last 15 years and the combination of their individual skills in asset allocation, financial mathematics and portfolio management respectively, has allowed them to innovate and implement novel solutions to practical problems they have encountered in the course of managing large pools of assets.

Pranay Gupta, CFA, has 25 years of experience in investment management, having worked in Europe, the UK, the US and Asia. As Chief Investment Officer for eminent asset management businesses in Asia, Pranay has been responsible for overseeing over US$85bn in institutional, retail and insurance assets across 11 countries. Pranay has also been the Portfolio Manager of a US$22bn multi-strategy multi-asset fund where he deployed innovative methodologies to deliver consistent positive performance, and has been awarded the title of *Best Discretionary Asset Manager in Asia*. Over the course of his career, Pranay has managed equity funds in every part of the world, emerging market debt funds, fund of hedge funds and systematic quantitative funds. Pranay was the Chairman of the Investment Committee of the CFA Institute Research Foundation, responsible for overseeing the asset allocation of the endowment, and a Research Fellow at the Centre for Asset Management Research and Investments at the National University of Singapore. Pranay is the Founder of the Global Association of Alternative Investors (GAAI), a global not-for-profit investment think tank of sovereign wealth funds, university endowments, and corporate and government pension plans, which debate issues on a wide range of topics in asset management. Pranay also currently helps the CFA Institute in directing the design of the Asset Allocation and Alternatives curriculum of the CFA Program. Pranay has lectured around the world on various subjects, and is a frequent guest on BBC World, Bloomberg TV, CNBC and CNN.

Sven R. Skallsjö, PhD is a finance expert specializing in mathematical techniques for asset allocation and risk management. Following a degree in mathematics he turned his interest to economics and financial markets. He earned his PhD in 2004 from the Stockholm School of Economics, where he investigated the interplay between monetary policy and the dynamics of the yield curve focusing on implications of the zero bound for policy rates. He is currently active in the field of risk management, and has designed and developed risk models at Ignis Asset Management, AGL Structured Finance and Shell Asset Management. In his work he uses mathematical techniques to help structure intuitive concepts. Sven has co-authored various papers on multi-asset class investment and risk management.

Bing Li, PhD, CFA is currently the president of BC Capital Management Ltd a Hong Kong-based firm that provides investment solutions for high-net-worth individuals in mainland China. After earning his PhD in Chemistry from the University of Western Ontario, Bing started his career in financial services as a quantitative developer at Greydanus, Boeckh & Associates, Inc., where he successfully developed bond trading strategies by modeling the movement of the yield curve and spread curve. During his 20 years of experience, Bing has been the Portfolio Manager and worked for several global asset management firms in Canada, Europe, the UK and Hong Kong, and managed institutional and retail funds of global bonds, equities, fund of hedge funds and multi-class asset allocation. As a long-time industrial practitioner, Bing has paid detailed attention to the implementation issues in constructing investment strategies, and consistently outperformed respective benchmarks.

CHAPTER ONE

An Introduction to the Multi-Asset Investment Problem

The last decade of financial market research and asset management has focused a great deal on the generation of alpha, the separation of return into alpha and beta, and in debating active versus passive management. Indeed, the majority of the investment industry across the world today is structured to support these facets of managing assets. The majority of market research carried out in investment banks is at the individual security level to advocate potential investments expected to generate excess return over the market benchmark. The majority of active asset managers in any asset class in any geographic region of the world claim to have skill in finding the "right" stocks and bonds, which would allow them to beat market benchmarks, and thus charge active management fees. Even asset owners, be it sovereign wealth funds, corporate and government pension plans or endowments have the majority of their effort and resources focused on selecting the right strategies and hiring and firing external managers.

This structure of the financial industry, however, seems to be at odds with a basic tenet that all of us have learnt over and over again – that asset allocation is responsible for 90% of the risk and return of a portfolio. While the actual number of 90% has been disputed by many, it is still widely accepted that asset allocation as a function accounts for a large part if not the majority of a portfolio's total return. Why then do we have the bulk of the global financial services industry structured to focus on the 10% related to research and investment strategies based on security selection? Meanwhile, the main meat of the investment problem, portfolio allocation, remains pitifully under-researched, under-innovated and remains the single biggest cause for asset owners, institutional or individual, failing to reach their portfolio objectives.

A realization of this fact has led to an interest in global multi-asset investing. Initially starting with a focus on asset allocation, the field of multi-asset investing has become diverse, and is called by different names and positioned differently in different organizations. Apart from multi-asset, this research area has been called asset allocation, risk allocation, factor allocation, risk budgeting, strategic asset allocation, tactical asset allocation, macro investing, investment solutions and policy portfolio creation, to name a few, and is used at almost all levels of the investment spectrum from asset owner strategic portfolio creation to creation of fund of funds.

In this text we examine the many facets of multi-asset investing and propose a generalized framework that puts the nomenclature of various market activities in this field into perspective. We argue that all assets today operate within a global multi-asset context, and the "real" active management skill required for the successful management of asset owner portfolios is one of allocation. What is represented today as active or passive management relative to a market benchmark is a problem of considerably smaller significance. However, the multi-asset absolute return problem is far more difficult than a relative return investment problem, and requires better tools and methodologies than are available in the investment world today. This book hopes to propose some practical suggestions in this continuing evolution.

1.1 WHAT IS MULTI-ASSET INVESTING?

We define multi-asset investing as any investment activity where more than one asset class is involved in the composition of an investment product, service or solution. This includes everything from the client requirement and product design, to the various components of the investment process and portfolio analysis required to manage such a product.

Figure 1.1 depicts a framework showing the broad architecture of all multi-asset activities covering this broad field. In the investment decisions category this covers asset forecasting, allocation, portfolio construction, implementation and risk diagnostics. A greater variety is emerging in the asset forecasting processes, both judgmental and systematic, along with greater introspection of the choice of buckets being used for allocation purposes. This variety of forecasts can then be formulated on the basis of return, risk or a combination of the two, at multiple investment horizons. Portfolio construction of a multi-asset portfolio is evolving to incorporate "real risk" constraints, along with greater focus on the management of tail risk. Implementation of the multi-asset portfolio is becoming more flexible, not only with active managers as is traditionally done, but with the newly available derivative instruments. This has brought back the active–passive debate, with the popularity of smart beta as a product category. Finally, the portfolio analysis or diagnostics framework needed to analyze issues and design improvements in the investment process is becoming a basic necessity. At the product decision level, there is greater effort to customize the investment product being offered. This has led to the creation of multiple multi-asset strategies, each of which is relevant to a category of asset owners, where their specific requirements and constraints are incorporated into the investment solution.

In this book, we challenge some of the long accepted beliefs in the management of global multi-asset strategies, and propose some heuristic solutions to problems that are

Figure 1.1 The variety of investment and product and decisions required in a multi-asset investment platform

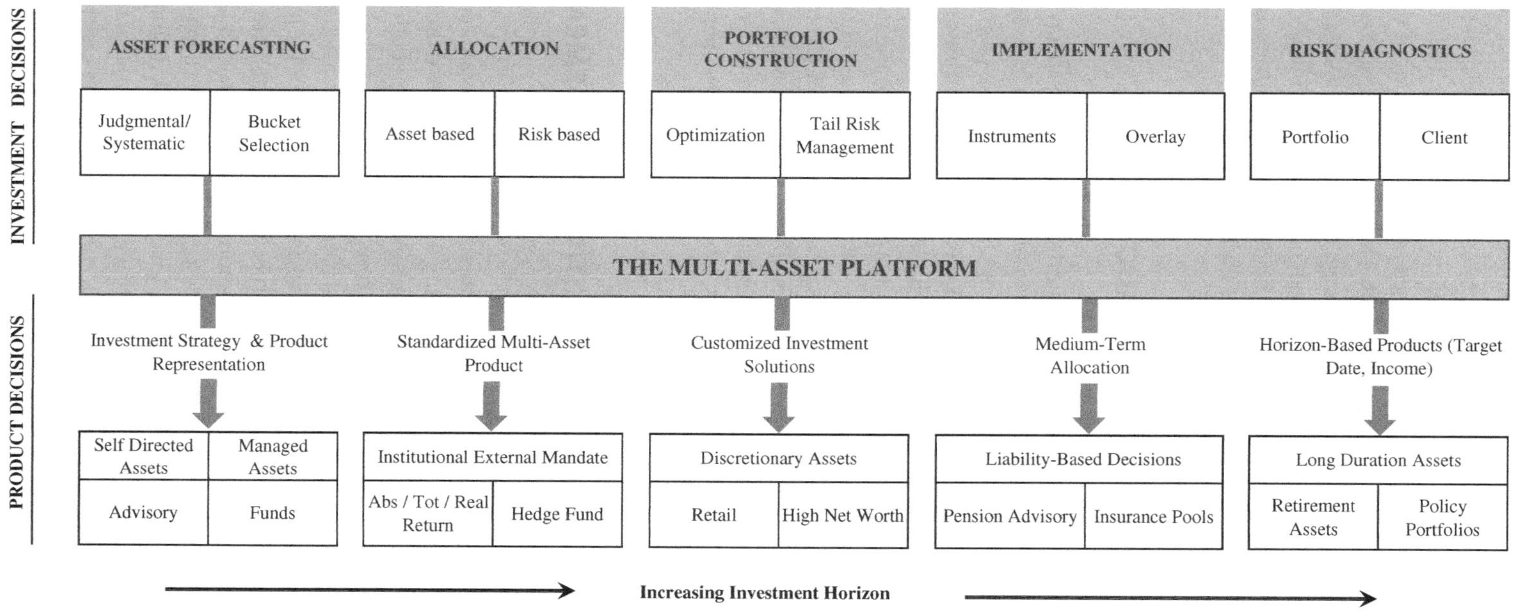

ASSET FORECASTING		ALLOCATION		PORTFOLIO CONSTRUCTION		IMPLEMENTATION		RISK DIAGNOSTICS	
Judgmental/ Systematic	Bucket Selection	Asset based	Risk based	Optimization	Tail Risk Management	Instruments	Overlay	Portfolio	Client

THE MULTI-ASSET PLATFORM

Investment Strategy & Product Representation	Standardized Multi-Asset Product	Customized Investment Solutions	Medium-Term Allocation	Horizon-Based Products (Target Date, Income)

Self Directed Assets		Institutional External Mandate		Discretionary Assets		Liability-Based Decisions		Long Duration Assets	
Advisory	Managed Assets	Abs / Tot / Real Return	Hedge Fund	Retail	High Net Worth	Pension Advisory	Insurance Pools	Retirement Assets	Policy Portfolios

Increasing Investment Horizon

INVESTMENT DECISIONS

PRODUCT DECISIONS

faced by practitioners. We propose tested non-standard solutions to some of the actual practical problems faced in global multi-asset investing. In many cases, it is difficult to prove with an academic level of rigor that the proposed solution is theoretically optimal; however, what we can say is that we have used each and every one of these tools successfully in the management of large asset pools. The techniques described here may not be the final end product of the investment process evolution, but seem to be a more robust solution than what is used in many investment processes today. Finally, we aim to provide a structure that can serve as the basis for the direction of future research initiatives in the many areas that encompass multi-asset investing.

 ## 1.2 THE CONVENTIONAL STRUCTURE

The original concept of investing across multiple asset classes in a portfolio was based on the premise that it provided diversification and that investing in equities would earn a risk premium. These two concepts of diversification and risk premium spawned the creation of multi-asset investing for asset owner portfolios. However, the two basic tenets of the traditional framework stand challenged today as cross-asset correlation is much higher and risk premium lower and more volatile. The basic requirements of an asset owner of a target return and managed drawdown risk are therefore more challenging to meet. This has led to greater focus on all aspects of the multi-asset investment process which can be improved. An evolution in the creation, management and deployment of multi-asset products is therefore underway in order to accommodate the more complex global financial markets, where hybrid instruments and derivatives are more readily available.

 ## 1.3 TRANSITIONING FROM ACTIVE MANAGEMENT TO EXPOSURE ALLOCATION

The concept of asset classes based on instruments used in corporate capital structure has been at the foundation of multi-asset investing. Having segmented the financial universe into these asset classes, the majority of investment resources in both asset owners and asset managers are focused on beating the respective asset class market benchmarks to create alpha. But is separation of alpha and beta necessary for a better investment outcome or simply for deciding what is an appropriate fee structure? We propose a structure which generalizes the concepts of alpha and beta, and argue that there is no clear distinction between alpha and beta. The demarcation is actually between commoditized and non-commoditized beta exposures, which changes as the market evolves. We believe that the implications of this framework for active investment and risk management processes, is that the investment management industry will transition to a structure where greater resources and effort are spent on allocation, compared to alpha generation.

Another ramification of the instrument-based asset class structure is that this categorization has also been used as the basis for asset allocation decisions. However, while allocation is improved by using uncorrelated silos, we know that there is a conceptual overlap between credit and equity as parts of a single corporate capital structure. Disentangling interest rate risk present in sovereign bonds, credit risk present in corporate bonds and equity risk present in equity securities, would allow the creation of a stacked structure for estimation of risk and risk premiums. We believe this may be a more appropriate structure for allocation decisions.

1.4 CREATING AN IMPROVED ALLOCATION STRUCTURE

Most plan sponsors formulate a single long-term asset allocation for their assets, and then spend a great deal of effort to select a number of active managers within each silo of asset class or style. While this diversifies alpha and manager risk, it ignores the fact that the single most important decision responsible for the risk and performance of the assets, the allocation decision, which remains as an undiversified single decision, is in many cases outsourced or done with minimal internal resources, and is the primary cause of many plans having funding gaps.

We argue that the traditional plan sponsor asset allocation process needs to be redesigned to become multi-strategy in design, and be implemented by asset owners using a range of approaches. Different views and methodologies will therefore reduce the plan's exposure to a single point of failure, and provide diversification where it's needed most. We discuss two such approaches – a fundamental process and a systematic process. Our fundamental allocation process is based on the concept of business cycles, and proposes that asset prices are impacted by six main cycles – the global business cycle, the local business cycle, the monetary cycle, the credit and capex cycles and the market cycle. Along with risk limiting factors, we have found that this assimilation of cycle information is useful in taking allocation decisions.

A second approach to allocation is grounded in quantitative techniques to create a strategic allocation stance against major asset classes. Using a risk budgeting framework, and adapting it to regimes caused by macroeconomic changes allows us to actively alter the allocation between the main asset classes. With the implementation of a drawdown management approach, we find that this modified active risk budgeting process yields better results across various evaluation parameters, when compared to a standard risk allocation process, or a 60/40 portfolio. We further confirm the stability of this approach by testing its viability in different historic time periods, and different bull and bear market regimes for equities and bonds.

Finally, we discuss a new approach to make the allocation forecasting process more efficient. An army of investment analysts at investment banks regularly analyze individual securities and publish earnings estimates for each company. These forecasts are disseminated widely through vendors, to the extent that market participants are able to find the mean consensus expectation for each company, as well as how surprising it would be if their individual forecast proved more accurate. However, no such mechanism for collation and distribution of the consensus of recommended allocations is available in the world today. Arguably, if one were to create a database of expectations of allocation buckets for each market strategist, then one could follow a similar process to corporate expectations for asset allocation purposes.

1.5 CONSTRUCTING A MULTI-ASSET PORTFOLIO TO MANAGE TAIL RISKS

Tail risk arises at multiple stages in the investment process – from the high level asset allocation decision down to the individual portfolio manager's process for selecting securities. While asset owners often cite that they have a long-term investment horizon, in practice they are very sensitive to intra-horizon drawdowns. Intra-horizon risk can represent a substantial part of the total risk, and thus needs to be managed explicitly when constructing a portfolio of assets, strategies or asset classes. However, conventional risk parameters and practices followed in portfolio construction processes largely ignore intra-horizon risk. This leads to sub-optimal assessment of asset risk and leads to the construction of portfolios which are not in sync with the risk aversion of the client.

We propose a composite risk measure which simultaneously captures the risk of breaching a specified maximum intra-horizon drawdown threshold, as well as the risk that the performance is not met at the end of the investment horizon. We believe this captures the "true" risk of a portfolio much better than traditional end-of-horizon risk measures. We also propose a portfolio construction process which uses the full return distribution, without the assumption of a normal distribution, and demonstrate how this can result in improved control over the tail risk of a portfolio.

The traditional approach to portfolio risk analysis is the use of a single methodology for risk estimation of a portfolio. We believe that risk by its very nature needs to be analyzed in a multi-dimensional manner. A diagnostic framework which disentangles the return of a portfolio in various dimensions, including between skill and luck, is critical to evaluating investment strategies and more importantly, re-engineering an investment process to deliver stable portfolio performance. We discuss examples of some of the important analysis in this regard.

1.6 MULTI-ASSET INVESTING IN EMERGING MARKETS

Emerging markets have historically been segmented into various sub-categories and regions for convenience. This is evident both in the debt universe, where separate market benchmarks exist for hard currency and local currency debt, and in the equity universe where countries are categorized into regions, without a definitive investment rationale. We propose that emerging market investments require an integrated multi-asset investment universe, where there is a synchronized classification across asset classes.

It is a fact that active managers in emerging markets on average have a poorer performance compared to those in developed markets. In Asia, the majority of active equity strategies claim to derive their value addition by focusing on security selection. However, we find that if a manager's skill in asset allocation and stock selection were the same, then two-thirds of the portfolio's return in Asia would come from asset allocation, not from security selection. This is in sharp contrast to a US equity portfolio, where this would be only 18%. We therefore propose that for Asian equity portfolios, a much greater emphasis is required on the allocation process; a facet which seems to have been missed by asset managers thus far.

1.7 FROM MULTI-ASSET STRATEGIES TO MULTI-ASSET SOLUTIONS

The investment industry has gone through three major disruptions in recent history – a fee-led disruption caused by the rise of index funds, a return-led disruption caused by the rise of hedge funds, and a distribution-led disruption caused by the choice by some financial institutions to be client focused and to market investment products in an open architecture, without necessarily manufacturing them as well. We believe that the industry will now go through an allocation process-led disruption, caused by a renewed focus on the allocation process, rather than the pursuit of alpha. This will impact the product structure manufactured by asset management firms and transition the industry to focus on client investment solutions, rather than the current focus on investment strategies.

For institutional asset owners, conventional active and passive strategies will then simply be implementation methods, the proportion of each being based on their own constraints of cost and skill in manager selection. The current active versus debate will become passé.

An individual or private wealth investment has the same portfolio objectives as that of any institutional asset owner: a requirement of absolute return from a global multi-asset, multi-strategy portfolio. However, the business model of private banking makes a direct application of institutional investment processes difficult. We propose a revised framework for private wealth investment management, which we believe overcomes some of the organizational challenges, yet allows better management of private wealth assets from an investment standpoint.

1.8 STRUCTURING A MULTI-ASSET BUSINESS

Asset managers across the world have initiated activities to enhance their multi-asset capabilities, with the increased interest and asset flow into this category. Each firm having analyzed its strengths and weaknesses has positioned its multi-asset offering in a market segment where they will be able to exploit competitive advantage. From a product standpoint, we look at the major product categories in multi-asset and the skills that are required to be successful in each. From an investment skill perspective, we identify the key areas where significant improvement is required in the investment process. Finally, from a client standpoint we analyze the areas where a mismatch exists today between the products supplied by asset managers and client expectations. We also examine the combination of skills that are required to run a successful commercial multi-asset business – thought leadership, investment process skill, market strategy advice, media presence and a broad knowledge of all component strategies.

We also analyze the business model of hedge funds which argues that incorporating a performance fee in asset management fees aligns the interests of the asset manager and asset owner. We study the implications of a typical hedge fund contract where the manager is allowed to adjust the activeness of the portfolio dynamically over time. Taking managerial compensation into account can have considerable consequences for the probability distribution of assets. In particular, in the management of allocation decisions, we find that a performance fee incentive structure leads to a greater propensity for taking large bets, to the detriment of the portfolio.

The text ends with a chapter from Willis Towers Watson Investment Services, which is one of the leading investment consultants and advises a large number of corporate and government pension plans, sovereign wealth funds and endowments on allocation issues.

CHAPTER TWO

The Traditional Allocation Structure

n the management of any pool of assets, the asset allocation decision is undoubtedly of fundamental importance. Brinson, Hood and Beebower (1986) claimed that asset allocation explains on average 93.6% of the variation in total plan return. While the number itself has been disputed, there is consensus on the importance of asset allocation in the investment process. A typical 60/40 allocation to equity and fixed income results in a volatility of around 10%. A common active management policy is to allocate a 3% tracking error limit for the asset manager. These two assumptions alone are sufficient to arrive at a variance contribution of the asset allocation decision in excess of 90%.

Apart from asset owner asset allocation, multi-asset funds also perform asset allocation as the mainstay of their investment process. Fraser-Jenkins et al. (2012) analyzed 529 multi-asset funds, and found that assets under management had increased from $100bn in 2004 to $600bn in July 2012. This compares to equity funds having a net outflow of $200bn over the same period, and fixed income funds having an inflow of $1200bn.

It is notable that in spite of its significance for total fund returns, the high-level asset allocation is often managed with less rigor than the active management component of any portfolio. Greater effort is generally devoted to diversifying the set of active portfolio managers, often hiring multiple managers within the same area, and well-formulated routines typically exist for evaluating and handling candidate investment processes.

This disproportionate attention to active management could be motivated if the asset allocation decision was a clear given, and had been "solved" with near certainty for a given pool of assets. However, experience over the last few decades with results is proof to the contrary. The funding gaps, which exist today in most plan sponsors, can be traced back largely to poor asset allocation decisions.

Secondly, it has been recognized that recent research in asset allocation methods could lead to the creation of possible alternatives. For instance, risk parity has been proposed as an alternative method for balancing between equities and fixed income. Also, within both equities and fixed income there are alternative ways for constructing the benchmarks, for example constructing country weights by GDP rather than market capitalization. Within equities there are also benchmarks allocating higher weight to stocks with low volatility.

Amid this richness in views on asset allocation, the asset base of plan sponsors has experienced significant variability over the past decade. This has spurred an increased focus on risk management, including a demanding growth in regulatory reporting. Therefore, it is not difficult to argue that focus should also be directed towards the asset allocation decision, since this is where the majority of the investment risk originates.

2.1 THE TRADITIONAL INVESTMENT PROCESS

The basic objective of any asset owner is to achieve a target absolute return (derived from liability analysis or inflation expectations), with a requirement of a 90% confidence level that the maximum drawdown does not exceed a pre-specified level, say 10%. Of course, one would like to achieve this with the highest portfolio efficiency. Figure 2.1 depicts this basic asset owner problem as a time series of assets and liabilities.

The question is then how to invest the assets while respecting the constraints. A very common investment approach used worldwide across asset owners and asset managers is a two-step process. First, deciding on a long-term strategic or policy portfolio. This is generally done by an in-house research group or in consultation with an external advisor, to arrive at an allocation to the major asset classes – equities, fixed income and alternatives. Second, finding investment managers or strategies within each of the asset class silos, and allocating assets to fulfill the allocation made.

Each of the managers is required to operate within specified tracking error limits calculated with respect to standard market indices. Monitoring of performance and risk, and rebalancing of the overall portfolio are done at appropriate intervals. Figure 2.2 depicts the overall plan sponsor investment process.

Figure 2.1   The basic asset owner problem

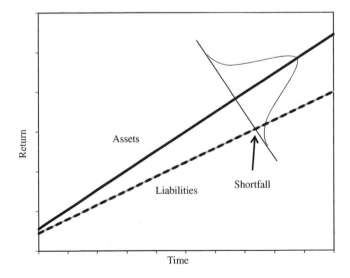

Figure 2.2 Schematic overview of the traditional plan sponsor investment process

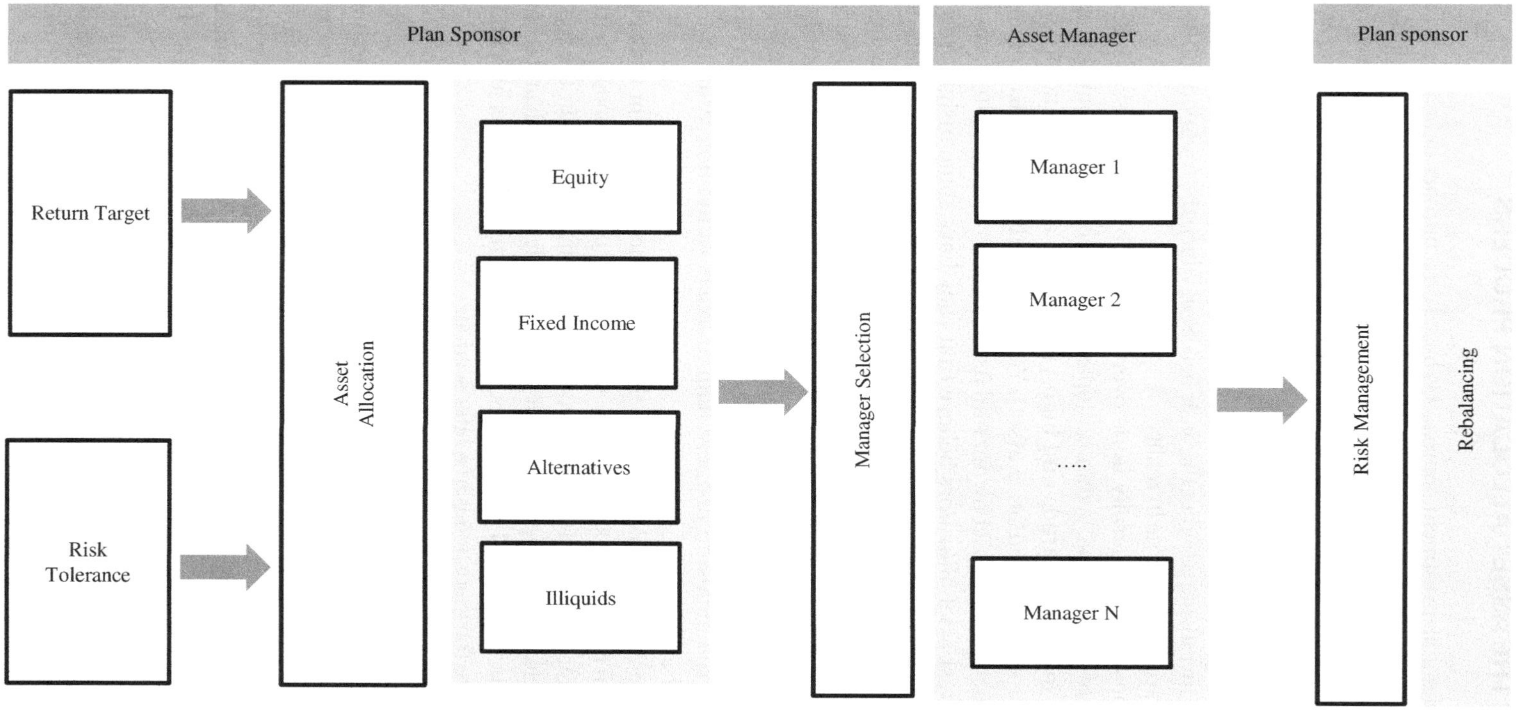

2.2 THE ASSET ALLOCATION PROCESS

The traditional investment approach is based on a number of beliefs and assumptions.

First, the basic belief is that investing in multiple asset classes delivers a diversified portfolio. Second, the belief that investing in equities enables the investor to harness a long-run equity risk premium and is a hedge against inflation. Third, an assumption that the definition of the silos provides a clear separation of asset class investment skills, and alternatives are a separate "asset class." Finally, the belief that creating an organization structure that neatly compartmentalizes each of the investment process steps is optimal. Here, we investigate whether the basic beliefs on which the traditional investment process is based are actually true in reality.

Allocation is generally done over eight major asset classes – the four equity regions of US, Europe, Asia and Japan, the three fixed income categories of sovereigns, investment grade and high yield bonds, and a commodity basket (we use gold here as a representative asset). Variation to this categorization exists based on the domicile of the asset owner and use of conceptual groupings, such as GEM and EAFE. Most asset allocators believe that they have some insight into the expected future return of asset classes, and hence take an active allocation decision to tilt towards the asset classes with the higher expected returns. They believe that this allocation skill will help the portfolio achieve the desired return. Further, it is also assumed that the resulting portfolio will be diversified, which would help in mitigating the maximum drawdown risk. Here, we exclude illiquid assets such as real estate and private equity, in order to facilitate a time series analysis illustration; however, the inclusion of these illiquid assets would not result in a substantially different outcome.

Figure 2.3 and Table 2.1 show the performance of the eight asset classes over the illustration period of 2000 to 2014. Also included are two composite portfolios – firstly, a perfect foresight portfolio, constructed as equally weighted in the top two performing asset classes over the subsequent year, annually rebalanced; and secondly, an equal weighted portfolio of all asset classes, signifying a zero skill asset allocation process. We will refer to these portfolios in a later section.

A point to note here is that the maximum drawdown of most of the asset classes exceeds, say, an allowed 10% threshold by far, the exception being global sovereigns. However, if the results were calculated over a longer period of time, sovereign yields would have also gone through a cycle, which would display the characteristics of a higher drawdown. Figure 2.3 also includes a statistic on the 10% maximum drawdown Value at Risk (VaR). This is the 10% quantile for the maximum drawdown over a 1-year horizon using monthly returns. The numbers are calculated by stochastic simulations using the historical mean and volatility estimates. Note that these also exceed the 10% maximum drawdown constraint in most cases.

The drawdown characteristics of asset classes emphasize that the asset allocation problem has poor quality ingredients at inception and it would require both

Figure 2.3   Performance of the eight asset classes defined in Figure 2.2

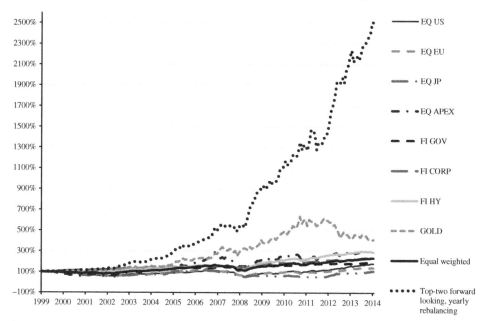

Notes: Thick dark line – equally weighted portfolio; Dashed line – perfect foresight portfolio constructed as an equally weighted portfolio of the top two performing asset classes over the subsequent year. Rebalanced end of January each year. Period: 2000–2014. '(H)' indicates FX hedged. Equity indices all FX unhedged. Mean calculated as arithmetic. Sharpe ratio use the 1-year UST yield.

Data Source: Bloomberg, Merrill Lynch, MSCI

high skill and diversification of drawdown risk for the problem to have a viable solution.

 ## 2.3 THE BELIEF IN DIVERSIFICATION

As we have discussed, a basic tenet of doing asset allocation is the belief that it results in diversifying risk. Figure 2.4 and Table 2.2 show rolling correlations of the four equity asset classes and high-yield (which bears characteristics similar to equity in the capital structure). It can be seen that the correlation generally ranges between 50–75% in the sample period, at which level the scope for diversification is lower than desirable. Among the four equity indices the first principal component accounts for 80% of total variance. This is not to say that equity allocation is irrelevant, and indeed a portfolio should be well diversified to be efficient, but these correlation levels show that when allocating to equities, we are basically taking a bet on global equity markets as a single factor.

Some researchers propose that while geographic diversification is failing, it is possible that other partitions of the investment space provide better diversification. There has

Table 2.1 Performance of the eight asset classes defined in Figure 2.2

Asset Class	Index	Mean Return	Volatility	Sharpe Ratio	Maximum Drawdown	Maximum Drawdown VaR (10%)
US Equities	MSCI USA	5.2%	15.4%	0.20	51%	14.5%
Europe Equities	MSCI Europe	3.4%	15.5%	0.09	54%	16.4%
Japan Equities	MSCI Japan	2.2%	18.0%	0.01	57%	21.0%
APEX Equities	MSCI AC Asia Pacific ex Jap	9.4%	21.2%	0.35	62%	17.8%
Global Sovereigns	ML GI Sovereigns (H)	4.5%	2.9%	0.86	3%	0.0%
Global Corporates	ML GI Broad Corp (H)	5.7%	4.1%	0.89	11%	0.0%
Global High Yield	ML GI High Yield (H)	7.6%	10.0%	0.56	34%	5.2%
Gold	Gold Spot Price	11.0%	63.6%	0.14	36%	70.5%

Notes: Period: 2000–2014. '(H)' indicates FX hedged. Equity indices all FX unhedged. Mean calculated as arithmetic. Sharpe ratio use the 1-year UST yield.

Data Source: Bloomberg, Merrill Lynch, MSCI

Figure 2.4   Rolling correlations of five major indices

Notes: Each line represents the average of the index's correlation with the other four, using monthly total returns over the preceding 24 months. Time period Dec 2001–Dec 2014, monthly returns.

Data Source: Bloomberg, Merrill Lynch, MSCI

been significant interest recently in proposing factor allocation methods as an improvement. Figure 2.5 and Table 2.3 show rolling correlations for six equity factor indices of size, value and growth. This depicts that factor correlation levels are even higher, suggesting that factor allocation also has the same challenges. One may try different variations of partitioning the investment space, and different periods may indeed have differing levels of correlation amongst asset classes; however, it seems relatively consistent that gains from diversification between equity asset classes are lower than is traditionally portrayed.

A second question is the extent of diversification possible within fixed income. Corporates and sovereigns differ in the amount of credit risk that is taken by the investor, which is analogous to the beta for equity market investments. A higher beta (i.e., more credit risk) implies a riskier portfolio, for which the investor expects to be paid an additional return. Within fixed income, the correlation of total returns of corporates and sovereigns over the examination period stands at 56%. However, if we extract the credit beta from

Table 2.2   Correlation matrix of the five major equity indices, Dec 2001–Dec 2014, monthly returns

	US Equities	Europe Equities	Japan Equities	APEX Equities	Global High Yield
US Equities	100.0%	75.7%	39.8%	57.1%	5.0%
Europe Equities	75.7%	100.0%	26.7%	52.4%	18.0%
Japan Equities	39.8%	26.7%	100.0%	26.3%	16.4%
APEX Equities	57.1%	52.4%	26.3%	100.0%	72.4%
Global High Yield	5.0%	18.0%	16.4%	72.4%	100.0%

Data Source: Bloomberg, Merrill Lynch, MSCI

Figure 2.5   Rolling correlations of six Standard & Poor's indices (All Countries)

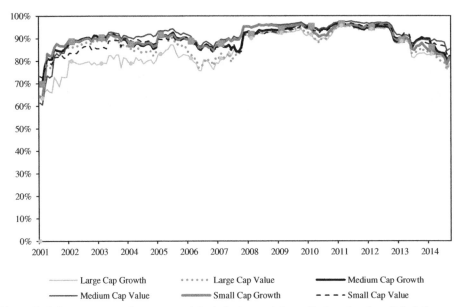

Notes: Each line represents the average of the index's correlation with the other five. Calculations based on monthly total returns over the preceding 24 months.

Data Source: Standard & Poor's

corporate returns, and then calculate the correlation within fixed income, we get an average correlation of 93.1%. This is depicted in Figure 2.6.

It is to be noted that, again in fixed income, the correlation of the sovereign and corporate asset classes is over 90%, signifying that there is minimal diversification possible within the fixed income silos, except for a decision on the level of credit beta in the portfolio.

Hence what is believed to be an asset allocation decision across eight asset classes leading to a diversified portfolio, is in reality a decision on how much equity risk and credit risk to take in a portfolio. Figure 2.7 and Table 2.4 depict the real and only diversification

Table 2.3   Correlation matrix of the six Standard & Poor's indices (All Countries). Dec 2001–Dec 2014, monthly returns

	Large Cap Growth	Large Cap Value	Mid Cap Growth	Mid Cap Value	Small Cap Growth	Small Cap Value
Large Cap Growth	100.0%	89.5%	83.5%	78.5%	71.2%	70.3%
Large Cap Value	89.5%	100.0%	72.2%	84.3%	69.8%	77.7%
Mid Cap Growth	83.5%	72.2%	100.0%	85.4%	88.2%	81.0%
Mid Cap Value	78.5%	84.3%	85.4%	100.0%	85.2%	92.8%
Small Cap Growth	71.2%	69.8%	88.2%	85.2%	100.0%	93.7%
Small Cap Value	70.3%	77.7%	81.0%	92.8%	93.7%	100.0%

Data Source: Standard & Poor's

Figure 2.6   Rolling correlations of sovereigns and corporates

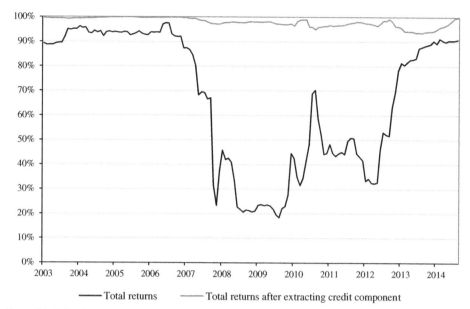

———— Total returns   ———— Total returns after extracting credit component

Notes: Black line based on total monthly returns. Grey line after extracting the credit component calculated as index duration X change in index asset swap spread. Calculations over the preceding 24 months. Period: Dec 2003–Dec 2014.

Data Source: Merrill Lynch

Figure 2.7   Rolling correlations of (1) Global Equities (MSCI World), (2) Global Sovereigns and (3) the asset swap spread of Global Corporates

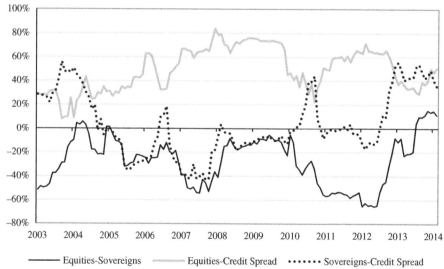

———— Equities-Sovereigns   ———— Equities-Credit Spread   •••••• Sovereigns-Credit Spread

Notes: Calculations based on monthly total returns over the preceding 24 months. Period: Dec 2003–Dec 2014, monthly returns.

Data Source: Bloomberg, Merrill Lynch, MSCI

Table 2.4 Correlation matrix of Global Equities (MSCI World), Global Sovereigns and the asset swap spread of Global Corporates, Dec 2003–Dec 2014, monthly returns

	Global Equities	**Global Sovereigns**	**Asset Swap Spread**
Global Equities	100.0%	11.5%	60.0%
Global Sovereigns	11.5%	100.0%	−29.6%
Asset swap spread	60.0%	−29.6%	100.0%

Data Source: Bloomberg, Merrill Lynch, MSCI

benefit that actually exists in an asset allocation process – shown as the correlation between equities and the credit spread.

The belief in achieving a diversified portfolio through traditional asset allocation therefore seems unfounded.

One is tempted to believe that having only alpha strategies within an asset owner portfolio may be a solution. Indeed alpha should theoretically be uncorrelated to beta, as per its definition. We use the HFR indices as a proxy for pure alpha strategies. The characteristics of these pure alpha strategies are shown in Table 2.5, and we display the rolling correlations between the four HFR indices in Figure 2.8.

Even through the drawdown characteristics of alpha strategies seem more favorable, the average correlation between these strategies, with the exception of macro, is in the 60–70% range, again a level at which meaningful strategy diversification is limited. Finally, we note that the 10% maximum drawdown bound is still breached in most cases, although applying the 10% VaR statistic, the number for the total portfolio is likely to come down below 10%.

Hence, it seems that while pure alpha strategies can be a partial solution for a small plan, it is unlikely to be the full solution for asset owners of a substantial size.

Table 2.5 Descriptive statistics for HFR sub-indices

HFR Sub-Index	**Mean Return**	**Volatility**	**Sharp Ratio**	**Maximum Drawdown**	**Maximum Drawdown VaR (10%)**
Equity Hedge	3.28%	7.23%	0.17	29.52%	5.99%
Event-Driven	4.46%	6.17%	0.39	25.80%	3.45%
Macro	3.84%	7.79%	0.23	24.49%	6.14%
Relative Value	3.51%	6.85%	0.21	38.74%	5.27%

Note: Sharpe ratio calculated using the 1-year US treasury yield.

Data Source: HFR

Figure 2.8   Rolling correlations of four HFR indices

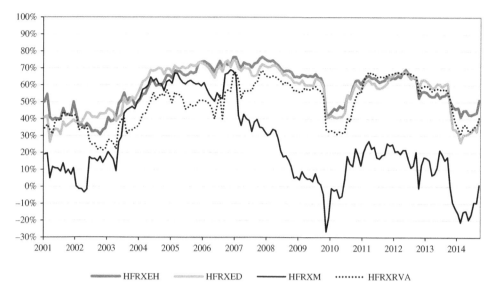

Note: Each line represents the average of the index's correlation with the other three, using monthly total returns over preceding 24 months.

Data Source: HFR

2.4 HARNESSING EQUITY RISK PREMIUM AND THE INVESTMENT HORIZON

An allocation to equities in a policy portfolio is done with the belief that the long-run return of equity market investments delivers a risk premium above the risk free rate. When asset owners create policy portfolios a 3-year horizon is commonly used.

Figure 2.9 depicts the rolling returns on the S&P 500 index over different investment horizons of three years, five years and 10 years. The fact that the mean of these charts lies comfortably above zero, serves to confirm the presence of an equity risk premium. However, what is less widely appreciated is that the actual return by an investor, who seeks this equity risk premium, can be significantly different from the long-run average. In reality, the actual return is largely a function of when the policy portfolio decision is made, and can range anywhere between +20% and −20%. Only if the asset owner were to maintain a constant equity exposure, despite interim drawdowns (which is both behaviorally and often legally challenging), would he succeed in earning the ERP.

Further, a critical parameter that determines the level of risk premium actually harvested is the investment horizon used for the asset allocation. The choice of the investment horizon and the schedule of when the decision is taken are therefore parameters which determine whether equity premium is actually harvested or not.

Figure 2.9 Rolling returns of S&P 500 index for 3 years, 5 years and 10 years, signifying the return an investor would have achieved by allocating passively to the equity market, while having the different investment horizons

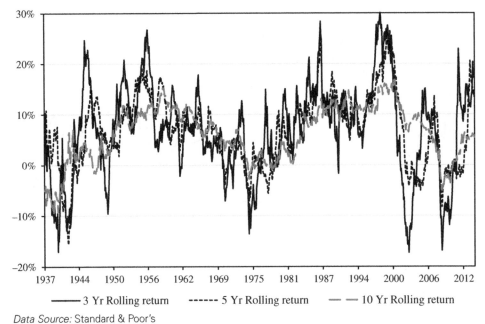

Data Source: Standard & Poor's

2.5 ASSET CLASSES AS MUTUALLY EXCLUSIVE SILOS

The concept of asset classes as buckets for asset allocation was conceived at a time when financial engineering was in its primitive phase. There were few hybrid and crossover instruments between these asset classes at that time. Today, however, there are a multitude of market instruments that are a hybrid of the old asset classes and live in between the original silos. The asset class framework, therefore, is not as neat a categorization structure as it may once have been. Further, it is evident that a large number of hedge fund strategies operate in the gaps between the asset classes, where they believe alpha is more prevalent. The alternatives category is a result of this structure as most of these strategies don't fall into one of the existing buckets.

It therefore seems that the concept of having equity and fixed income categories as neat allocation categories needs revision.

2.6 ORGANIZATION STRUCTURE AND RESOURCE ALLOCATION

While over 90% of the risk and reward of the portfolio comes from the top level asset allocation decision, in most organizations 90% of the resources are devoted instead to the selection and replacement of managers. This structure is ingrained in the asset management and investment banking industries, and generally in the investment profession. There is a fundamental resource allocation mismatch between where risk and return are generated, and where resources are allocated in an organization.

2.7 IMPLICATIONS FOR SKILL REQUIRED IN ASSET ALLOCATION

It is obvious that not getting the diversification we originally believed makes the task of the asset allocator more difficult, i.e., a higher skill is required to construct a portfolio with the same maximum drawdown threshold, than if the portfolio diversification was more readily available.

Figure 2.10 depicts the return profiles of various asset allocators with different assumed levels of allocation skill. Note the Top portfolio is the perfect foresight portfolio depicted in Figure 2.3. The remainder of the profiles represent lower skill in the asset allocation decision, as the assumption of perfect foresight is relaxed, the Bottom being the worst possible skill in asset allocation.

A point to note is that while the perfect foresight portfolio unsurprisingly has an extraordinary return, its maximum drawdown is 29.8%. Even if we apply the 10% maximum drawdown VaR statistic the number is still 12.1%. This implies that it is impossible to construct a portfolio within these asset classes that would meet the

Figure 2.10 Performance of portfolios with perfect foresight over the following year, rebalanced yearly end September

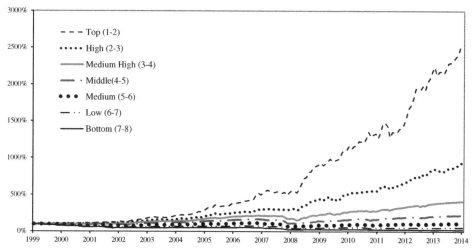

Note: Each portfolio is equally weighted in two asset classes – the solid black line invested in the top two performers, down to the dashed line invested in the worst two.

Figure 2.11 Frequency diagram for the 12-month max drawdown, based on 10,000 simulations of 12 monthly returns with annual volatility and mean as of Top (1-2) from Figure 2.2

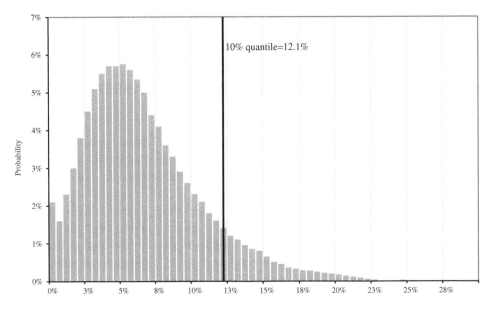

constraint of a 10% maximum drawdown with a 90% confidence level. Figure 2.11 shows the probability distribution of the 12-month maximum drawdown, and the 10% quantile drawdown of 12.1%.

We therefore find that there are significant challenges, both from the return and risk side of an allocation portfolio, in meeting the general requirements of any asset owner.

2.8 REQUIREMENTS FOR A REVISED ALLOCATION SOLUTION

Given the importance of asset allocation in the investment process, the poor characteristics of the individual asset classes and the risk and return requirements of asset owners, developing an improved solution is essential. For any revised solution, the minimum criteria for success are:

1. The dependence of the portfolio on the singular decision of the level of equity exposure in the portfolio needs to be reduced. The structure cannot rely on skill in timing equity markets. We discuss a potential solution to this issue in Chapter 3.
2. The definition of risk needs to cater for intra-horizon drawdown, which is a significant risk faced by asset owners or asset managers during the period that the assets are invested. We propose a solution to this issue in Chapter 10.
3. The structure should facilitate a mechanism to manage the drawdown beyond a pre-specified drawdown threshold. We illustrate a possible implementation in Chapter 11.

4. The structure should facilitate appropriate positioning of hybrid asset products and alternatives in a robust manner. We propose a framework for this in Chapter 3.
5. Analysis of the level of alpha and beta in a product or portfolio segment needs to be undertaken, so that fees can be calibrated appropriately, but this does not necessitate the portfolio being segmented in this manner.
6. The risk of the portfolio in any dimension should be known at any time.
7. The structure should be flexible enough to allow changes relatively quickly.

2.9 PARALLEL DEBATES CREATED IN THE SEARCH FOR A REVISED ALLOCATION SOLUTION

This search for a revised allocation solution has created a debate amongst participants on many subjects, some of which are listed below:

- **Asset Forecasting: Fundamental or systematic**
    Asset forecasting is done primarily either as a fundamental "view-based" process, or as a quantitative process. While there is a philosophical divide between the two approaches, in reality the demarcation is more obscure, as, in general, all processes of asset forecasting use skills from each domain. At the extremes of the spectrum, a constant debate and tension exists between these forecasting methods.
- **Allocation Silos: Geographies, sectors or risk factors**
    Another contentious area is the definition of the silos on which allocation is done. Traditional methods have favored geographic allocation (into regions and countries) as the predominant style, primarily because economic cycles of countries were different. This transitioned to a more sector- or industry-based approach as the world economy globalized, and sector linkages proved stronger determinants. Recently, as market and behavioral phenomena have dominated, greater effort has been expended on risk factor allocation. This debate is prevalent today.
- **Asset Allocation or Risk Budgeting**
    Both asset managers and researchers seem to view the allocation of assets and the allocation of risk (risk budgeting) as two different disciplines. In reality, one goes hand in hand with the other, as risk and return are inseparably related. The only difference is what comes first in the allocation process and what comes second – risk or return. As a corollary of this fact, it seems that managers who advocate a purist stance of only using pure fundamental allocation judgment, as well as those who view risk parity as the panacea to the allocation problem, are both failing to account for one whole side of the investment problem.
- **Implementation: Active managers or exchange-traded funds (ETFs)**
    Debate exists on the choice of implementation vehicles in a multi-asset portfolio. Commercial interests drive the use of in-house active funds; client interests dictate using both in-house and an open architecture for all managers to be incorporated; market efficiency advocates propose ETFs; and index funds and others propose also the use of delta one derivatives.

CHAPTER THREE

Transitioning from Active Management to Exposure Allocation

J ust as "efficient and diversified portfolios" were the buzzwords of the 20th century, the one term, which has come into fashion over the last decade and been used (or misused) infinitely is "alpha." Whether it is pension funds or hedge funds, institutions or individuals, academicians or practitioners, there seems to be an ever more continuous and intensifying effort to find this elusive entity. But is there a common understanding of the terms alpha and beta?

A common practitioner definition is that beta return is the market return (the market being represented by a benchmark) and alpha is the return above or below the market return. This definition requires the prior definition of what is the market return and how best to represent it. The most common representation of the market is the market capitalization weighted benchmark. In a multi-asset context this discussion becomes even more complicated. Unlike single asset class portfolios – where the market capitalization-weighted benchmark is traditionally accepted as the product benchmark – in multi-asset space, definition of the benchmark is a decision of the investment manager. Hence, the subsequent decision of what is alpha and what is beta (both of which depend on the benchmark choice) becomes all the more difficult.

In multi-asset strategies, the strategic or policy asset allocation decision is often used synonymously with the beta decision. The implementation of this allocation into active strategies is then considered as the portion responsible for the generation of alpha. From an asset owner's standpoint, however, the strategic asset allocation decision itself is an active decision with respect to the return objective of absolute return. The subsequent decision of investment in active strategies has a far smaller impact in this overall context.

We believe that the demarcation between alpha and beta is only in the eye of the beholder, but changes as the market evolves and as variety in instruments to access various segments of financial markets increases. We present here a generalized framework for looking at alpha–beta demarcation and its progressive implications for the active investment process in single and multi-asset space.

 ## 3.1 A HISTORIC RATIONALIZATION OF ALPHA AND BETA

An active manager's challenge has always been the quest for excess return. Given that most listed exchanges created stock indices even from the early days, attaining return above this exchange benchmark was always the objective. Although it was not labelled as alpha specifically, this is the common meaning of the term even today, and is loosely related to the portfolio manager's ability or skill.

Sharpe (1964) created a parsimonious model to represent Markowitz's (1952) portfolio theory of diversification, with the single factor Capital Asset Pricing model (CAPM). This formulation formed the basis of development of future academic research. Grinold and Kahn (1993) popularized the extension by stripping out market beta from portfolio return and labelling the residual as alpha:

$$r_p(t) - r_o(t) = \beta.r_M(t) + \varepsilon_p(t)$$

Where, $r_p(t)$ is the portfolio return, $r_o(t)$ is the return on a risk free asset and $r_M(t)$ is the market excess return. Although this was correct, it made the inherent assumption that market direction was not forecastable, and thus not intended as an active decision by an active manager. Hence, even if an active manager were skilled at timing market direction as a variable, he would have created no alpha, or no excess return, according to this formulation. For example, a portfolio which consists of all stocks in an index with a beta greater than 1, on the specific basis of an active positive view on the overall market return, would have a portfolio beta well above 1. If the investment view turned out to be correct, the portfolio would generate a return well above the market index. However, by use of the above equation it would be deemed that the value addition by the active manager was minimal as only the return net of the beta adjusted market return would be deemed to be on the basis of skill.

Subsequent research did not challenge the demarcation of alpha and beta that was thus created, but focused on finding other variables which could be classified in the systematic risk category, and were not captured by CAPM. Chen, Roll and Ross (1986) used macroeconomic factors to represent the systematic returns in the market. Fama and French (1992) added size and value as common factors in stock returns:

$$r_p(t) - r_o(t) = \beta_{1p}r_M(t) + \beta_{2p}SMB(t) + \beta_{3p}HML(t) + \varepsilon_p(t)$$

Where *SMB (t)* is the risk premium of small stocks over large stocks in period *t*, and *HML (t)* is the risk premium of high B/M (value) over low B/M (growth) stocks.

And of course, the definition of alpha was now demoted to the residual after all these factors were extracted.

The demarcation of alpha and beta has remained with us even today, and the assumption of not being able to forecast returns for systematic or beta factors has remained an inherent assumption. The task of finding factors which explain the alpha component or non-systematic return has been left to the active investment manager. However, if indeed an active process has the skill and takes beta as an intended bet, why should it be penalized for generating excess return by timing beta? Why can a manager not generate excess return by forecasting beta factors and if, indeed, one is able to do this, why is the resulting excess return not called alpha?

3.2 PROGRESSION OF ACTIVE MANAGEMENT

Market beta, value and size having been extracted from return by academicians; practitioners looked for other factors, which would seek to differentiate their portfolio, in a bid to exploit inefficiencies as part of active management. These included balance sheet characteristics, market characteristics, geographic or industry-based characteristics or combinations of these. This enabled the skilled managers to generate alpha in the eyes of all concerned, even when the benchmark evolved to incorporate so-called systematic factors within the benchmark. The driving motivation, of course, was the additional benefit of being able to retain clients, and hence their revenue stream.

Concurrently, the 1990s saw the increased development of structured products and derivatives. Of these products, some became popular and hence liquid and cost efficient. Soon derivative products were available to most investors as levered instruments to get exposure to broad stock indices, stock sectors and industries, currencies, size categories and even style, the traditional beta factors. What was once considered an investment process by an active manager to gain alpha was now commoditized into an instrument to which anyone could have access. The ramification being that as access to exposure was easy and could be obtained at a low cost, active managers found it difficult to charge management fees for such a product. Furthermore, the greater use of these instruments made markets more efficient, such that any structural payoff to these factors diminished and only timing the exposure to them could result in excess return.

In order to continue charging management fees and to portray that they were truly generating alpha and not beta return, some managers claimed to have market neutral portfolios. These so-called hedge funds were, however, neutral to only the first form of beta – market beta, and not neutral in all respects.

3.3 GENERALIZING THE BETA CONCEPT

We believe that in the generalized form, portfolio return is the result of the payoff to risk exposures, which have been taken by a portfolio. These exposures may be the result of active intended decisions by the portfolio manager as part of his investment process to attempt to outperform the market benchmark, or be unintended and a result of other active intended decisions in the portfolio. As markets become more efficient, active

managers evolve their investment process by increasing the complexity of these exposures to try and keep outperforming. They augment this by decisions on when to enter
and exit from an exposure. Concurrently, as intermediaries seek to profit from the barter
of exposures, they develop instruments which enable easier and cheaper access to exposures, and in effect commoditize them.

In theory, if it was possible to determine a complete variable list without error,
we can formalize this concept similarly to the Arbitrage Pricing Theory (APT) of Ross
(1976), except that we use the formulation in active return space of a portfolio, as
below:

$$r_p(t) - r_0(t) = \underbrace{[\lambda_1(t)b_1(t) + \cdots + \lambda_p(t)b_p(t)]}_{\substack{\text{Not commoditized beta} \\ \text{Traditional alpha space} \\ \text{Alpha} = \text{f (not commoditized beta)} \\ \text{Risk factors}}} + \underbrace{[\lambda_{p+1}(t)b_{p+1}(t) + \cdots + \lambda_K(t)b_K(t)]}_{\substack{\text{Commoditized beta} \\ \text{Traditional beta space} \\ \text{Beta} = \text{f (instrument availability)} \\ \text{Exposures}}} \quad (3.1)$$

Where, $r_0 = \lambda_0$ or the return on a risk free asset, b_k is the factor loading and λ_k are
the risk premiums, $k = 1, \ldots K$.

This essentially means that the demarcation is not between alpha and beta, but
between betas that are commoditized and those that are not. Those that have been commoditized are classified in traditional literature as betas, and the rest are classified as
alpha. As markets evolve, market instruments become available for exposure to non-
commoditized betas, in effect moving that risk premium from traditional alpha to traditional beta space.

We label the betas that are commoditized as "exposures", as, dependent on the level
of risk that a portfolio is exposed to, these exposures can be managed independently
using market instruments. We label the non-commoditized betas as risk factors, as these
cannot be managed independently, since no market instruments are available to manage
this risk. Both exposures and risk factors would be present in any given portfolio.

Hence, in the simplest form, use of a market capitalization benchmark for segregating alpha and beta simply means categorizing the beta related to market capitalization
in the Exposures category, and everything else as Risk Factors. Similarly with the incorporation of Fama-French factors, one is simply advocating that size and value are the
two additional betas which should fall into the Exposures category, apart from market
capitalization. Note that as we believe that the level of portfolio risk to an exposure or
risk factor is time varying, we are not seeking to create a segregation into systematic and
unsystematic variables based on statistical significance over a given test period.

3.4 THE DEMISE OF ASSET CLASS DEMARCATED ALLOCATION

The traditional demarcation of asset classes has led to the whole investment industry deciding to wed themselves to a fixed rigid categorization for all purposes. This has

resulted in an asset class demarcated world for organization structures, active and passive investment products and risk analysis. In our framework, however, asset classes are simply an exposure in a portfolio. The grouping of all equity exposure investments into one box is then labelled as equity, and similarly the group of all fixed income instruments is labelled as fixed income. Asset class demarcation in itself, therefore, is just another way of grouping the betas of a portfolio. We illustrate this as:

$$r_p(t) - r_0(t) = [\lambda_1(t)b_1(t)] + [\lambda_2(t)b_2(t)] + \underbrace{[\lambda_3(t)b_3(t) + \cdots + \lambda_K(t)b_K(t)]}$$

$$\underbrace{}_{\text{Equity}} \quad \underbrace{}_{\text{Fixed Income}} \quad \underbrace{}_{\text{Other}}$$

(3.2)

Cross asset class instruments such as CDS and convertible bonds, then, are instruments that allow an investor to have a combination of exposures, such as equity, fixed income and volatility in a single instrument. While these instruments are difficult to incorporate neatly in a traditional asset class framework, they fit seamlessly in the exposure and risk factor framework.

While an asset class demarcated framework was adequate in a world without hybrid instruments, it seems that, as different instruments proliferate, it is becoming more and more inadequate as the solitary basis for handling investment structures.

3.5 IMPLICATIONS FOR THE ACTIVE INVESTMENT PROCESS

For the active manager this framework has several implications:

1. As risk factors become commoditized into exposures, the space to generate alpha (from the remaining risk factors) decreases, and the space for beta return increases.
2. Any active investment process that today generates return by taking exposures will become obsolete progressively, as the exposure premium reduces as the exposure is commoditized.
3. Even those risk factors, which today seem impossible to commoditize, will become commoditized as and when sufficient investor demand results in creation of liquid cheap market instruments.
4. The alpha investment problem, which originated in deciding when and what risk factor to have in a portfolio, will gravitate towards becoming an allocation process across a multitude of exposures, and when to increase or decrease a specific exposure.

In effect this means that in our formulation, if we were able to conclude a set of exposures, which could collectively explain the complete movement of the market, the alpha versus beta debate is actually quite irrelevant. Alpha is simply the exposure premium in the portfolio, from risk factors that have not as yet been commoditized. What has been commoditized is categorized as beta.

Where does the final investment process then go? The eventual investment problem is therefore not an alpha generation issue, but a beta allocation issue – how to allocate effectively to the betas of the existing exposures as a function of time. We therefore believe that active management will devolve to an exposure-based allocation process, where the objective is largely to allocate to different forms of beta, and where alpha is only that component of portfolio return that the active manager has chosen to ignore from the beta allocation process. Portfolio diversification is just the diversification obtained by applying the forecasting process to more than one beta.

3.6 INVESTMENT STRATEGY CATEGORIZATION

Active investment managers take great pains to distinguish their product from their peers by attempting to convince investors of the greater wisdom of their investment process. In effect, what they are attempting within our framework is focusing their skills on a defined set of betas, which they believe are crucial to add value, and where they profess to have forecasting skill. They attempt to forecast the trajectory and payoff of these betas and attempt to position the portfolio towards or away from these betas on an ongoing tactical basis.

As investors require a simple structure to assimilate the abundance of active asset managers, they categorize the managers in multiple ways, thus resulting in a label for each category, which managers then wear to describe themselves. What is, however, important to note is that all such labels simply represent a method of grouping the betas and ascribing a label to each group. We discuss a few of the common labels below, and how they fit neatly into our structure.

$$r_p(t) - r_0(t) =$$
$$\underbrace{[\lambda_1(t)b_1(t) + \cdots + \lambda_p(t)b_p(t)]}_{} + \underbrace{[\lambda_{p+1}(t)b_{p+1}(t) + \cdots + \lambda_q(t)b_q(t)]}_{} + \underbrace{[\lambda_{q+1}(t)b_{q+1}(t) + \cdots + \lambda_K(t)b_K(t)]}_{}$$

Passive indexing	Active management	Alternatives
Fundamental	Quantitative	Technical
Top-down allocation	Bottom-up security selection	Relative value

$$(3.3)$$

3.6.1 Fundamental, Quantitative and Technical

Fundamental investment processes inherently assume either a trend or a reversal in characteristics to arrive at an investment decision. For example, a fundamental investor may assess the P/E of an equity security to be cheap, when he compares it to what it has been in the past. Alternatively, fundamental investors forecast a disruption (such as a merger, new product development or change in management direction and restructuring), to arrive at the forecast value of a characteristic. In either case, they are forecasting the level of risk to take against the "P/E" exposure or risk factor in a portfolio.

Quantitative investment processes tackle the same issue through back-testing methods, primarily with the assumption of continuity in the original time series or a moment of the time series.

Technical analysis also is not dissimilar to either fundamental or quantitative analysis. Whereas technical analysis tries to forecast the time series of security prices, fundamental analysis tries to forecast the time series of fundamental variables, and quantitative analysis is a composite of both of the above with a more structured process.

3.6.2 Top-down, Bottom-up and Relative Value

A similar argument can be made about investment managers who claim skill in top-down analysis or bottom-up stock selection or relative value processes. In effect, they have chosen the set of betas where they believe they have skill in forecasting and assigned a label to that style of investing.

Any investment strategy can thus be articulated in our framework, where the investment manager focusses on a certain set of betas to arrive at his investment decision.

3.7 POSITIONING OF ALTERNATIVE INVESTMENTS

Much has been said in literature about whether hedge funds, or other strategies classified as alternatives, form an asset class of their own. Researchers have also attempted to analyze the returns of hedge funds to decipher whether they are delivering alpha or beta, and are thus worth the fees that they charge investors.

In our framework, these questions themselves become somewhat obsolete. Hedge funds and traditional active managers have the same variables available to them as risk factors or exposures. As such, since we disagree with the basic concept of the existence of asset class demarcation in the first place, hedge funds, of course, are not an asset class. Furthermore, leaving the fee structure aside, what these strategies deliver is the return harnessed from risk factors and exposures, again like any other traditional strategy. The "alternatives" label is therefore not only misplaced, but is also a function of an incorrect framework to analyze investment strategies, as hedge funds would not fit neatly into an asset class-based framework.

The only two areas where hedge funds have an advantage over traditional funds is their ability to use leverage and the ability to short. Hence, while traditional investors are limited to an exposure or risk factor of between zero and one, hedge funds have the ability for this to be negative or greater than one. Their fit into our framework, however, is seamless, without the necessity to create an exception.

It is also to be noted that the scarcity and consequent higher fees for alpha are a result of greater market efficiency within asset classes, which is where traditional strategies are domiciled. In recognition of this, and because of the fact that inefficiencies continued to exist between asset classes, hedge funds exploit the opportunity by taking cheap commoditized exposure in an asset class that was not present in the client determined benchmark, and hence pretending to generate alpha. The use of CDS for credit exposure in equity portfolios, or the use of volatility derivatives in equity or fixed income portfolios, are examples of this phenomenon. The composite exposure framework thus effectively resolves the issue of active managers pretending to generate alpha by taking exposures that are commoditized in another asset class.

3.8 OBSOLESCENCE OF PORTABLE ALPHA

It is clear that no organization, investment process or team of individuals will be able to develop skills to successfully target the forecasting and management of all possible exposures and risk factors. Hence, there will always be a set of chosen skills that investment processes and organizations can research successfully, which then determines the investment strategies that the asset management organization sells. Similarly, given that asset owners have largely structured their organization along asset classes, their internal skill set is focused to outperform the given asset class benchmark.

The use of portable alpha strategies has allowed investment managers to transport these skills to any different underlying exposure. For an asset manager, this enables them to target a pool of assets that they would not have access to, as they may not have the skill to target inefficiencies in that space. For the asset owner employee, as the target and vision is limited to the particular asset class he is responsible for, it is additive to port the alpha from outside his asset class, thus creating a diversifying return stream. Both parties benefit, and it becomes difficult to challenge their logic in the conventional framework as it matches their objectives. It has therefore suited both the asset manager and asset owner employee to advocate the use of portable alpha strategies in the portfolio.

In a broader context for the asset owner organization, however, the use of portable alpha strategies results in distorting the analysis of their actual risk because what is thought to be alpha (and risk) from fixed income strategies, for example, may actually have underlying investments in equity ported to a fixed income universe. This issue can be resolved in our exposure-based integrated framework, as it focusses not on a pre-decided categorization, but on the exposures and the skill in managing those exposures that any asset manager possesses.

3.9 POSITIONING OF FUNDAMENTAL INDEXATION AND SMART BETA

There is no real difference between a smart beta strategy or fundamental indexation strategy and the quantitative enhanced indexed strategies of the 1990s. However, by positioning themselves as a passive strategy by using the term "beta" they have neatly avoided scrutiny of their actual performance to the same degree to which active managers are subjected. For the asset owner employees within an asset class, these strategies have allowed them to claim that they are passively managed (at supposedly a low cost), while in reality deploying active management.

In an exposure-based framework, just as a passive indexing strategy delivers exposure to a single variable (market capitalization for traditional passive), a fundamental indexation strategy delivers exposure to a different variable (for example, corporate earnings), along with market capitalization. Effectively, it is the same set of securities in the portfolio, but weighted differently. Which weighting methodology is a better representation of the market is a debatable question. Similarly, smart beta is also the same set of securities but weighted to provide exposure to two variables (for example, market capitalization and earnings).

$$
r_p(t) - r_0(t) =
$$
$$
\underbrace{[\lambda_1(t)b_1(t) + \lambda_2(t)b_2(t)]}_{\text{Equity 'Smart' Beta}} + \underbrace{[\lambda_3(t)b_3(t) + \lambda_4(t)b_4(t)]}_{\text{Fixed Income 'Smart' Beta}} + \underbrace{[\lambda_3(t)b_3(t) + \cdots + \lambda_K(t)b_K(t)]}_{\text{Other}} \quad (3.4)
$$

In an asset class-based framework with market cap weighted indices, both smart beta and fundamental index strategies claim to add value above the benchmark. In reality, however, their function is simply to provide exposure to a different variable, without the necessity of any skill that is the hallmark and necessity for an active manager. In an exposure-based framework, therefore, both strategies would fail to convince that they add value apart from as an instrument for a different exposure and thus demand any fees higher than those of a traditional passive product. More importantly, the exposure-based framework would be in a better position to analyze and manage their overall exposure if all strategies were analyzed within a common framework.

3.10 RISK IN AN EXPOSURE-BASED FRAMEWORK

Just as the analysis of returns has been done on the basis of alpha and beta, the investment process itself has also traditionally been demarcated between return generation and risk management. Risk matrix calculations, being time and resource intensive, have been standardized by various vendors, whereas return generation was left to the asset manager. Because clients were demarcated by asset class, vendors perforce had to do the same. Hence, their efforts were directed to create single asset class risk matrices with the highest possible explanatory power. These are still the industry standard today. However, these are of limited use in a multi-asset class world, which is actually where the portfolios of all asset owners reside. Further, in an effort to differentiate themselves, vendor risk philosophies have ranged from using top-down macro factors, to bottom-up style factors, or statistically created principal components. However, as none of them knows the intended exposure of the investment process of any portfolio, the concept of demarcation into intended and unintended risk being managed in the risk system did not arise.

In our exposure-based framework, it is evident that exposures or risk factors have to be managed from the perspective of which are forecastable (and hence part of the alpha generation or intended risk) and which are not forecastable (and hence are part of the risk exposures that need to be curtailed). Therefore, for risk management to truly happen, the risk model must be created in parallel with the alpha model and be synchronized to the investment process. Vendor-developed risk models can never be truly representative of portfolio risk. We elaborate on an evolved process for risk evaluation later in the text.

3.11 HORIZON-BASED ORGANIZATIONAL DEMARCATION

Most organizations demarcate functions in asset management implicitly on the basis of the investment horizon. Asset owners traditionally have had a separate group performing studies to develop a long horizon policy portfolio, from the group which researches the same assets on a shorter horizon. Portfolio managers tend to be involved in decisions with a medium-term investment horizon. Trading desks implementing investment decisions also attempt to forecast the same assets over a very short-term time horizon. All of them in reality are simply deploying an exposure allocation process to gain exposure premium along their respective investment horizons.

In our framework, this simply is a categorization of risk premiums based on their horizon, as below:

$$r_p(t) - r_0(t) =$$

$$[\lambda_1(t)b_1(t) + \cdots + \lambda_p(t)b_p(t)] + [\lambda_{p+1}(t)b_{p+1}(t) + \cdots + \lambda_q(t)b_q(t)] + [\lambda_{q+1}(t)b_{q+1}(t) + \cdots + \lambda_K(t)b_K(t)]$$

Short-term betas	Medium-term betas	Long-term betas
Implementation skill	Active management skill	ALM & Policy portfolio

$$(3.5)$$

A horizon demarcated organization structure is plausible if one believes that forecasting at different investment horizons requires different skills. However, the structure may be improved if one were to align groups targeting the same exposure across investment horizons. This has the benefit of resolving issues such as the evaluation benchmark that should be given to each of the groups and creating synergies in multi-horizon portfolio construction while minimizing excess turnover.

3.12 TRANSITION FROM AN ASSET-BASED TO AN EXPOSURE-BASED ORGANIZATION

Implementing an exposure-based framework requires the transition of an organization from the traditional asset class-based structure to an exposure-based structure. Figure 3.1 illustrates a four-step process for any organization to transition from the incumbent asset class-based approach (Stage 1) to an exposure-based approach (Stage 4).

Figure 3.1 Transitioning the investment process from an asset-based to an exposure-based approach

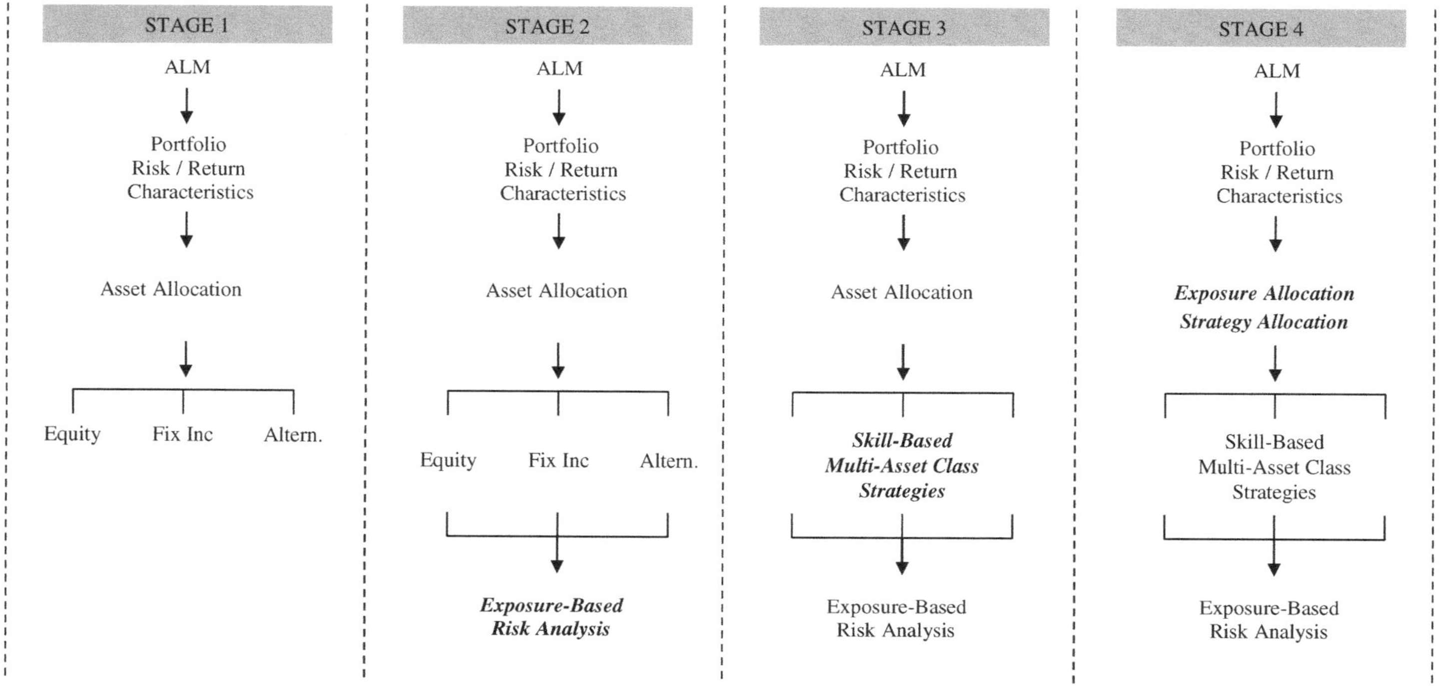

Stage 1 is the current state, where allocation is made to conventional product categories. Products are managed using conventional benchmark philosophies. The likely result is a low probability of alpha for the portfolio manager, and a less than diversified portfolio with a high probability of a shortfall in return objectives for the asset owner.

The first and most crucial step in the transition is to create a risk analysis process that is able to analyze all asset types in an exposure framework (Stage 2). This is the fundamental foundation on which the whole transition needs to be based. While this is a never-ending process, sufficient ground needs to be covered here to be able to explain at least the existing portfolio of asset and strategies in exposure terms. Creation of an exposure-based risk analysis framework allows for a stronger input into the selection of new asset strategies into the portfolio. We discuss this further in Chapter 13.

Stage 3 requires the full deployment of the exposure-based risk analysis into the investment process of selecting new portfolio assets, and retiring some of the existing ones. The primary consideration here is the evaluation of all assets on the basis of contribution to exposures by the asset, the analysis of skill in managing the time varying exposure and the ability to constrain risk factors for the overall plan portfolio. Asset owners continue to allocate to benchmarked products as they do now. Asset managers reorganize their investment philosophies to a skill-based structure, such that they are able to exploit inefficiencies anywhere and port alpha from various sources to this product. Effectively, while the product demarcation for market digestion remains intact, the underlying investment structure is free from the demarcation restrictions, using a skill-based multi-strategy approach. Portfolio diversification increases substantially, and it is more likely that return objectives are met, as inefficiencies can be addressed more successfully.

The final step of Stage 4 requires the creation of a forecasting process for exposure management and strategy allocation (rather than asset class allocation), which would create a determining input to the skill-based strategy selection process. Asset allocation is no longer done to conventional asset class demarcated benchmarks, but to multi-asset class skill-based products. Inefficiencies between traditional asset classes can now be targeted. The asset owner has true diversification to exposures, and maximum return potential. In its most evolved state, we believe this can only happen when assets are allocated not to generic benchmarked products, but to skills, which focus on specific inefficiencies. At the same time, asset managers have to provide products, which also focus on skills.

From an implementation standpoint, it is difficult today to implement multiple beta factors simultaneously, as instruments are either not available or expensive. Hence, while we seek to create a generalized allocation process for analysis and forecasting of beta factors, we believe the transition will happen progressively. We propose augmenting the traditional allocation structure depicted as Stage 3 in Figure 3.1, with three other betas, so as to progressively move toward Stage 4. Some betas, which are possible to add today as allocation buckets, are depicted in Figure 3.2, which displays a practical structure that would create multiple betas progressively, based on level of importance. Level 1 of the exposure management process is discussed further in Chapter 6. Level 2, which is the sub-allocation decision to geographies and factors, is discussed further in Chapter 7.

Figure 3.2   Levels of exposure management

Level 1 : Exposure Management	EQUITY BETA	CREDIT BETA	RATES

Level 2 : Geographic Allocation	US Equities	US Credit	Carry
	European Equities	European Credit	Currency Bias
	Japanese Equities	Japanese Credit	
	Asia / EM Equities	Asia / EM Credit	

Level 3 : Factor Allocation	Economic Sector	Economic Sector	Duration
	Size	Credit Duration	
	Value		
	Volatility		

Level 4 : Risk Factor Management	Commodity Prices	Expected Loss on Default	Inflation
	Risk Aversion		

Concurrently, we propose implementing the complete analysis of strategies into its component exposures and risk factors. This bottom-up analysis would result in the betas which need to be managed by the top-down exposure allocation process.

3.13 CONCLUSION

We present a generalized framework for incorporating the various facets of alpha and beta, using an exposure-based formulation. We argue that the return of a portfolio is the premium earned as a result of taking specific risks. As markets become more efficient, some of the risks become commoditized into instruments, which have easier access and lower cost. This has traditionally been classified as beta return, and here we label it as exposure premium. Non-commoditized risk in portfolios or risk factors is what has traditionally been labelled as alpha. We argue that the categorization as alpha and beta is obsolete as the generation of alpha is effectively also the premium earned by taking a non-commoditized risk. In this context, we argue that portable alpha, smart beta and fundamental indexation need to be repositioned, and the traditional organization demarcation by investment horizon needs to evolve to an exposure-based structure.

CHAPTER FOUR

Redefining Risk Premium for Multi-Asset Allocation Decisions

I n the recent past, as correlation between asset classes has increased, drawdowns experienced in the attempt to gain equity risk premium (ERP) in any multi-asset portfolio have become higher and more painful to sustain. As equity markets moved up and down, the single biggest determinant of the success or failure of a multi-asset portfolio has become the percentage of equity risk exposure in the portfolio. Both simple and smart investors have suffered alike, as attempting market timing has either not been possible, or been unsuccessful. This issue has impacted the gamut of areas where multi-asset strategies are present: in plan sponsor policy portfolios, balanced portfolios for individuals, institutional multi-asset strategies, and in strategic and tactical asset allocation decisions.

Portfolio theory defines equity risk as the volatility in equity prices over a given time period. This approach, while easy to calculate, comes from the perspective an investor takes in buying a financial instrument. Similarly, ERP has been defined as the total return on equity investments above the risk free rate, where the risk free rate is a short-term sovereign rate, and is considered to be risk free.

In this chapter, we attempt to revise the definition of equity risk and equity risk premium from the perspective of an asset allocation investment process in a multi-asset portfolio. We believe this revised framework is more suitable for application to asset allocation decisions – strategic and tactical. It is important to note that here we are not proposing any specific allocation methodology as being superior. We propose that the building blocks of risk and risk premium estimation, currently being used for alloca-tion decisions, need to evolve to cater for the real constraints present from a practical standpoint.

4.1 INCUMBENT RISK AND RISK PREMIUM FRAMEWORKS

There are broadly three incumbent empirical philosophies to estimate ERP:

1. Extrapolation from long-term historical returns.
2. Demand side modeling, where risk premium is estimated as a function of risk taken.
3. Supply side modeling using forward-looking proxies, like earnings, dividends or valuation.

In practice, extrapolation is popular in allocation and asset management, as it requires minimal explicit assumptions on the validity of current market valuations or on aspects such as dividend payout ratios. Supply side modeling is popular in aca-demic studies, as it is often believed to be more forward-looking, although its accuracy is largely dependent on the skill in forecasting the chosen proxy to financial markets. Differences have arisen between researchers on aspects such as the time period used for estimation, the use of arithmetic or geometric return and the choice of asset used to represent the risk free rate. Researchers have also used historical analysis to estimate ERP, as well as a variety of forward looking proxy characteristics such as dividend yield, valuation ratios and economic growth. Largely the US equity market has been used as the base case for calculating ERP, and ERP for other global markets is estimated as a function of the US market. However, to the best of our knowledge, all literature assumes a scenario where only two assets coexist – risk free and equities, and all results are made with the assumption that mark to market intra-horizon drawdowns do not constitute risk for the investor. We do not believe these two assumptions are realistic in a practical multi-asset setting, and seek to create a framework where these assumptions would not be necessary.

In practical asset allocation, all global asset markets exist concurrently in a portfo-lio, with the base market being determined by the domicile of the investor rather than always the US. Furthermore, in practice, the path taken by the portfolio is paramount in portfolio choice, rather than the end point alone. The incumbent framework therefore needs to be adapted to account for:

a. The fact that equity, credit and risk free assets are always present concurrently in any portfolio, just as they are in corporate capital structure, where debt and equity risk are related with debt being superior; and
b. The intra-horizon risk of drawdowns of the investment.

4.2 FRAMEWORK FOR THE CONCURRENT PRESENCE OF ALL ASSET CLASSES

Corporate financing is done using a variety of capital market instruments, all of which are part of a seniority structure for the purposes of their claim to a part of the income of the issuer company or on the assets of the company in the event of bankruptcy. In a simple capital structure, comprising only of debt and equity, the debt holders have seniority, both for payment of interest from annual income and for repayment of principal in the event of bankruptcy. In both cases, equity holders are subordinate to debt holders. As such, an investor in the equity of a company de facto bears the full credit risk of the company first and foremost, in addition to the risk for holding the equity. We therefore argue that equity risk, in fact, includes the risk arising from the debt issued by that company, and the risk of the country where the company is domiciled. In order to calculate the true risk for equity alone, the component of risk arising from debt must be extracted from the risk parameter.

Similarly, we argue that debt issued by a company already includes risk that would be present as a result of the company's country of domicile, i.e., country credit risk. Thus corporate credit risk should be estimated after removing the country risk. We believe this concept needs to be applied for the estimation of both risk and risk premium for the various asset classes. Figure 4.1 depicts the risk and risk premium structure that we argue for.

Figure 4.1 Illustration of incumbent and proposed risk, and risk premium calculation for asset classes

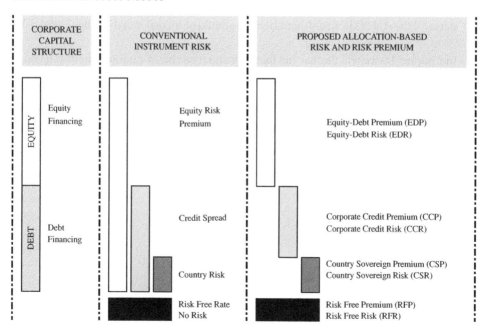

The concept of stacking premiums was first proposed by Siegel, Ibbotson and Riepe (1988); however, we note that to the best of our knowledge, all historic work treats equity and bonds as independent assets, and equity risk premium is derived after removing duration risk premium, not corporate credit premium, as we suggest here. As we specifically focus on asset allocation, where equity and debt coexist in a portfolio, and most often an allocation towards equity assets is at the expense of debt rather than risk free, we highlight that the incumbent framework doesn't address this scenario.

While this framework can be challenged, we believe that evaluating the risk of an instrument after extracting the risk component of other instruments which are senior in the capital structure is a more appropriate structure for asset allocation decisions, where it is preferable to have allocation silos which are mutually exclusive.

4.3 INCORPORATING INTRA-HORIZON RISK

An asset's return volatility is the common measure used as the proxy for risk. We emphasize two shortcomings of this measure –

a. Investors consider a drawdown within the investment horizon as real risk, and manage this by having a stop-loss threshold to preserve part of the initial investment. The risk of capital loss intra-horizon should therefore be a component of any risk measure.

b. Investors consider bearing risk, with the objective of earning a positive risk premium at the end of the investment horizon. Risk is not symmetric under this context, and the partial positive moment should be considered less risky than the partial negative moment. As such, the probability that the realized return falls below the target premium at the end of the investment horizon should be incorporated in calculating risk.

In Chapter 10 we will discuss the fact that the true risk of an investment is a composite of intra-horizon risk and end-of-horizon risk, and have formulated asset risk as the composite of the probability that the intra-horizon return X_T falls below a threshold x and end-of-horizon return Y_T will fall below expected risk premium x. We reproduce this result here for our current discussion:

$$\psi\,(x,y) = \mathbb{P}\,(X_T \leq x \text{ or } Y_T \leq y)$$

$$= N(d_1) + e^{\frac{2y\mu_{log}}{\sigma^2}} N(d_2)$$

Where

$$d_1 = \frac{x - \mu_{log}T}{\sqrt{\sigma^2 T}}, \qquad d_2 = \frac{2y}{\sqrt{\sigma^2 T}} - d_1, \qquad \mu_{log} = \mu - \frac{\sigma^2}{2}, \text{ and}$$

$N(*)$ denotes the standard normal distribution function.

Intra-horizon risk: $\psi_{IH}(y) = \psi\,(y,y)$ and End-of-horizon risk: $\psi_{EH}(y) = \psi\,(x,y) - \psi\,(y,y)$

Here, $X_t = \log\left(\dfrac{P_t}{P_0}\right)$, $Y_t = \min_{0 \leq s \leq t} \log\left(\dfrac{P_s}{P_0}\right)$ where P_t is the value of the portfolio at time t, and X_t is simply a normalization of the portfolio, where expressing it as the logarithm of the portfolio somewhat simplifies the exposition. The variable Y_t represents our notion of intra-horizon loss – the minimal value that X_t assumes intra-horizon, where we focus on loss since inception.

We use this framework to calculate the risk of the various asset classes in a multi-asset portfolio. We also note and rationalize conceptually that:

a. The short-term sovereign instrument used as the risk free asset may have zero default risk, but in reality also has intra-horizon risk, which is non-zero. This can be as a result of the change in expectations of interest rates.

b. The end-of-horizon risk for a debt instrument (sovereign or corporate) is the risk of not meeting the instrument return target, i.e. maturity redemption, and is thus equivalent to the issuer default risk.

4.4 RISK AND RETURN PREMIUM FOR ALLOCATION SILOS

We apply our stacking framework to calculate risk and risk premium for the various asset classes in a multi-asset portfolio, while incorporating both intra-horizon and end-of-horizon risk of the asset class. For each of the new mutually exclusive risk buckets, we calculate both premium and risk indices which would represent the return potential and true risk of that bucket. The application leads to a construct for the indices delineated in Table 4.1 below.

We illustrate this formulation for the US financial markets as a base case. The same framework can however be applied to any country. The Standard and Poor's 500 index is used as the representation of US equity markets, and we use the Merrill Lynch Bond Indices for the US fixed income market. The Merrill Lynch US Treasury Master is used as the global risk free rate rather than the short-term US T-bill, as it is preferable to match the investment duration where possible. We use the 5-year bond as this is similar in duration to assets in the broad credit market. A monthly frequency is used from December 30, 1988 till September 30, 2014.

The indices, which would represent asset class returns, are straightforward. Equity return is calculated using the S&P 500 total return series. For representing the return on US corporate credits, we match the security composition for the creation of a synchronized asset base for both asset classes, using the constituents of the S&P 500 equity universe. We classify the companies by the issuer credit rating, and the returns of each credit rating are taken from the Merrill Lynch bond indices, and weighted in the ratio present in the S&P 500 index. A US Corporate Credit Index is then created by subtracting the Risk Free Index return from this return series. This is depicted in Figure 4.2 below.

Table 4.1 Construction of risk and risk premium indexes for each allocation bucket

Asset Class	Type	Index Name	Index Construct
Risk Free	Return	Risk Free Premium (RFP)	US Long Bond ytm
	Risk	Risk Free Risk (RFR)	RFP index intra-horizon risk (equivalent to interest rate risk)
Sovereign	Return	Country Sovereign Premium (CSP)	Sovereign ytm – RFP
	Risk	Country Sovereign Risk (CSR)	SRP index intra-horizon risk + Country default risk
Debt	Return	Corporate Credit Premium (CCP)	Debt ytm – CSP – RFP
	Risk	Corporate Credit Risk (CCR)	CCP index intra-horizon risk + Corporate default risk
Equity	Return	Equity Debt Premium (EDP)	Eq Tot Retn – CCP – CSP – RFP
	Risk	Equity Debt Risk (EDR)	Equity Total Return intra-horizon – CCR – CSR – RFR

Figure 4.2 The US Corporate Credit index

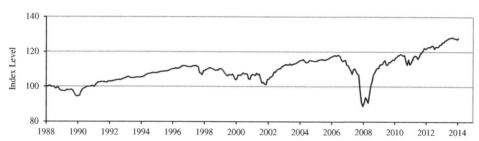

Notes: Constructed with components matched to US Equities, using the S&P 500 index composition. Monthly frequency. Base of index = 100 at Dec 31, 1988.

Data Source: Bloomberg, Merrill Lynch, Standard & Poor's

To estimate the end-of-horizon risk for sovereigns, we use the long-term yield premium (5-year rolling average) that the market demands for investing in that country as a proxy of country default risk. Similarly, we estimate the end-of-horizon risk for corporate credits as the 5-year average yield premium for that grade of corporate issuer. For estimating intra-horizon risk, we calculate the return threshold which would be breached with a 10% probability intra-horizon, for a defined period of rolling return. The intra-horizon risk is sensitive to the choice of investment horizon, and depends specifically on the review period of the client/management. We choose here an investment horizon of 12 months at which frequency we believe governance decisions are made in practice. We also show results for a 36-month investment horizon at which policy portfolio allocation is often done, but in practice a shorter period is often followed. If portfolio reviews are made quarterly, as is often the case with asset managers, then a 3-month rolling period needs to be chosen to estimate intra-horizon risk.

4.5 ASSET CLASS PREMIUMS – COMPARISON OF TRADITIONAL AND PROPOSED METHODS

Using the asset class indices, we can estimate the risk premium for each asset class, using our philosophy. A 12-month investment horizon is used here, reflecting a period over which a review is usually done. The results are shown in Figure 4.3.

No surprises were expected for RFP. For CCP, we find also very little difference, given that the components of S&P 500 are all mostly high grade credits. We believe that CCPs of different countries would show a marked difference from conventional calculations. EDP results indicate that the convention definition of equity risk premium results in higher values than our estimation, as the credit premium of companies is removed from being labelled equity risk. Again we expect this difference to be higher for less creditworthy companies.

Figure 4.3 Asset class premiums

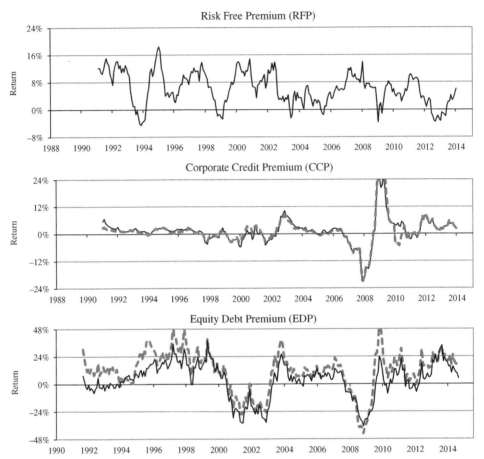

Note: Solid line shows asset class premiums in a multi-asset portfolio for a 12-month investment horizon, using a 12m rolling return, compounded geometrically. Dotted line shows premiums for each asset class using the conventional definition of risk premium.

Data Source: Bloomberg, Merrill Lynch, Standard & Poor's

 4.6 ASSET CLASS PREMIUMS – IMPACT OF DIFFERENT INVESTMENT HORIZONS

We illustrate the impact of using a different investment horizon in forecasting and in reviews. Policy portfolios are generally made with a 36-month horizon, and result in the graphs shown in Figure 4.4. We illustrate that if in such a case, review and governance leads to decisions on a 12-month frequency, rather than 36 months, the premiums can be significantly different.

As such, we emphasize that a matched investment horizon for forecasting and review is paramount, to be able to synchronize expectations of risk and return.

Figure 4.4   Premiums for various asset classes in a multi-asset portfolio

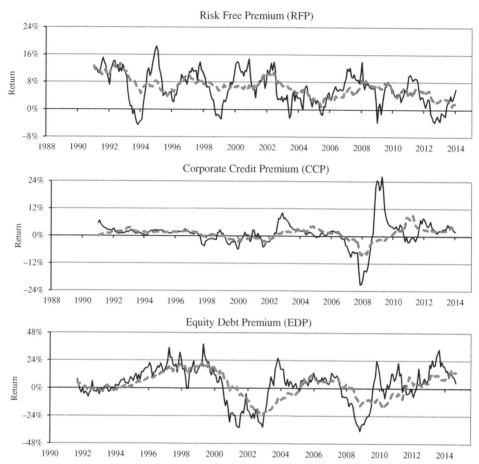

Notes: Solid line shows a 12-month investment horizon; dotted line shows a 36-month investment horizon. Period rolling return is compounded geometrically.

Data Source: Bloomberg, Merrill Lynch, Standard & Poor's

4.7 ASSET CLASS RISK – COMPARISON OF TRADITIONAL AND PROPOSED METHODS

We note that using a 12-month investment horizon, the broad shape of the risk variation is similar to that of traditional calculations, as shown in Figure 4.5. However, there are a few notable differences. Conventional methods assume the risk free asset to be zero risk, whereas we demonstrate that the risk free asset also has a drawdown risk. Secondly, we show that taking intra-horizon drawdowns into consideration, corporate credit risk can lead to an average drawdown of 2%, and can even reach above 8%. This is higher than traditional estimates for the same period. Finally, for equity markets we are able to incorporate intra-horizon risk into equity risk. The impact of this is however more evident as investment horizon is varied, as shown in the next section.

Figure 4.5 Risk of various asset classes in a multi-asset portfolio for 12-month investment horizon (i.e., using a 12-month rolling return)

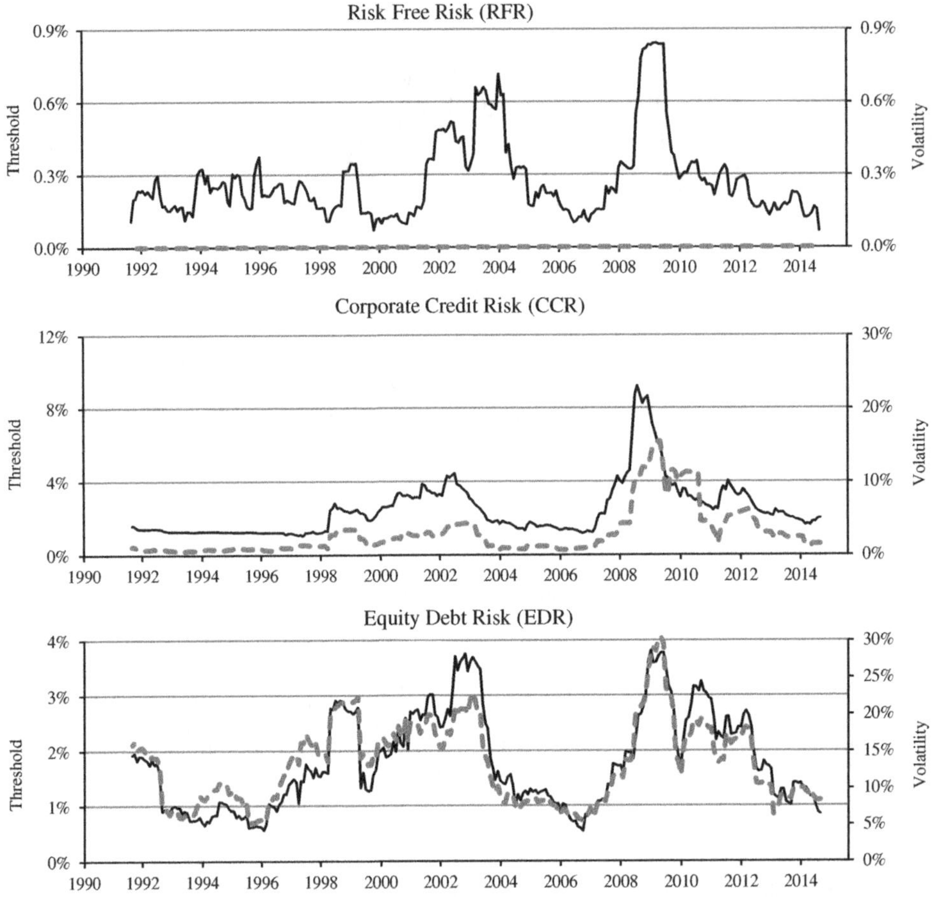

Notes: Drawdown probability threshold set at 10%. Solid line shows proposed method of drawdown threshold; dotted line shows traditional method of volatility.

Data Source: Bloomberg, Merrill Lynch, Standard & Poor's

4.8 ASSET CLASS RISK – IMPACT OF DIFFERENT INVESTMENT HORIZONS

Variation in the investment horizon from 12 months to 36 months shows a marked increase in asset risk, as a result of the higher probability of intra-horizon drawdown. In particular, we note that equity risk drawdown thresholds increase from a high of about 4% to about 10%, with the increase in investment horizon. The results are shown in Figure 4.6.

Figure 4.6 Risk of various asset classes in a multi-asset portfolio

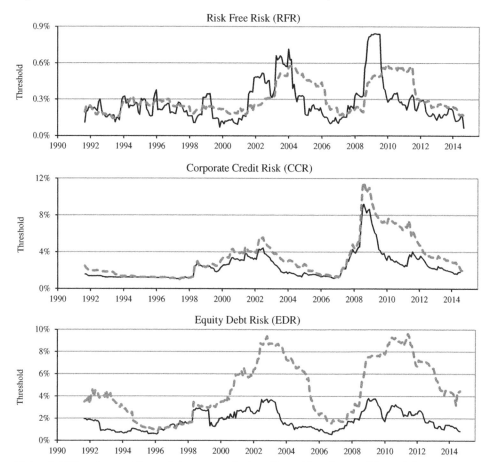

Notes: Solid line shows a 12-month investment horizon. Dotted line shows a 36-month investment horizon. Drawdown probability threshold set at 10%.

Data Source: Bloomberg, Merrill Lynch, Standard & Poor's

 ## 4.9 SOVEREIGN RISK AND RISK PREMIUM

In a US-only structure, we assume zero sovereign risk. However, for all other countries, we need to incorporate sovereign risk into our framework. We use the UK as an example to illustrate Country Sovereign Risk and Country Sovereign Premium, but a similar method can be applied to the estimation of CSP or any country.

The Merrill Lynch UK Gilts Index is used to represent the return on UK sovereign bonds, which is shown in Figure 4.7, and the Country Sovereign Risk and Premium are shown in Figure 4.8.

Figure 4.7 United Kingdom sovereign index. Base of index set at 100 at December 31, 1988

Data Source: Bloomberg, Merrill Lynch

Figure 4.8 Country sovereign premium and risk for the United Kingdom for a 36-month investment horizon

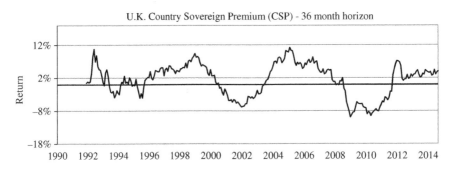

Note: Dotted line shows premiums for each asset class using the conventional definition of risk premium.

Data Source: Bloomberg, Merrill Lynch

4.10 APPLICATION TO VARIOUS MULTI-ASSET INVESTMENT PROBLEM SCENARIOS

Having created indices to represent the facets of risk and potential premium for each allocation silo, we can articulate which of these indices can be used in the various types of multi-asset problems.

- **Scenario 1: Long investment horizon, two asset classes, no mark to market.**
  A portfolio scenario where only equities and risk free assets are possible, where the investment horizon is very long, and where there is no mark to market assessment of the portfolio intra-horizon, leads us to the classic base case calculation of ERP. In such a scenario, the use of existing methods where a long-term risk free rate is subtracted from long-term equity returns would suffice. However, while this is the most widely used scenario, we believe that in practice this is precisely where there is a mismatch between the assumptions inherent in conventional ERP calculation and a practical portfolio investment and review process.

- **Scenario 2: Long investment horizon, three asset classes, no mark to market.**
  If we introduce the presence of the third asset class of credit, while retaining the facets of long-term investment horizon and no intra-horizon mark to market risk, we would arrive at a long-term equilibrium weight for equities, credits and risk free assets in a multi-asset portfolio. Here, we would utilize the risk premium indices we have created in the previous section; however, risk would still only be calculated as end-of-horizon risk, without the intra-horizon component. This scenario accommodates the presence of credits, but still assumes a utopian view of portfolio review.

- **Scenario 3: Long investment horizon, three asset classes, presence of mark to market risk.**
  While retaining the construct of Scenario 2, and introducing the fact that the investor is also risk averse towards mark-to-market intra-horizon drawdown, we change the calculation of risk to each asset class to include intra-horizon risk. The risk premium calculations done in Scenario 2 would, however, remain unchanged. This scenario depicts the realistic version of how we would envision strategic asset allocation in a multi-asset portfolio, or for the creation of an asset owner policy portfolio.
  This scenario still assumes that the investor does not have any investment skill in forecasting asset prices in the short and medium term, and allocation is done for the long term based on a pre-specified methodology such as a 60/40 portfolio or a risk parity allocation portfolio. This therefore sets the base case of the results possible in a multi-asset portfolio of zero forecasting skill.

- **Scenario 4: Short–medium investment horizon, three asset classes, presence of mark to market risk.**
  If we further assume that the investor has a non-zero skill in forecasting asset prices in the short or medium term, this skill can be additive to the portfolio in Scenario 3 either in terms of addition to portfolio return or a decrease in portfolio risk.

This scenario represents a realistic view of a multi-asset investment strategy, where both long-term and shorter term allocation decisions are taken, and where the portfolio review process is much shorter, highlighting the presence of intra-horizon risk.

4.11 CONCLUSION

Asset allocation methodologies today base their process on two fundamental tenets – the presence of an equity risk premium available over a risk free asset, and the belief that investing strategically with a long-term investment horizon will eventually enable them to harness this premium as portfolio return.

While we do not disagree with either of these tenets, we believe that the current process of asset allocation omits three critical aspects. First, even though asset owners are willing to have a long investment horizon, they are seldom willing to accept the intra-horizon drawdown risk that accompanies this. Second, the estimation of equity risk and equity risk premium does not acknowledge the presence of credit instruments, and is always done above a risk free asset. We believe that from an allocation perspective this makes the allocation silos significantly overlapping. Finally, the bond universe used to estimate any credit index is constructed independently of the stock universe used for an equity index.

We have attempted to accommodate these aspects and create a framework that we think is more appropriate for asset allocation decisions in a multi-asset setting. We create a credit premium index which matches the universe of issuers of the S&P 500 index used for equity indices. We further redefine the calculation of risk to incorporate both intra-horizon and end-of-horizon risk. And finally, we disentangle interest rate risk present in sovereign bonds from credit risk present in corporate bonds and from equity risk present in equity securities. Making these three sources of risk layered above one another reflects in our opinion a more accurate depiction of allocation silos, which thus become more segregated. We demonstrate that the revised framework results in different results for risk and risk premiums for each asset class, which become dependent on the investment horizon chosen. This further highlights the fact that it is critical to match the investment horizon for asset allocation decisions with the portfolio review horizon, to achieve the highest probability of meeting the risk and return objectives of the asset owner.

CHAPTER FIVE

A Multi-Strategy Allocation Structure

An aspect of the traditional allocation and implementation structure described in Chapter 2 is that there is a single allocation process that impacts the total asset base of an asset pool. The process generally assumes a single forecast horizon and a minority of organization resources are devoted to this effort. However, significant organizational effort and resources are instead devoted to selecting and monitoring the set of external managers in the portfolio. Multiple managers are selected within each allocation bucket to ensure that alpha risk is diversified. But this mind-set of diversification across strategies isn't applied to the allocation process, which is actually responsible for the majority of portfolio return and risk. In most firms the allocation decision continues to be a single decision (point of failure), which remains undiversified from a team or investment process perspective.

The allocation process generally involves a decision over eight liquid asset classes, each of which has had a maximum drawdown in excess of 10%. Equity asset classes are far more correlated between themselves than is anticipated. Fixed income asset classes are the same. This results in the allocation decision devolving to a simple decision of how much equity and credit risk to take in the portfolio. Given the low breadth of this decision, it is almost equivalent to market timing. History has taught us that market timing is an almost impossible task to perform consistently over time. Thus the scope for diversification using a traditional allocation process is limited. As we have seen in Chapter 2, for a large plan sponsor, even a portfolio with a perfect foresight allocation will breach a reasonable 12-month maximum drawdown threshold of 10% at the 90% confidence level. The lack of diversification thus also results in drawdowns which breach an asset owner's risk tolerance threshold.

Alpha strategies can form part of an overall solution to the diversification and drawdown issues, as they may have good benchmark relative drawdown characteristics and a low correlation with other asset classes. The disadvantage is the limit on their capacity, which can make it difficult to fill the entire allocation. This capacity constraint on their availability prevents them being the full solution for a large plan sponsor. As they can only be a part of the total solution for a large fund, we perforce would still need to have a beta allocation investment process, in order to have a large corpus invested.

5.1 CATEGORIES OF ALLOCATION APPROACHES

We begin by seeking a categorization of the various allocation approaches where each category represents a set of methods unified by a common philosophy, and where the categories are somewhat mutually distinct. These will form the building blocks for the allocation framework. A broad classification of allocation methodologies is presented in Figure 5.1. Our proposal, while subject to debate, groups the variety of methodologies into a succinct set. We have specifically used investment horizon as a distinct parameter for the classification, as time diversification is a key objective of the overall structure. The three main categories are:

1. *Long-Term/Predetermined* – where the weight of each asset class is either fixed or predetermined by a defined fixed methodology, without interim subjective views.
2. *Medium-Term* – views generally between six months and three years, which are rebalanced periodically.

Figure 5.1 Classification of allocation approaches

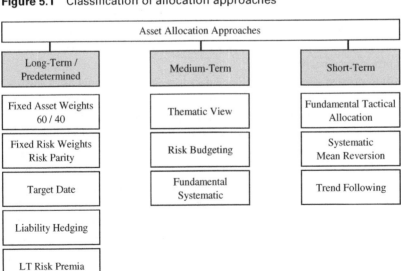

3. *Short-Term* – where allocation is done with an investment horizon of less than six months.

The asset classes on which all of these methodologies operate is generally the same, although it is seen that in long horizon strategies, investors tend to group the smaller asset categories together.

The allocation methodology categories which result are detailed below:

1. **Fixed Asset Weights**

    The traditional fixed asset weight portfolio that has been popularized by academia is a 60/40 portfolio. Variations of this weighting scheme have arisen over time, where the weight of each asset class is varied over time based on parameters such as client risk aversion and income requirements.

2. **Fixed Risk Weights**

    Here the weight of each asset class is predetermined on a risk basis. Risk-based approaches disregard expected returns and focus entirely on the risk characteristics of the investment decision. Notably these include the risk parity portfolio, where the allocation is determined such that the risk contribution from each asset class in the portfolio is equal.

    Risk parity contradicts the classical 60/40 allocation mix, directing a significantly higher proportion to fixed income assets, with an approximate resulting mix being a weighting scheme of around 20/80 of equities versus bonds, respectively. While this allocation has performed well over the past decade, a major criticism of risk parity is that most studies that advocate this approach test the evidence only in a period when bond yields have been declining and fixed income securities have been buoyant. In the current scenario where global interest rates have reached close to zero, and the risk of bond performance is skewed to the downside, the approach may be challenged in the future. This observation does not rule out the risk parity approach altogether, but reinforces the fact that this is not the panacea to the allocation problem.

    Among risk-based approaches we also find the minimum variance portfolio. The minimum variance portfolio seeks those weights in asset classes which minimize the overall portfolio risk or variance. This technique is often used when there is a constraint on the overall risk budget, and the allocator needs to free up risk budgets to allocate elsewhere.

    Risk-based approaches allow the investment of a larger asset base; however, as the results of this approach require frequent small rebalances, even on a daily basis, their turnover and maintenance can be challenging and expensive. Moreover, these approaches, being mechanistic, become difficult to implement in periods when there is a dramatic rise or fall in market volatility.

3. **Target Date Funds**

    Based on the life cycle concept, here the asset allocation changes systematically in a predetermined manner, during the fund's life until a target date of the fund's termination. These techniques are often used to justify the allocation for an individual over his life, based on changes in risk appetite that happen with age.

4. **Liability Hedging**

Here the assets are invested such that the cash flow generated by the investments, matches the expected liability cash flow requirements. The objective is simply to immunize the portfolio, rather than take any views on risk or return.

5. **Long-Term Risk Premium**

Long-term risk premium allocation relies on estimates of risk and reward over a longer historical time period, typically 50–100 years. These are then used as a basis for development of allocation policy, along with assessments about the economy's long-term growth potential and inflation rate. This method has long been used by consultant firms in recommending an asset allocation for pension funds' allocation policies, and is an approach with broad acceptance among both academics and practitioners. The empirical foundation of this process makes a case that expected returns would be realized over the long term, thus making it well-suited for pension funds which typically have longer investment horizons. A problem, however, is that performance tends to come at the cost of significant intra-horizon drawdowns, which requires that the asset owner has a high tolerance for drawdown. In practice this tolerance is greatly overestimated and both managers of the firm and regulators impose decisions even when a far smaller intra-horizon drawdown threshold has been breached. It is therefore ironical that while this is the most popular single method followed by plan sponsors to perform allocation, it is also almost certain that the plan breach its risk tolerance limits at some point, and thus fail to realize the very benefit of the methodology.

6. **Strategic Allocation**

Allocation based on a fundamental view of expected returns of financial market assets on a long-term investment horizon allows for a broad macro view of the world to be reflected in the strategic asset allocation of an asset owner's portfolio. Generally these views incorporate concepts such as development of economies, globalization and demographics.

7. **Thematic View**

Judgmental views of the current themes on an economic or micro basis, which are generally medium term in tenure, can be built into an allocation structure. Thematic approaches identify a set of investment themes or factors, each of which is expected to carry a premium. Typical examples of thematic concepts can be economic turnaround at the country, region or global level, disruptive ideas such as technology or medicine, innovative ideas and trends, natural resources and new markets. Thematic ideas can vary not only on the basis of where to implement, but also their investment horizons and expected risk and return characteristics. Apart from single theme allocation structures, there are also investment processes which follow a combination of multiple themes in creating a portfolio allocation.

8. **Risk Budgeting**

Similar to medium-term fundamental thematic views, one can articulate views on expected risk in the medium term. This can then allow the allocator to determine the proportion of risk that should be allocated to each asset class segment.

9. **Fundamental Systematic Allocation**

Fundamental systematic strategies are those where the investment idea is generated fundamentally, but implemented systematically. The majority of fundamental systematic approaches are allocation strategies based on systematic rules applied to observable economic fundamentals. A typical example is a benchmark where the component securities are weighted according to GDP rather than market capitalization. Another example is where assets are weighted by the income that they generate.

10. **Fundamental Tactical Allocation**

Generally based on economic views of the macro environment, along with bottom-up financial market expectations. Economic views rely on subjective assessment of the economic environment to forecast future economic parameters. Economists and market strategists then attempt to translate these predictions into the expected movement of asset prices. While one could argue the lack of consistency over time of this top-down approach, the process does have the advantage of being able to apply "common sense" to identify market disruptions which are not easily uncovered by other methods. In general, while the economic parameter forecasting process is often modelled quantitatively, the process to translate this to allocations is generally qualitative and subjective. Furthermore, it would be fair to say that most such allocation decisions tend to focus on expected returns of the allocation buckets, rather than a quantitative analysis of their risk contributions.

While concrete evidence is hard to come by, most allocation processes across the world use such a fundamental economic top-down approach for allocation decisions, especially over a medium-term investment horizon. Collection of evidence of the actual value addition of this approach from historic allocation decisions is however not done by any known source.

11. **Systematic Mean Reversion**

Hedge funds such as managed futures funds and CTAs often use systematic techniques to decide allocation to various asset class exposures. These are a defined set of rules which often tend to follow a mean reversion approach to asset prices, and are used in higher frequency allocation decisions.

It is also to be noted that each approach we have discussed here has a natural investment horizon at which it operates. In many cases they use a different dataset to the other methods and often require different skills and different processes to function. Conceptually, therefore, the various approaches are likely to be uncorrelated to each other.

Further, despite the fact that the risk and return objectives of all these approaches are the same, the allocation methods in the long-term category are not thought of as active views, and investors tolerate much greater risks in these methodologies than when using the methods in the medium and short terms. Investors in the medium and short-term methods have a much lower tolerance for drawdowns, and are willing to liquidate these methods at a much shorter notice period.

From a nomenclature standpoint it is also ironical that the long-term methods are thought of as beta allocation processes and the medium and short-term methods are

thought of as alpha generation. Not only are the yardsticks for their evaluation different, but the people and departments that allocate at different horizons are also different.

Finally, another approach to the allocation problem is to steer away from traditional
asset class allocation altogether, and instead seek exposure to alpha strategies only. This
sounds appealing, as in theory alpha strategies have minimal or zero correlation to beta
factors, and the Sharpe ratios of traditional betas tend to be much lower than that of pure
alpha strategies. At first glance, therefore, it would appear that a composite alpha-only
portfolio would have better risk reward characteristics. However, we have seen in Chapter 3 that the alpha beta divide is one of nomenclature rather than reality, and several
empirical studies have shown that there is a substantial amount of beta in traditional
alpha strategies. Hence, coupled with the fact that true alpha strategies are generally
capacity constrained, the alpha strategies only structure can form part of an overall
investment solution, but is unlikely to be the full solution by itself.

5.2 A MULTI-STRATEGY FRAMEWORK FOR THE ALLOCATION PROBLEM

Gupta and Straatman (2006) demonstrated the gains in diversification when one applies
multiple investment strategies within a portfolio. Figure 5.2 shows a stylized framework

Figure 5.2   Evolution of risk and return in a multi-strategy fund, as number of
strategies (N) moves from 1 to infinity

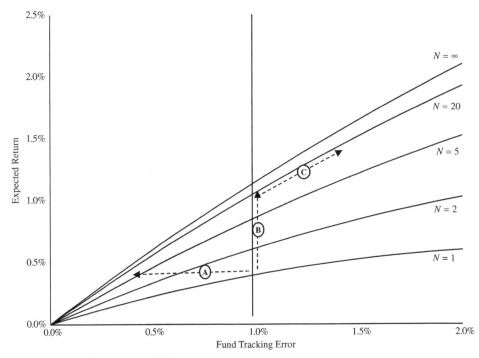

Source: Gupta and Straatman (2006)

of how a portfolio's characteristics improve as uncorrelated strategies are included in a portfolio. Increasing the number of strategies can lead to a decrease in overall portfolio risk at the same level of return (line A), an increase in portfolio return at the same overall portfolio risk (line B) or a combination of these two extreme cases. Furthermore, one is always allowed the option of increasing overall portfolio risk levels, to increase the level of returns.

We also know that multiple types of allocation investment processes exist, which have different investment horizons; different characteristics are conceptually uncorrelated with each other. Given the definitive benefit that exists in deploying multiple strategies for an investment decision to increase diversification and reduce risk, we see few reasons to support the incumbent structure of a single allocation process for the full portfolio of an asset owner. This single investment process for the allocation decision, irrespective of which type of allocation process is chosen, will have the highest contribution of risk and return of the overall plan, compared to all other investment decisions taken in the portfolio.

We propose that multiple investment processes should be applied to the allocation decision for any portfolio. Having multiple allocation processes would allow for incorporating diversity in allocation approaches, would reduce the plan's exposure to a single view, and would allow the allocation decision to be done at multiple horizons within the same plan, thereby facilitating time diversification. Apart from the benefit of not embedding a single process for the whole portfolio, this structure also has the advantage of an additional allocation layer in the structure: the ability to perform allocation to the allocation methodologies which allocate to market asset classes. This allows capital to be better allocated to each allocation category based on its expected performance in the current market regime, or where the conviction level or skill is higher.

5.3 THE BENEFITS OF STRATEGY DIVERSIFICATION

In its most simplified form, the allocation decision involves only three assets, equity-related securities or equity risk, credit related securities or credit risk and interest rate related securities or duration. We have seen that, in reality, investment breadth is not increased significantly simply by an increase in the number of sub-asset classes. Neither is it increased by an increase in rebalancing frequency, since the mere size of the asset base imposes natural bounds on the turnover. Breadth instead can be increased from an increase in the number of decision-making processes on the same assets, each of which uses a different set of information sources, has unique investment horizons, rebalancing frequencies, and is each independently viable. Increase in breadth is regularly applied in portfolio management investment processes, when a broad range of signals are blended together to create a composite view on the attractiveness of a given asset. However, based on our experience, this approach has never been applied to allocation decisions. At all levels, be it at the plan sponsor policy portfolio allocation, or the allocation within a multi-asset fund, allocation tends to be done using a single methodology with a single investment horizon. With a multi-strategy approach to asset allocation we have the ability to express a range of views on a very narrow set of assets. This is a setting where diversification takes a somewhat different shape as compared to when applied through a direct broadening of the investment universe.

In the current setting the benefit of diversification resembles the concept of Bayesian blending. Different views on how to perform asset allocation are taken into consideration. Each view is associated with a range of possible outcomes for long-term performance, but by averaging across them, the range of possibilities is narrowed down. Provided the average view is positive, the likelihood of positive performance overall is increased.

Ideally diversification should also assist in moderating intra-horizon volatility, drawdowns and exposure to event risk. In part this benefit is achieved by the averaging across investment approaches, but it is also something that can be addressed by complementing the set-up with an allocation layer managing the allocation between the various methodologies used. We can illustrate this using event risk as an example. Forecasting the timing of an event is often not possible, even for the best forecaster. However, it is generally feasible to anticipate with some degree of confidence the impact of a given event on asset prices.

At the time of writing this book, an event that is anticipated to happen in the medium term, is a rise in short-term interest rates initiated by the US Federal Reserve. This event can be related directly to the market price of US Treasuries. This is advantageous because for a given allocation we can in principle calculate its beta against the corresponding shift in market prices. This in turn makes it possible to impose bounds on the allocation's event beta exposure. In Chapter 9, we apply this methodology in the portfolio optimization for a multi-asset fund. By gradually adjusting the level of the constraint it is possible to see how the allocation responds to event exposure.

Apart from the diversification benefits that result from the ability to allow for multiple allocation frameworks, there are several other issues that automatically get resolved. Both academics and practitioners argue on the merits and fallacies of asset allocation versus risk allocation. Asset allocation ignores risk; risk allocation ignores views. Is there a best of both worlds? In our framework, we are not forced to select one over the other. In practice, neither of the two methodologies can claim to be perfect at all points of time. There are bound to be periods when one will be more successful than the other and vice versa. Our ability to concurrently allow for both methodologies, with the additional lever of allocating the amount of risk or capital to each methodology, makes the asset allocation versus risk allocation discussion somewhat obsolete.

Other questions, which are the subject of much debate, are: Which silos should you allocate to – asset classes, geographies or factors? Should one be active or passive? Should allocation be top-down or bottom-up? Our framework allows for all of these methods to be concurrently viable. We propose a diverse set of exposure allocation methodologies in a multi-strategy framework to achieve process diversification, making the portfolio become more stable in all market regimes. In addition, this gives the ability to allocate more capital/risk to the methodology which is more likely to work in the current market regime, giving an additional layer of control.

5.4 INDIVIDUAL ALLOCATION METHODOLOGY REQUIREMENTS

While the creation of a multi-strategy allocation framework creates a more flexible and sustainable allocation process, it still requires strong individual allocation processes as an input. Adding a new allocation methodology to the framework creates diversification and changes the overall Sharpe ratio of the investment process. A question which then arises is: What should be the minimum Sharpe ratio of an allocation methodology, for it to be useful for inclusion in the multi-strategy framework? We model this question below in general for a multi-strategy setting.

Assume the existing allocated portfolio is normal with mean μ_B and standard deviation σ_B. There is an additional allocation strategy normal with mean μ_A and standard deviation σ_A. The correlation between the active strategy and the portfolio is ρ. The Sharpe ratios of the strategy and the portfolio are respectively $\lambda_A = \mu_A/\sigma_A$ and $\lambda_B = \mu_B/\sigma_B$.

The combined portfolio allocates w to the new strategy and $(1 - w)$ to the existing portfolio. We seek to find the minimum Sharpe ratio of the new allocation methodology, such that the Sharpe ratio of the combined portfolio is greater than that of the existing portfolio.

The Sharpe ratio of the combined portfolio can be derived as

$$\lambda_C = \frac{w\mu_A + (1-w)\mu_B}{\sqrt{w^2\sigma_A^2 + 2w(1-w)\rho\sigma_A\sigma_B + (1-w)^2\sigma_B^2}}.$$

Using the individual Sharpe ratios and the modified weights ω

$$\omega = \frac{w\sigma_A}{w\sigma_A + (1-w)\sigma_B}, \quad 1-\omega = \frac{(1-w)\sigma_B}{w\sigma_A + (1-w)\sigma_B}$$

we get

$$\lambda_C = K \times (\omega\lambda_A + (1-\omega)\lambda_B),$$

where

$$K = \frac{1}{\sqrt{1 - 2\omega(1-\omega)(1-\rho)}}.$$

This says that the Sharpe ratio of the combined portfolio is a linear combination of the individual Sharpe ratios, modified by the factor K. The factor represents a gain from diversification. The factor K is always greater than or equal to unity, and equality obtains only if the new allocation methodology and the existing portfolio are perfectly correlated (provided w is strictly between zero and one). Thus, even if the Sharpe ratio of the new strategy is lower than that of the existing portfolio, the Sharpe ratio of the combined portfolio may still be higher. To deduce the exact condition we find the condition on λ_A for which the inequality $\lambda_C \geq \lambda_B$ obtains.

Provided the Sharpe ratio of the combined portfolio is positive, the condition can be written as

$$\frac{1}{1-2\omega(1-\omega)(1-\rho)}\left(\omega\lambda_A+(1-\omega)\lambda_B\right)^2 \geq \lambda_B^2 \qquad (5.1)$$

or

$$\lambda_A^2+2\kappa\lambda_A\lambda_B-\left(1+2\kappa\rho\right)\lambda_B^2 \geq 0$$

where

$$\kappa=\frac{1-\omega}{\omega}.$$

The expression on the left hand side of (5.1) is a quadratic function of λ_A with zeros given by

$$\lambda_A=\lambda_B\left(-\kappa\pm\sqrt{\kappa^2+1+2\kappa\rho}\right).$$

The expression under the root sign is non-negative for all κ and ρ, ensuring that the zeros are real. We select the positive root since λ_C is positive monotonic in λ_A. The condition is now obtained as

$$\lambda_A>\lambda_B\left(-\kappa+\sqrt{1+2\kappa\rho+\kappa^2}\right) \qquad (5.2)$$

The condition is both necessary and sufficient provided $\lambda_C > 0$. However, under (5.2) we have

$$\omega\lambda_A+(1-\omega)\lambda_B=\omega\left(\lambda_A+\kappa\lambda_B\right)$$
$$>\omega\lambda_B\sqrt{1+2\kappa\rho+\kappa^2}$$

which is always greater than zero. Therefore (5.2) is necessary and sufficient.

We can therefore conclude that the Sharpe ratio of the combined portfolio is greater than that of the existing portfolio if

$$\lambda_A>\lambda_B\left(-\kappa+\sqrt{1+2\kappa\rho+\kappa^2}\right) \qquad (5.3)$$

where

$$\kappa=\frac{1-\omega}{\omega} \quad \text{and} \quad \omega=\frac{w\sigma_A}{w\sigma_A+(1-w)\sigma_B}.$$

Furthermore, consider the limiting case as $w \downarrow 0$ which corresponds allocating only marginally to the new strategy. In this case $\kappa \to \infty$. A Taylor expansion shows that

$$\sqrt{\kappa^2+2\kappa\rho+1}=\kappa+\rho+o(1/\kappa)$$

where o represents a term approaching zero as $\kappa \to \infty$. The limiting condition on λ_A therefore becomes $\lambda_A > \rho\lambda_B$. If the new strategy has a low correlation with the existing

Figure 5.3 The factor $-1+\sqrt{2(1+\rho)}$ as a function of ρ

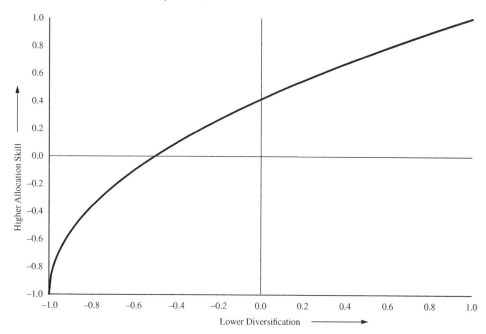

portfolio, then the condition is very weak. Indeed, if $\rho = 0$ the Sharpe ratio of the new allocation methodology only needs to be positive.

Secondly, consider the limiting case $w \uparrow 1$, where everything is allocated to the new methodology. Then $\kappa \downarrow 0$ and the condition is simply that $\lambda_A > \lambda_B$. Allocating everything to the new methodology is beneficial if, and only if, this strategy has a higher Sharpe ratio.

Lastly we consider the role of ρ. Suppose that $\sigma_A = \sigma_B$ and that $w = 1 - w = 1/2$. Then $\kappa = 1$ and the condition reads

$$\lambda_A > \lambda_B\left(-1+\sqrt{2(1+\rho)}\right).$$

The factor $-1+\sqrt{2(1+\rho)}$ is plotted in Figure 5.3.

This depicts that the minimum Sharpe ratio required for low correlated, diversifying new allocation methodology decreases monotonically. Hence, a highly diversifying methodology need only have a low Sharpe ratio, whereas a highly correlated methodology needs to have much higher skill in order to justify inclusion.

 ## 5.5 EXAMPLE OF A MULTI-STRATEGY ALLOCATION APPROACH

With the allocation categories defined, we demonstrate the viability of the multi-strategy allocation framework with an example of how it may perform in practice. However, the results here need to be treated as indicative, as we do not have a good proxy for the economic views, where we simply rely on simulated return series. Furthermore, it is obvious that the time period for this study is far too short for a meaningful conclusion; hence the results are meant as an illustration of the proposed structure, rather than a conclusive justification.

The common and established method for such an illustration is to look at historically realized performance. However, justifying the structure on the basis of historical performance has its limitations. Any investment philosophy can prove successful for a long period of time, only to then reverse. For example, although risk parity has performed well over the past 20 years we still question its reliability for the next two decades. However, despite the limitation on uses of historical performance, we could still investigate diversification benefits by focusing on the correlation structure between the various allocation approaches.

We choose five allocation methodologies, and propose to construct a portfolio using an equal asset weight in these five methods to arrive at our final portfolio. To enable a broad range of investment horizons, we use the following five strategies in our example: alpha only, risk budgeting, tactical asset allocation, fundamental systematic and long-term risk premium. To arrive at the characteristics of each individual methodology, we use the assumptions listed in Table 5.1.

From this analysis we get the methodology characteristics depicted in Tables 5.2 and 5.3. While the results are indicative, we can see that the different strategies have a correlation structure which ranges from −9.8% to 87.9%. This appears to confirm that there are substantial diversification benefits to be gained by using multiple approaches.

Further, the Sharpe ratios of the different approaches are obviously a function of the simulation and the time period of the test, and vary from 0.09 to 0.82. Most importantly, it is noticed that the long-term approaches have a higher maximum drawdown of 32.0% and 24.6%, compared to the short and medium-term allocation approaches.

Table 5.1   Time series used to approximate the allocation categories

Strategy	Simulation methodology
Alpha Only	50% HFRX Macro Index + 50% HFR Macro / CTA
Risk-Based Approach	Risk parity between MSCI AC World and Barclays Global Aggregate (FX hedged). Annual rebalancing with covariance matrix calculated over the preceding 5 years, monthly returns
Economic View-Based Approach	Simulated as a random walk, uncorrelated with the other strategies. Volatility set equal to 7% and realized information ratio to 0.09. The information ratio is based on the assumption of a portfolio manager investing in 500 uncorrelated stocks having a composite Sharpe ratio of 0.7. Translating this to an 8 asset universe decreases breadth by a factor of Sqrt(500/8) ~ 8. This implies a Sharpe ratio of 0.7/8 = 0.09
Fundamental Systematic	40% MSCI AC (GDP) + 60% Barclays Global Aggregate, GDP weighted. The 40/60 allocation based on the relative market capitalization of the two indices
Long-Term Risk Premium	60% MSCI World + 40% Barclays Global Aggregate (FX hedged)

Table 5.2 Performance and risk statistics for the five allocation methodologies, Period Sep 2000–Sep 2012, monthly returns

	Mean Return	Volatility	Sharpe Ratio	Maximum Drawdown	Max Drawdown VaR (10%)
Alpha Only	5.6%	6.2%	0.60	9.5%	6.8%
Risk-Based	5.5%	4.3%	0.82	13.2%	4.1%
Economic Views	2.6%	7.0%	0.09	13.4%	8.1%
Fundamental Systematic	6.2%	8.0%	0.53	24.6%	9.3%
Long-Term Risk Premium	3.7%	9.0%	0.19	32.0%	12.1%
Equal Weighted	4.7%	4.6%	0.59	14.4%	5.1%

We construct the composite portfolio as an equally weighted composite of the various allocation methodologies. The risk and performance for this multi-strategy structure is given in Figure 5.4.

As seen from Figure 5.4 and Tables 5.2 and 5.3, the composite portfolio has a realized drawdown of 14.4%, which primarily results from a significant equity exposure. While this still exceeds the 10% bound, note that it is less than half that of long-term risk premium. Moreover, the 10% maximum drawdown VaR statistic is now down to 5.1%. The Sharpe ratio over the sample period is 0.59, about the same as alpha only.

The average realized Sharpe ratio among the categories is 0.44, implying that the proposed structure improves upon the average by a factor of 1.32. If we were to not rely on the historically realized Sharpe ratio, but instead make an assumption that they are equal and positive across the categories, then this is sufficient to show that the equally weighted structure improves upon the average by a factor of 1.49.

Note that the results are based on the equally weighted allocation, which need not be optimal. Complementing the structure with an allocation layer above the allocation silos can also add significantly to improving the risk–return characteristics of the asset allocation decision.

Table 5.3 Correlation between the five allocation methodologies, Period Sep 2000–Sep 2012, monthly returns

	Alpha Only	Risk-Based	Economic Views	Fundamental Systematic	Long-Term Risk Premium
Alpha Nnly	100.0%	28.2%	2.2%	28.7%	12.3%
Risk-Based	28.2%	100.0%	3.3%	84.4%	72.0%
Economic Views	2.2%	3.3%	100.0%	−1.2%	−9.8%
Fundamental Systematic	28.7%	84.4%	−1.2%	100.0%	87.9%
Long-Term Risk Premium	12.3%	72.0%	−9.8%	87.9%	100.0%

Figure 5.4 Performance graph for the equally weighted composite of five allocation methodologies, period 2000–2012

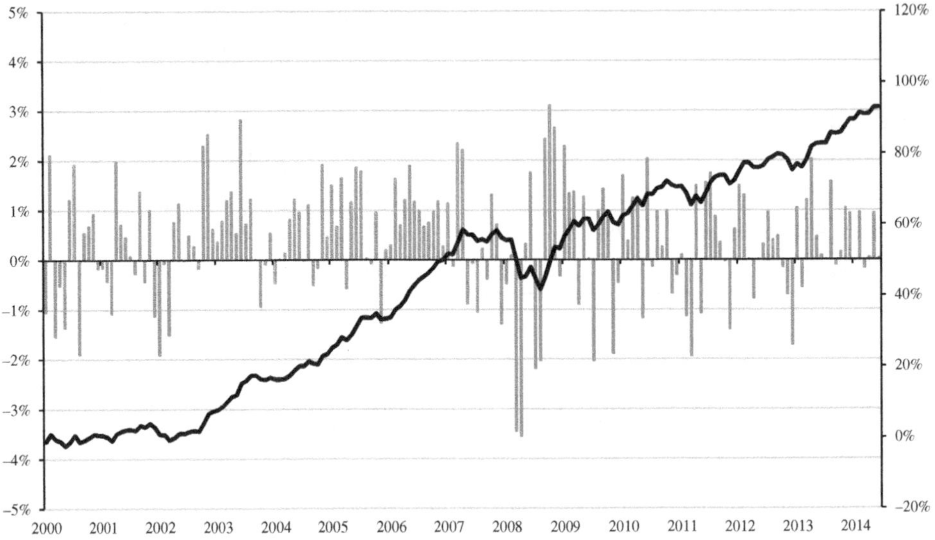

Data Source: Bloomberg, HFR, MSCI, Barclays

5.6 CONCLUSION

Traditional asset class allocation typically results in downside characteristics that exceed the risk tolerance of asset owners. Moreover, the asset class correlation structure results in diversification being limited, and allocation becoming a market timing strategy, which is unreliable. Alpha strategies may be utilized only up to a certain point, due to capacity constraints.

We propose that a multi-strategy approach should be used in the allocation problem and demonstrate that an allocation framework that utilizes multiple different methods of allocation in a portfolio is likely to harness greater diversification benefits and result in a better risk–reward portfolio.

In the next two chapters we detail two specific allocation methodologies, which are very different from each other in concept, dataset and implementation. The first is a fundamental approach and the second a systematic one.

CHAPTER SIX

A Fundamental Exposure Allocation
Approach – Business Cycles

O ne of the basic investment philosophies used for allocation is a fundamental judgmental process based on macroeconomic outlook. While it is difficult to explicitly articulate the mechanism of a fundamental investment process, we describe below such an approach based on the concept of business cycles, which has proved useful in practice.

The concept of business cycles proposes that various segments of economic activity progress over time in a cycle. A cycle consists of four phases – trough, expansion, peak and contraction. The sequence of events is recurrent but not periodic. Nor is the magnitude and duration of each cycle the same. Various economic indicators such as GDP, employment, consumer spending, capital spending, inflation and others, can be seen going through cycles.

6.1 THE PASSIVE ECONOMIC MODEL

For almost a century, economists have argued the presence or absence of economic cycles. The prevalent thesis prior to the Great Depression was a belief in neoclassical analysis, which argued for a general equilibrium. It argued that free market forces create a price for all goods and services such that supply will equal demand and all markets will operate at equilibrium. If a shock of any kind were to happen, causing demand or supply to change, the economy would adjust quickly to reach a new equilibrium via lower interest rates and lower wages. Government intervention was thus not necessary. Neoclassical views lost favor, as in their paradigm a crisis such as the Great Depression was not possible, because it does not allow for cyclical fluctuations around economic activity apart from temporary disequilibria.

The Austrian school evolved the neoclassical approach by including the role of government and money, while retaining the general equilibrium concept. This argued that cyclical fluctuations were caused by the actions of governments when they seek to increase GDP or employment, by adopting expansionary monetary policies. By lowering the interest rate, governments induced private enterprise to overinvest in capital expenditure which then does not match the demand. On the realization that they have overinvested, companies stop investing, which depresses demand. Prices and wages must now readjust to reach a new equilibrium, thus creating a cyclical fluctuation.

From an allocation standpoint, both the neoclassical and Austrian beliefs would lead to a fixed weight allocation decision based on the risk tolerance and return requirement of the asset owner. It is interesting to note that current allocation philosophies, which advocate near static asset class weights, such as 60/40, or long-term strategic asset allocation, are similar in concept to a passive economic belief.

6.2 AN ACTIVE ECONOMIC APPROACH

In reality, financial markets have experienced several major crises, even since the Great Depression. One would therefore find the neoclassical and Austrian models unpalatable, in comparison to the Keynesian model. The Keynesian approach fundamentally disagreed with the previous approaches in three main respects:

a. It is argued that the generalized price and wage reduction that would be necessary to reestablish general equilibrium would be difficult to obtain in practice and even if it were possible, could result in a downward spiral of lower salaries, lower demand and lower investment.
b. It highlighted the fact that risk aversion during a recession could deteriorate business and consumer confidence to an extent that lower interest rates would fail to reignite the cycle, as happened in Japan in the 1990s.
c. It held that in times of crisis, government should intervene in markets to retain employment rates and investment rates, while running a larger than normal fiscal deficit, in order to limit the damage from major recessions.

While Keynes accepted that in the long run, markets could reach equilibrium, he is also famous for the quote "in the long run we are all dead." Critics of the Keynesian model argue that it is focused on the short term, that fiscal policy takes time to implement and that there is a danger that government finances are uncontrollable as higher fiscal deficits mean a larger government debt has to be serviced.

The Monetarist school of Milton Friedman, while agreeing with the Keynesian view of market cycles, added that it does not recognize the importance of money supply and lacks a representation of utility maximizing participants in the markets. He believed that business cycles occur not only because of government intervention, but also because of exogenous shocks.

Hyman Minsky contributed to the cycle theory by the fundamental belief that excesses of any kind in markets lead to a period of the opposite trend subsequently, i.e., a turn in the cycle. This exacerbates economic fluctuations. In practice, we see this in every aspect of financial market behavior. A period of rapid credit growth is often followed by a period where credit contracts, or a period of excessive risk taking is followed by a period of risk aversion. These turning points in business cycles are often referred to as Minsky moments.

6.3 A FIVE CYCLE ASSET ALLOCATION APPROACH

Any forecast of financial markets must necessarily be based on both macroeconomic drivers impacting the market, as well as micro drivers on each of the corporate components of the market index. However, creating a robust mathematical deterministic model of future financial market returns is a very ambitious task. Much of financial market dynamics is impossible to model, let alone using historical data. Further, even the most mathematical of models require a considerable amount of judgment in the creation of the model itself. As such, we do not seek to create an all-encompassing model structure, but only to synthesize the market drivers of asset prices into a tangible set of indicators, which can then be viewed judgmentally to arrive at an allocation decision. This in itself is a step forward in rationalizing the considerable amount of information that needs to be digested to arrive at an investment decision.

We seek to encapsulate the "best of breed" ideas into an implementable allocation approach, and attempt to crystallize the behavior of asset prices in five driver cycles and two risk cycles.

6.3.1 Cycle I – The Global Business Cycle

Significant components of the world economy have globalized to an extent that they drive a global business cycle which impacts asset prices across all countries to varying extents. We call this the global business cycle and an illustration of it is depicted in Figure 6.1. The major economic indicators that define any business cycle are GDP, unemployment, production and investment, in accordance with the identity:

$$GDP = Consumption + Investment + Net\ Trade \tag{6.1}$$

In attempting to model the business cycle we focus on those indicators which are predictive of financial markets, and those which may prove predictive of the business cycle, and hence for financial markets. We choose four components to represent the business cycle: the real GDP growth rate minus real interest rates; the annual growth rate of households' consumption (real terms); the annual growth rate of gross fixed capital formation (real terms); and the annual growth rate of exports (USD, nominal terms).

Our work shows that the second derivative of most of these series provides considerable predictive ability for financial markets. Demeaning and standardizing all variables

Figure 6.1 Illustration of Cycle I – The Global Business Cycle

GDP Growth

Output Gap ⟶

Business cycle

- - - - - Long-term trend

———— Shorter term flutuation driven by policy, productivity, terms of trade, inventory

Time

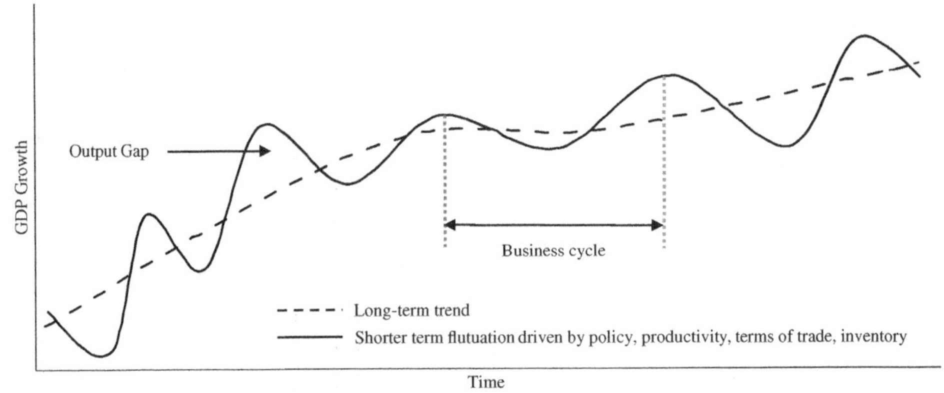

allows us to compare time series with different amplitude and provides us with a picture of the business cycle compared to the long run average. We then use this information to decipher whether the stage of the cycle is likely to benefit bonds or equities. Markets tend to misprice both asset classes at the turning points in the cycle, which creates investment opportunities.

6.3.2 Cycle II – The Local Business Cycle

While all economies in the world have an economic linkage to the global business cycle through aspects such as external trade, they also each have a component of their economy driven by local variables. Factors such as domestic consumption and investment are therefore also significant factors in the economic cycle of an economy. We distil these factors into a formulation of a local business cycle, in a similar way to the global business cycle, as shown in Figure 6.2. A combination of both the global and local

Figure 6.2 Illustration of Cycle II – The Local Business Cycle

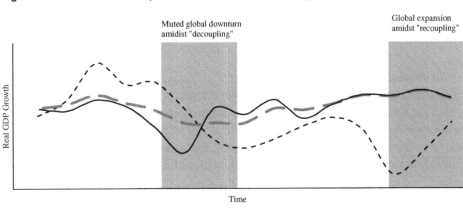

Real GDP Growth

Muted global downturn amidist "decoupling"

Global expansion amidst "recoupling"

Time

- - - Global   ▬▬ Country 1   ——— Country 2

business cycles would thus determine the economic cycle of a country. The diversity in economic cycles of various countries creates investment opportunities for global investors using country allocation.

6.3.3 Cycle III – The Monetary Cycle

The business cycle of an economy and monetary indicators are obviously linked inextricably. During a business cycle expansion, the business sector's need of financing increases. The business accumulates inventories to ensure sales, and needs financing for increased capital expenditure and investment. This increases the demand for money, constrains money supply, and tends to raise interest rates. Thus in making investment decisions, investors try to forecast monetary policy and the monetary cycle and couple this with various factors such as inflation expectations, fiscal policy and long-term interest rates. Conversely, during a business cycle contraction, central banks attempt to stimulate growth by the use of monetary policy tools, in order to stimulate demand, investment and growth. This relationship is depicted in Figure 6.3. Having said that, in our framework we have attempted to segregate the impact of real business cycle and the monetary cycle. We further divide the monetary cycle into four subcomponents, the composite of which is used for the purpose of impact on the financial markets.

Figure 6.3   Illustration of Cycle III – The Monetary Cycle

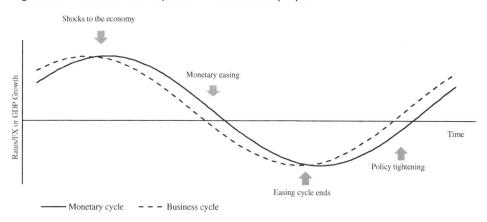

a. **Central Bank Liquidity Indicator**
The stylized central bank balance sheet can be written as:

FX Reserves + Domestic Loans = Currency in Circulation + Commercial Banks' Deposits

The right hand side of this equation is broadly equal to the monetary base. In other words, FX reserves and domestic loans are the counterpart of the monetary base. Moreover, the change in FX reserves equals the surplus/deficit in the balance of payments, and hence the change in total external liquidity.

The fundamental quantitative theory of money demand states that:

$$\text{Money stock (M)} * \text{Velocity of Money (V)} = \text{Price (P)} * \text{Output (Y)}.$$

Taking the natural logarithm of the above expression and the total first difference, we get:

$$\Delta M - \Delta P = -\Delta Q - \Delta V.$$

The difference "$\Delta M - \Delta P$" represents the concept of real growth of the monetary base. Assuming some price rigidity, this "deflated monetary growth rate" is different from zero, which is the case in the real world. Although we recognize that this concept is derived from the theory of money demand, our work suggests that it also proves useful from a money supply perspective.

We therefore use the annual growth in FX reserves and the deflated annual growth rate of the monetary base as indicators. We compute the t-statistics of both of these variables and then compute the simple standardized and centered average to formulate a Central Bank Liquidity Index.

b. **Domestic Excess Liquidity Indicator**

The above money demand equation can be rewritten as:

$$1/V = M/PQ$$

$1/V$ is usually called the Marshallian-K, which reflects the money stock in excess of nominal output, which is a potential driver for stock markets. However what matters from a forecast standpoint is the deviation from trend of the Marshallian-K, rather than the value itself, which tends to exhibit a rather stable behavior.

Time deposit, saving deposit and other deposits constitute the main difference between M1 and M2. A shift of funds towards these deposits generally puts a drag on liquidity available for equity markets and marks an increase in risk aversion. Whereas it is time-consuming to keep track of the changes in these deposits, it proves much easier to compute the difference between the growth rate of M1 and that of M2 (for which consensus forecasts are widely available). Hence we use the cyclical component of the Marshallian-K and the difference between M1 (yoy %) and M2 (yoy %) to create a Domestic Excess Liquidity Index.

c. **Market Liquidity Indicator**

The excess of M2 over the market capitalization gives an indication of the affordability of equities relative to domestic money stock. Our indicators are market ownership (M2/market cap) and the four-week moving average of mutual fund flows. We compute the t-statistics of both of these variables and then compute the simple standardized and centered average to get the Market Liquidity Indicator.

d. **Money Price Indicator**

A decline in real short-term interest rate reflects an increase in liquidity and is a net positive for stock markets. A rise in the term-spread (long-term interest rate minus short-term interest rate) captures improvements in expectations. Our indicators are real short-term interest rate and the term-spread. We compute the t-statistics of both of these variables and then compute the simple standardized and centered average to get the Money Price Index.

6.3.4 Cycle IV – The Credit and Capex Cycles

While the monetary cycle is a supply side measure of the impact of asset prices, a demand side measure is the consumption of individuals and institutions in an economy. The demand side function can be formulated as a composite of the credit growth in an economy and by the propensity of companies to invest in capital expenditure. This is illustrated in Figure 6.4.

Figure 6.4   Illustration of Cycle IV – The Credit and Capex Cycles

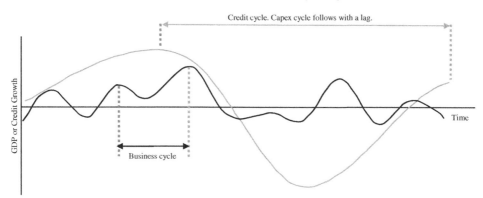

6.3.5 Cycle V – Market Cycle

Finally, a cycle endogenous to the financial markets itself is the market cycle. This is broadly composed of parameters related to market valuation relative to bottom-up corporate expectations. A simple and widely used yardstick to gauge the equilibrium value of stocks is P/E (price–earnings ratio). Gordon and Shapiro (1956) showed that P/E (more exactly price-to-dividend) is a function of the risk free interest rate, the risk premium, and expectations on earning growth.

 ### 6.4 CYCLE LIMITING RISK PARAMETERS

While macroeconomic and market cycles impact asset prices, a risk parameter that is relevant is policy risk and geopolitical risk. The political calendar of each country can bring with it substantial policy changes which could spur or act as a detriment for capital markets and the corporate environment. Using this as a risk factor is more appropriate as forecasting political outcomes is prone to error in most cases. Policy changes are often specific to sectors of the economy. They can effect asset prices in the short term through tax and trade related measures, and in the medium term through industry incentives, and in the long term through government expenditure plans.

6.5 SEGREGATING THE CORE AND CYCLICAL COMPONENTS

We hypothesize that economic cycles manifest themselves in financial markets in two ways: a long-term core trend in asset prices, and a short-term cyclical trend in asset prices. In asset allocation decisions, this is akin to strategic asset allocation, where the investment horizon is long, and tactical asset allocation, where the implications are for short-term advantage. For the long investment horizon, the core component trend is relevant, while for the shorter time frame, it is necessary to focus on the cyclical component.

Researchers have constructed models that explain up to 70% of the fluctuations in the Standard & Poor's stock price indices. By doing so, they confirm the existence of persistent chaotic cycles whose non-linear pattern may not be wiped out by market competition under non-equilibrium situations with trend evolution and frequency shifts. This so-called color-chaos model of stock market movements may establish a potential link between business cycle theory and asset pricing theory.

We have found it useful in practice to segregate the cycle into a core component and a cyclical component using a Hodrick–Prescott (HP) filter. The HP filter acts to remove a trend from the data. Other researchers have also used this to study the cycle effect in markets. Usually, the HP filter is used to provide an approximation of business cycles and to compute the output gap or the equilibrium exchange rate. It has seldom been applied to extract the cyclical component from stock markets.

We split a given series y_t into a growth (trend) component g_t and a cyclical component c_t, such that

$$y_t = g_t + c_t.$$

The growth component is determined by solving the following equation:

$$\text{Min}\left\{\sum_{t=1}^{T}(y_t - g_t)^2 + \lambda \sum_{t=2}^{T}[(g_t - g_{t-1}) - (g_{t-1} - g_{t-2})]^2\right\} \quad (6.2)$$

where the cyclical component is the deviation from the long-run path (core organic growth), and smoothness of the growth component is measured by the sum of squares of its second difference (rhs sum). The value of λ is not determined, in principle, by optimization but it is a matter of choice for empirical investigators based on "prior beliefs." Practitioners usually set λ at 7 for annual data, 1,600 for quarterly data and 126,400 (sometimes 129,600) for monthly data. As λ approaches infinity, the first difference $(g_t - g_{t-1})$ tends towards a constant, and the solution of the problem tends towards a least square fit of a linear trend.

This method does have drawbacks. It creates "border effects," as the filter is symmetrical. Indeed, to smooth a given point, the filter uses data that precedes and postdates that point, and then at the end of the period, it becomes asymmetrical again, generating a trend estimation bias.

An important part of applying the five cycle framework is to distinguish which of the cycles have a longer wavelength and thus impact the core trend of an economy, and which are shorter wavelength cyclical trends. The HP filter is a useful tool in that respect.

6.6 THE COMPOSITE FIVE CYCLE FRAMEWORK

While it is virtually impossible to create a framework where all known information can be digested logically in a structured manner, the cycle framework attempts to structure the majority of the data into a logical structure. Assessment of the impact of each variable may well be done purely quantitatively, although in practice this faces many challenges given that economic environments don't necessarily repeat over time.

To create a composite assessment, we prefer to digest the information into a heat map which is then assessed qualitatively. While this does create variability and possible behavioral biases, it has the benefit of not regimenting a structured quantitative mix of the various cycles at play.

CHAPTER SEVEN

A Systematic Exposure Allocation Process – Active Risk Budgeting

The two allocation approaches that have traditionally been used systematically for strategic asset allocation are the balanced 60/40 portfolio and an allocation using risk parity. Both approaches have one feature in common – they have approximately fixed weights between equities and bonds in all market conditions. A 60/40 portfolio always rebalances to a 60/40 allocation irrespective of market conditions, and a risk parity portfolio always rebalances to equal risk (which translates to roughly a fixed allocation between equities and bonds), irrespective of expected returns. Any solution that is superior to these approaches must therefore be adaptive to market regimes while not attempting to time equity markets, which we know is not possible. We want the revised process to be systematic in nature, without interim subjective views, grounded in the logic of risk diversification (budgeting) and adaptive over market regimes in order to have a better overall return and drawdown profile than the static weight methods.

We propose here one formulation for creating a strategic portfolio as an example. We continue to use the concept of the business and monetary cycle in this systematic framework to specifically illustrate that the allocation process can be significantly different even when the input information is largely the same for different forecast methodologies. Moreover, as discussed earlier, any allocation methodology is itself an active investment skill, where much innovation and expertise is demanded.

The present methodology is restricted to the US for two reasons. Firstly, the US has been and still remains a principal driver of the global economy. Secondly, historical data with well-functioning capital markets is available which makes it easier to illustrate and demonstrate relationships. As long as we stay with basic and established concepts the analysis should carry over to an international setting. Some adjustments can, however, be expected for emerging economies.

Table 7.1   Characteristics of US asset classes

Full Period (1932–2013)	Risk Free	Treasury	Corp	Equity
Annual Return	3.5%	5.2%	6.9%	11.5%
Excess Return		1.7%	3.3%	8.0%
Volatility	0.9%	5.7%	5.8%	15.0%
Sharpe Ratio		0.29	0.57	0.53
Maximum Drawdown		−16.8%	−18.0%	−48.9%

Data Source: US Federal Reserve, Standard & Poor's, Moody Investor Services, Deutsche Bank

For US equities, we use the total returns series of the S&P 500 index, gross dividends. For the risk-free rate, we consider a monthly rebalanced investment in a 3-month T-bill, data for which extends back to 1934. For government bonds, we use total returns, monthly reinvested in a hypothetical par yield bond with a 5-year maturity. Yields for maturities at three months, and one and five years are obtained as the constant maturity treasury yields, and from these a zero coupon curve is constructed using linear interpolation. A total return series is then constructed by buying a hypothetical par bond at the end each month, and selling it the month after at a price according to the new yield curve. This data extends back to 1954. For the period 1930–1954 a proxy for the 5-year rate is constructed by regressing its level on the 3-month rate and the composite yield for long-term treasuries. A proxy is then constructed assuming that parameter estimates obtained for the post-1954 period also hold prior to 1954. A total return series corresponding to the 5-year maturity is constructed in a similar way using the level and the monthly change in the long-term treasury yield as explanatory variables. The methodology appears to work well and regression R squares are generally high. For corporate bonds, we make use of yields on a monthly frequency of the Moody's Yield on Seasoned Corporate Bonds – All Industries, Aaa and Baa. These are used to proxy a total return series by matching the yield levels and changes with total returns reported in a study by Deutsche Bank (2008). Parameter estimates are highly significant and the overall fit is good.

The basic characteristics of the asset classes from 1932–2013, the period under investigation, are given in Table 7.1. Over the full sample period the equity premium in excess of the 3-month T-bill is 8.0%. For bonds the corresponding number is 3.3%. Equities exhibit a volatility almost three times that of bonds, and its Sharpe ratio is comparable. However, equities experience a maximum drawdown about three times that of bonds.

7.1 MODELING THE BUSINESS CYCLE

The Taylor rule is a universally accepted method for the analysis of business and monetary cycles. It combines views on long-term real growth (thus inflation), deviation from target inflation, and the output gap (or employment gap) to produce the appropriate level of policy rate for a given economy. We also use this model for our analysis of the business cycle. In its original form from 1993 it formulates an approximation for the federal funds rate as

$$p+0.5y+0.5(p-2\%)+2\%,$$

where, p is the rate of inflation and y is the output gap. The underlying assumption of an inflation target of 2% and an equilibrium real rate also equal to 2%, can be adapted to the relevant economic environment, as can the 0.5 weights given to the output gap and deviation from target inflation. Implementations also differ in how they measure inflation and the output gap, such as measuring the output gap as deviation in employment from its natural rate. Collectively these rules have been found to apply to a wide range of countries. Empirically we find that the resemblance of the Taylor rule results to actual rates historically is remarkable.

We focus on the output gap, and examine its relationship with asset prices in a two-regime analysis. When the output gap is high, the policy rate tends to be higher than normal, while the converse holds in times of a low output gap. The relationship is directly tied to asset returns as recessions tend to see asset returns with higher volatility and greater drawdowns. Isolating time periods into two regimes corresponding to the sign of the output gap uncovers two distinct sets of asset return distributions. The regime corresponding to a negative output gap exhibits higher volatility and negative skew. Because the sample extends back to 1930, this could in part be a result of the Great Depression, but the overall pattern remains if we restrict the sample to the post-war period. Figure 7.1 depicts how large the drawdowns can be, in times of a negative GDP gap.

If this relation between the business cycle and asset returns is used productively in taking a strategic allocation decision, the portfolio is likely to exhibit an improved risk profile. The observation is consistent with findings on risk and expected returns more generally, with a good overview provided by Ilmanen (2012). A positive relation

Figure 7.1   Total returns of the S&P 500 index one quarter forward, in regimes based on the sign of the GDP gap

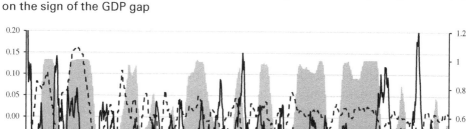

Data Source: Standard & Poor's, Congressional Budget Office

between risk and reward is present and effective up to a point, after which it deteriorates sharply. This has been found to apply to a broad range of cases and has in fact also been applied as a rationale for risk parity; see, for example, Asness, Frazzini and Pedersen (2012).

If we restrict attention to recessions as defined by the National Bureau of Economic Research, the statistics show that economic recessions are associated with a significantly higher volatility on the S&P 500, while the average return is even negative. This suggests avoiding equities altogether in times of recession, but in practice this is not easy to do. However, adjusting exposure as a function of the GDP gap is a weaker condition which can be implemented.

The business cycle component is measured as the GDP gap – the difference between actual and potential GDP. We measure this as the year on year percentage growth one year forward. While we have used historic actual numbers, using expected GDP from consensus estimates, which are available on a monthly frequency, could improve results.

We use the year on year growth in real GDP over the previous year, based on estimates by the Bureau of Economic Statistics. This is forward-looking in the sense that official GDP numbers are published with a lag, but backward-looking in the sense that we use last year's GDP growth as a proxy for expected growth over the next year. For potential GDP we apply the estimates by the Congressional Budget Office. From 1991 onward publications include a trajectory for historical potential GDP, which extends back to 1953 (and in recent years back to 1949). For the period 1991–2013 we use the publications as available at the given point in time. The period 1954–1991 is backfilled using the 1991 estimates. The period 1930–1953 applies a constant equal to the 1953 growth estimate.

7.2 MODELING THE MONETARY CYCLE

An extension of the Taylor rule is that central banks tend to adjust rates only gradually to changing economic conditions and the rule uses the previous period's policy rate as an additional determinant of today's rate. This gives rise to a degree of inertia in short rates, which avoids overly volatile paths, and we see extended periods of rising and falling interest rates. Periods of rising interest rates increase companies' borrowing costs, which weakens their creditworthiness. Similarly, periods of falling interest rates ease debt burdens and act as a stabilizing factor on the balance sheets. For allocation purposes we find it useful to extract the monetary component separately. The relationship between the direction of interest rates and general conditions for debt financing ties it closer to the allocation between governments and credit.

Table 7.2 shows the risk and return statistics for corporates in the two regimes. The two leftmost columns report numbers when returns are taken in excess of the 3-month T-bill. The two rightmost columns show the performance of corporates' relative 5-year government bond. Each set of columns has been beta-adjusted to account for the difference in duration. Regardless of how the excess returns are calculated we observe lower returns and equal or higher volatility when yields are trending upwards.

Table 7.2 Performance statistics of corporates in market regimes based on rising or falling interest rates

	Relative 3-month Treasury		Relative 5-year Treasury	
	Falling Yield	**Rising Yield**	**Falling Yield**	**Rising Yield**
Number of Observations	178	163	167	163
Mean Return	2.10%	4.30%	−0.40%	1.90%
Volatility	12.00%	8.60%	6.20%	5.80%
Sharpe Ratio	0.17	0.49	−0.06	0.32

Notes: Returns calculated as one quarter forward. The two leftmost columns refer to returns in excess of 3-month treasuries. The two rightmost perform the analysis relative to a 10-year treasury. Beta-adjustment performed using excess returns in excess of the 3-month treasury for both indices.

Data Source: US Federal Reserve

Figure 7.2 Total returns of corporates in excess of governments' one quarter forward and the rate trend

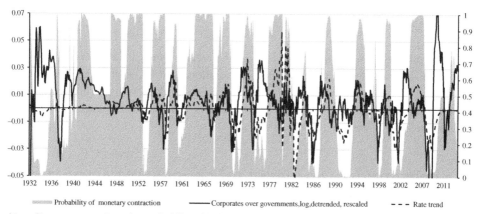

Note: The grey area gives the probability of being in the monetary contraction cycle regime.

Data Source: US Federal Reserve, Moody's, Deutsche Bank

We create a monetary cycle indicator constructed from the time series change in the 3-month T-bill. The trend in the yield is measured as the difference between a 1-year and a 3-year moving average. When the trend is positive, it indicates tightening monetary policy. A negative trend indicates easing monetary policy. Figure 7.2 displays how the indicator has evolved since 1930.

7.3 RISK ADJUSTMENT FOR EQUITY VALUATION

Although the business and monetary cycles outline the basic allocation methodology, we find it beneficial to include a precautionary measure against excessive valuation in equity markets. Shiller (2000) documents in the book *Irrational Exuberance* how high

Figure 7.3   Total returns of S&P 500 one quarter forward and the P/E ratio of S&P500

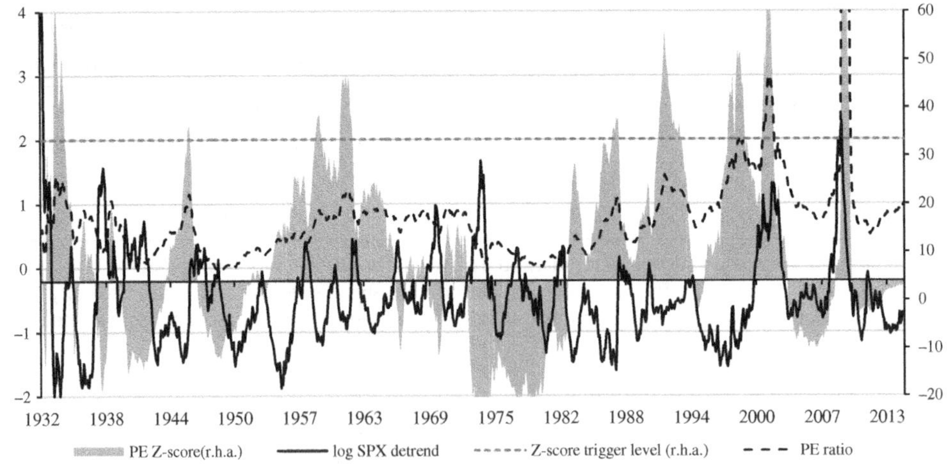

Note: The grey area gives the P/E Z-score.

Data Source: Robert Shiller, Standard & Poor's

equity valuations, relative to earnings fundamentals, tend to be followed by large draw-downs. The methodology therefore applies an additional risk layer which reduces equity exposure in times when valuations are high relative to fundamentals. To ensure against excessive equity valuations, we look at the P/E ratio of S&P 500, with price and earnings taken from Shiller's website (Figure 7.3).

7.4 CREATING AN ADJUSTED RISK BUDGETING ALLOCATION METHODOLOGY

We assume the risk parity allocation as a starting point. When applied to the basic equity-fixed income allocation this weighs the asset classes inversely to their volatilities. If, for example, equity markets are three times as volatile as fixed income markets, then the weight of equities is set to one third that of fixed income, thus leading to a 25/75 allocation. Risk parity generally performs well in back-test in terms of risk adjusted performance. Its main theoretical support is that if the asset classes have equal Sharpe ratios, it also forms the Markowitz tangent portfolio.[1] This might appear a restrictive assumption at first glance, but does in fact offer a good perspective on what is reasonable. For instance, in the above example a 50/50 allocation forms the tangent portfolio only if the Sharpe ratio of equities is three times that of fixed income. A practical drawback of using risk parity as an allocation methodology is that it results in a rather conservative portfolio. While it is possible to leverage the portfolio with futures contracts, in general we seek a non-leveraged solution.

---

[1] The claim holds under certain assumptions about the assets' correlation matrix, which are trivially satisfied in the case of two assets.

For a non-leveraged portfolio, as the only way to reach further out on the risk-return frontier is to increase the weight to risky assets, we propose that this allocation is made in a risk budgeting framework, i.e., that a volatility contribution target is set for each asset class, which is allowed to differ between the asset classes. As increasing the weight to risky assets irrevocably exposes the allocation to higher drawdowns, we make the process adaptive to the market environment using the previously described market regimes. Each regime is associated with a particular risk budget for the asset classes. The business cycle regime determines a risk budget for the main allocation between equities and fixed income. The monetary cycle specifies a budget of corporates versus governments.

We apply risk budgets as displayed in Table 7.3. However, if we were to define regimes based directly on the indicators, the allocation would display large swings as the indicators change sign. This is undesirable for at least two reasons. Firstly, from an implementation standpoint large reallocations are costly and demanding. Secondly, there is an issue of reliability. For instance, as we move from a negative to a positive output gap, it is clear that small differences in the methodology could easily shift the allocation decision one or a few quarters back or forth. Note that the rate trend does not influence the equity-fixed income allocation but only applies to the relative risk budget of governments versus corporates.

Instead we view each indicator as an imperfect observation of the current regime. For example, the larger the observed output gap, the more likely it is that we are in the positive output gap regime. Similarly, the higher the rate trend, the more likely it is that we are in the positive rate trend regime.

Practically, we proceed by first constructing a Z-score for each of the indicators. Histograms of the indicators are displayed in Figure 7.4. Per construction each is approximately centered on zero, so to obtain a Z-score all that is required is to divide each observation by the overall volatility. This results in two scores, Z_{BUS} and Z_{VAL} for the business cycle and the monetary cycle respectively.

The main indicator is Z_{BUS}, which is used for the risk budgeting of equity versus fixed income. The second indicator, Z_{MON}, is applied to determine the risk budget of governments versus corporates. Confidence indicators are constructed assuming a normal distribution by setting

$$p_{BUS} = \mathcal{N}\,(Z_{BUS}),\ p_{MON} = \mathcal{N}\,(Z_{MON}),$$

where $\mathcal{N}$ denotes the standard normal distribution function. The confidence indicators thus represent the probability that we are in a given regime.

Table 7.3   Risk budgets assumed for various regimes

	Equity	Fixed Income	Governments	Corporates
Positive output gap	70%	30%	–	–
Negative output gap	20%	80%	–	–
Positive rate trend	–	–	80%	20%
Negative rate trend	–	–	20%	80%

Figure 7.4 Frequency diagrams for the indicators – (a) Output gap (b) Rate trend

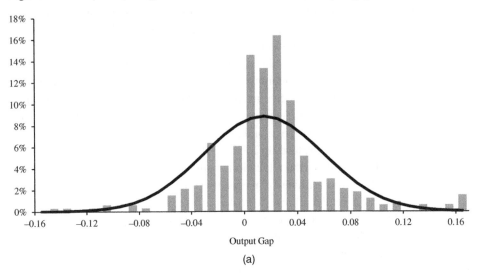

Output Gap

(a)

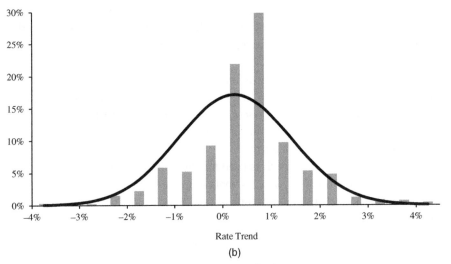

Rate Trend

(b)

Data Source: US Federal Reserve, Moody's, Deutsche Bank

The risk budgets for equities and fixed income are then set according to

$$w_{EQ} = 20\% + p_{BUS}\,50\%,$$
$$w_{FI} = 80\% - p_{BUS}\,50\%.$$

Following the same reasoning, within the fixed income the budget split is

$$w_{GOV} = w_{FI}\left(20\% + p_{MON}\,60\%\right),$$
$$w_{CORP} = w_{FI}\left(80\% - p_{MON}\,60\%\right).$$

As calculated, the risk budgets are still too jittery to serve as actual investment directives. The implementation therefore smooths weights by applying a moving average over the past four quarters.

For the equity valuation indicator, a Z-score is constructed in a similar way. From the P/E ratio a Z-score is constructed according to

$$Z_{PE} = \frac{PE_t - \mu_{PE,t}}{\sigma_{PE,t}},$$

where $\mu_{PE,t}$ and $\sigma_{PE,t}$ are the 10-year moving average and standard deviation of the P/E ratio. A rule is applied to cut the equity risk budget by half whenever $Z_{PE} > 2$, i.e., when the P/E ratio is at least 2 standard deviations above its 10-year historical average. This alters only the relative risk budget between equity and fixed income, while the budget ratio of corporates versus governments is kept constant.

In addition to the creation of a dynamic allocation, portfolio characteristics can be improved by implementing a rules-based drawdown management process. We use the Constant Proportion Portfolio Insurance (CPPI) methodology to limit drawdown risk. This drawdown management process monitors the weekly change in asset prices and adjusts the allocation between risk free (cash) and the risk taking portfolio when the portfolio value falls below a predetermined level.

Figure 7.5 summarizes the whole process in a flowchart.

7.5 SIMULATED PERFORMANCE RESULTS

We compare our proposed allocation methodology, Adjusted Risk Budgeting (ARB), to five major allocation methodologies as below:

- ▨ A 100% allocation to the risk free asset.
- ▨ A 100% allocation to equity.
- ▨ A 100% allocation to fixed income.
- ▨ A quarterly rebalanced allocation of 60% equity and 40% fixed income.
- ▨ A quarterly rebalancing allocation with equal risk contributions from equities and fixed income.

In order to compare the basic allocation methodologies against each other, we first simulate the portfolio without the use of drawdown management. This would allow us to make a preliminary judgment if the allocation rules of ARB, as created by the use of the business and monetary cycles, are adding any value above the other techniques in a meaningful manner.

Summary statistics for the full sample period 1930–2013 are reported in Table 7.4, and displayed in Figure 7.6. The 60/40 allocation stands out as the riskiest, both in terms of volatility and maximum drawdown. It is about twice as volatile as risk parity, while its

Figure 7.5 Flowchart for the implementation of an Adjusted Risk Budgeting
Allocation methodology

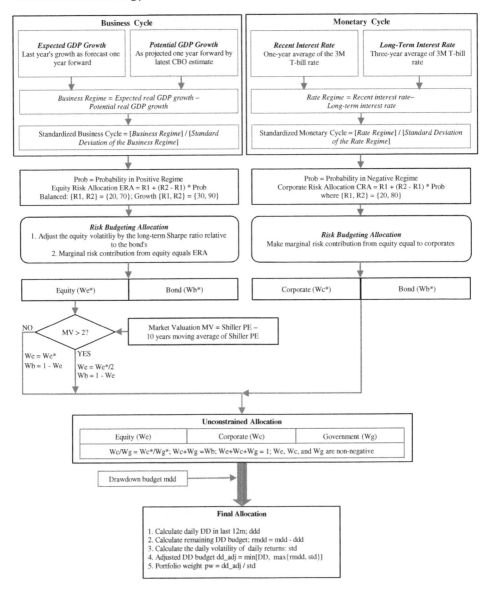

maximum drawdown is about twice as high. ARB exhibits a volatility and a maximum
drawdown which is slightly higher than that of risk parity. Realized returns however are
better than risk parity on a risk-adjusted basis.

Because the different allocation methodologies target different excess returns,
comparison between them can be challenging. Table 7.5 gives statistics after applying
leverage or deleverage of the allocations so as to keep realized excess returns constant
at 5.8%, corresponding to that of the 60/40 allocation. This allows a fair comparison

Table 7.4 Performance characteristics of various allocation methodologies, relative to the 3m T-bill

Full Period (1932–2013)	ARB	Risk Parity	60/40
Annual Return	7.5%	6.2%	9.4%
Excess Return	3.9%	2.7%	5.8%
Volatility	5.6%	4.5%	9.8%
Sharpe Ratio	0.70	0.59	0.60
Maximum Drawdown	−17.7%	−13.4%	−30.7%

Figure 7.6 Annual excess return, volatility and Sharpe ratio of main asset classes and allocation methodologies, relative to the 3m T-bill

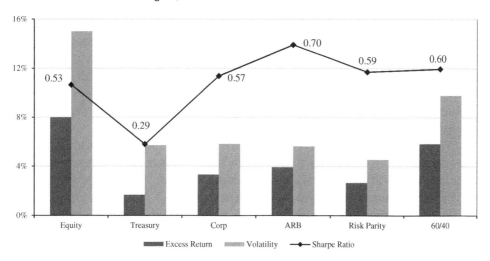

Table 7.5 Performance characteristics of asset classes, and various allocation methodologies, relative to the 3m T-bill with excess returns aligned

Full Period (1932–2013)	Equity	Treasuries	Corporates	ARB	Risk Parity	60/40
Excess Return	5.8%	5.8%	5.8%	5.8%	5.8%	5.8%
Volatility	11.0%	20.1%	10.3%	8.4%	10.0%	9.8%
Sharpe Ratio	0.53	0.29	0.57	0.70	0.59	0.60
Maximum Drawdown	−35.8%	−58.9%	−31.7%	−26.4%	−29.4%	−30.7%
Leverage	0.73	3.51	1.76	1.49	2.20	1.00

Figure 7.7 Cumulative returns of the 60/40 allocation, risk parity and ARB

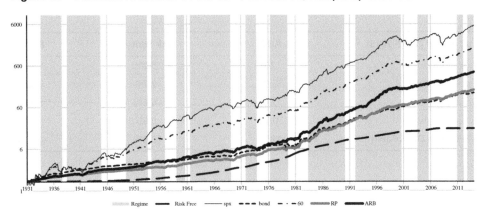

of the risk taken by methodologies to achieve the same risk premium. As we can see from the table, risk parity is comparable to the 60/40 in risk profile, with a volatility slightly higher and maximum drawdown, which is slightly lower. This implies that one can achieve near risk parity by holding a 60/40 constant ratio in equities/bonds and 40% in cash (i.e., deleverage 60/40 by 0.71). Both methodologies are superior to standalone asset classes (equities and bonds), with a lower maximum drawdown and/or lower volatility. ARB exhibits the best result from all risk measures (volatility, maximum drawdown, Sharpe ratio), by the fact that the methodology adapts itself to the business cycle.

We see from the cumulative returns over the full sample period shown in Figure 7.7 that adaptive risk exposure allows the ARB allocation to reduce equity exposure in times of elevated risks, which acts to moderate drawdowns over time. ARB allocations over time are depicted in Figure 7.10. Drawdowns depicted in Figure 7.8 show that compared with the 60/40 allocation ARB successfully avoids several periods of excessive drawdown, although risk parity still comes out as the safest allocation methodology. The difference

Figure 7.8 Drawdown for the various investment methodologies

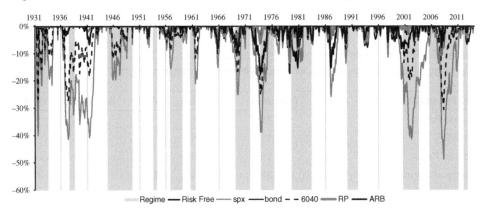

Figure 7.9　Comparison of performance drawdown between ARB & 60/40 and ARB & risk parity

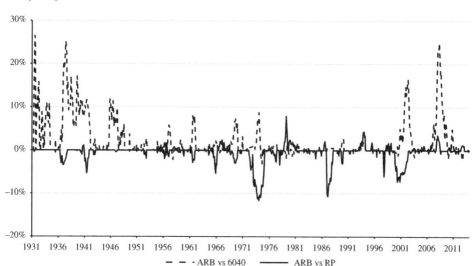

of performance drawdown between ARB and 60/40 and risk parity is shown in Figure 7.9. ARB is better off when the curve is above zero and is worse than 60/40 when the curve is below the zero line. In most cases, ARB is better than 60/40 by a big margin, and is worse in a few cases by 3–4%. Compared to risk parity, ARB has a similar downside performance. The turnover is plotted in Figure 7.11, which includes rebalancing caused by both the change in allocation due to market conditions; and due to differences in asset returns, shows that there are about 10 cases where the ARB turnover is more than 11% in a single rebalancing over the 80-year testing period. The average turnover is about 2% per month, and the 12-month moving average ranges from 0% to 5%.

Figure 7.10　ARB asset class allocations over time

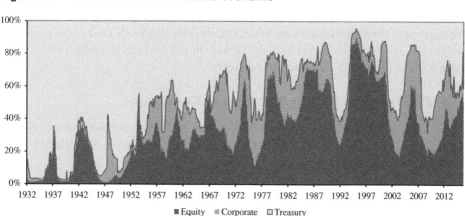

Figure 7.11 ARB allocation methodology turnover over time

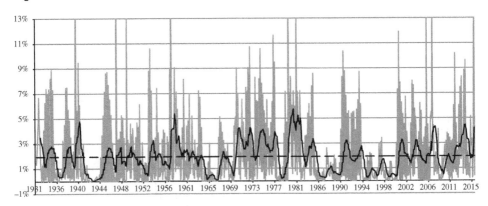

Various aspects of the simulated ARB allocation methodology give us the confidence that improvements are possible over the static weight 60/40 or risk parity methodologies, without the assumption of skill in forecasting ability. This illustration of the methodology thus helps us confirm that allocation is an active skill in the absolute return context, and simple rules-based techniques can provide significant improvements to a portfolio, when compared to static allocation techniques.

7.6 CONFIRMING ROBUSTNESS OF ARB ALLOCATION METHODOLOGY

While the composite simulation over the full 80-year period is positive for ARB, in order for the methodology to be considered robust it must display similar superiority in different market periods and different market regimes. We can analyze this by segregating the simulation results into different time periods of economic regime and market regime and comparing performance of the allocation methodologies.

7.6.1 Performance in Different Time Periods

We segregate the results into four time periods: Pre-1946 (1932–1945), post-war (1946–1982), the bull market (1983–2000) and the dot com and beyond (2001–2013). Table 7.6 and Figure 7.12 display these results.

7.6.2 Performance in Different Market Conditions

The regimes used are the bond bear market (1980–81), the bond bull market (2000–2003), the equities bear market (2007–2009) and the equities bull market (1994–1997). Figure 7.13 displays these results.

Results of the ARB are generally superior to both the 60/40 and the risk parity allocation process in almost all market periods. With the exception of the bond bull market, ARB also outperforms its peers in the other three market regimes. These results are of

Table 7.6 Simulated performance results of various allocation methodologies and asset classes in different time periods

Pre-1946 Period (1932–1945)	ARB	Risk Parity	60/40	Equity	Bonds	Risk Free
Annual Return	4.8%	3.9%	10.7%	13.7%	6.1%	0.3%
Excess Return	4.5%	3.6%	10.4%	13.4%	5.8%	0.1%
Volatility	2.3%	0.8%	16.2%	24.8%	3.6%	0.1%
Sharpe Ratio	1.95	4.36	0.65	0.54	1.60	
Maximum Drawdown	−6.7%	−1.9%	−27.3%	−41.4%	−5.0%	

Post-War Period (1946–1982)	ARB	Risk Parity	60/40	Equity	Bonds	Risk Free
Annual Return	3.8%	2.2%	9.2%	14.0%	1.8%	1.7%
Excess Return	2.1%	0.6%	7.6%	12.4%	0.1%	
Volatility	2.4%	1.7%	6.8%	11.3%	1.8%	0.3%
Sharpe Ratio	0.87	0.33	1.11	1.10	0.08	
Maximum Drawdown	−17.7%	−13.4%	−24.9%	−39.0%	−17.4%	

Bull Market Period (1983–2000)	ARB	Risk Parity	60/40	Equity	Bonds	Risk Free
Annual Return	14.5%	12.1%	13.7%	15.8%	10.6%	6.1%
Excess Return	8.3%	6.0%	7.6%	9.7%	4.4%	
Volatility	7.4%	5.8%	7.5%	10.5%	5.9%	0.6%
Sharpe Ratio	1.13	1.04	1.01	0.92	0.75	
Maximum Drawdown	−15.3%	−6.2%	−15.6%	−26.0%	−8.3%	

Dot-Com & Beyond (2001–2013)	ARB	Risk Parity	60/40	Equity	Bonds	Risk Free
Annual Return	6.7%	6.3%	6.1%	6.0%	6.1%	1.5%
Excess Return	5.1%	4.8%	4.6%	4.5%	4.6%	
Volatility	4.9%	4.8%	8.4%	13.7%	5.1%	0.5%
Sharpe Ratio	1.04	1.01	0.54	0.33	0.89	
Maximum Drawdown	−8.0%	−10.6%	−30.7%	−48.9%	−8.3%	

Figure 7.12 Simulated cumulative performance of various allocation methodologies and asset classes in different time periods

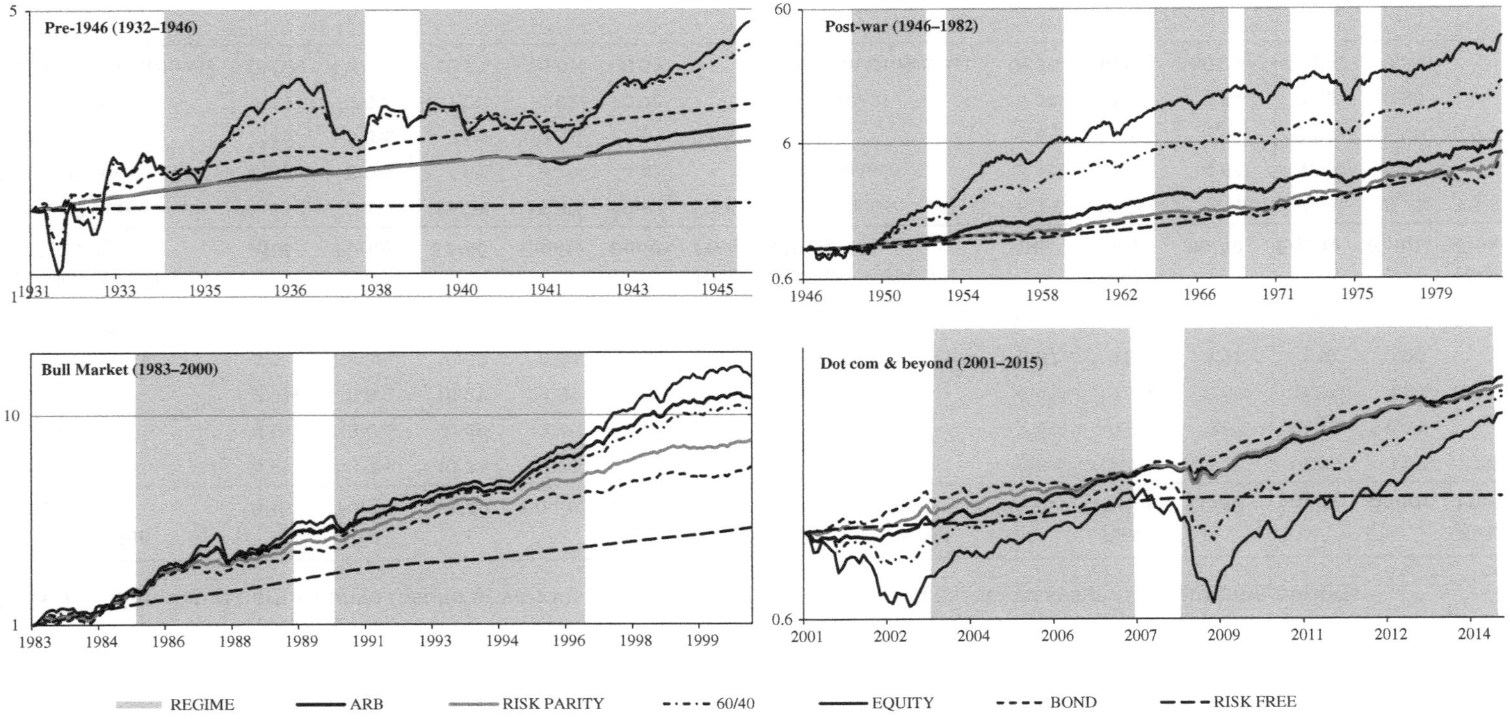

REGIME ——— ARB ——— RISK PARITY - - - 60/40 ——— EQUITY - - - - BOND - - - - RISK FREE

Figure 7.13 Simulated cumulative performance of various allocation methodologies and asset classes in different bull and bear markets

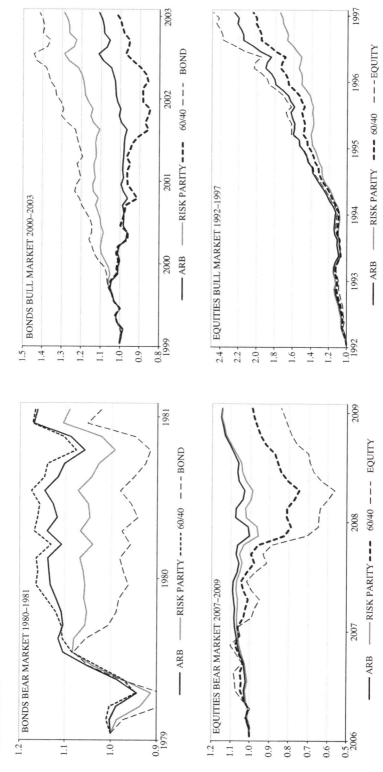

course susceptible to look-ahead bias, and can potentially be specific to the dataset; however, they do highlight the importance of creating an active strategic allocation process, which may be superior to traditional static approaches.

7.7 IMPLEMENTATION OF A DRAWDOWN MANAGEMENT PROCESS

In the implementation of the drawdown management process, we set this drawdown level at 8% in the simulation. Results of the allocation after implementation of the drawdown management process are detailed in Table 7.7 and Figure 7.14. In addition, Figure 7.15 shows the resulting portfolio volatility and Sharpe ratio over time. Given the fact

Table 7.7 Comparison of performance of ARB and risk parity allocation methodologies, with and without drawdown management

	ARB	ARB with DD Mgmt	Risk Parity	Risk Parity with DD Mgmt
Annual Return	7.48%	8.00%	6.21%	6.53%
Excess Return	3.93%	4.45%	2.66%	2.98%
Volatility	5.65%	5.20%	4.55%	4.28%
Sharpe Ratio	0.70	0.86	0.59	0.70
Max DD	−17.73%	−6.93%	−13.39%	−7.30%
Mean DD	−1.34%	−0.84%	−0.78%	−0.61%

Figure 7.14 Comparison of performance of ARB and risk parity allocation methodologies, with and without drawdown management process

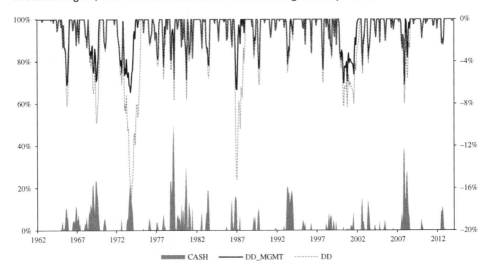

Figure 7.15   Portfolio volatility and Sharpe ratio of ARB allocation methodology after implementation of drawdown management process

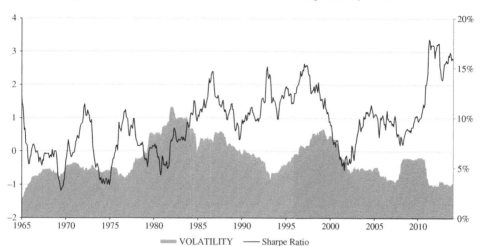

that the drawdown management has to happen at a higher frequency, in this case weekly, the test period is reduced to 50 years from 1962–2013.

While simple in its construction, this systematic allocation approach illustrates how it is possible to improve upon a static allocation approach, in a practical setting. The robustness of the solution is confirmed with its stability in different market periods and market conditions, and its drawdown characteristics seem to be better than the static allocation alternative. Finally, we note that the turnover is a limited amount, which is a constraint in any large asset pool implementation. We reiterate that an allocation approach which combines this systematic process with the previous chapter's fundamental approach is likely to have further improved characteristics due to strategy diversification.

CHAPTER EIGHT

Estimation of Asset Allocation

The business model of investment banks has historically created an army of research analysts, who pour over corporate financial statements to estimate future expected corporate earnings. This practice has led to the availability of an abundance of earnings expectations data, reflecting the investment view of various market researchers. With the availability of database technology many years ago, several companies began to collect this data and distribute it to subscribers, so that they could use the information to arrive at better investment decisions. With the knowledge of expectations of different analysts, investors benefitted from the depth and breadth of the data, and its analysis, for an improved expectation analysis. In fact, the estimation and analysis of corporate earning has developed to such an extent that the basic data is available almost for free to most investors today, and a much more detailed dataset and its analysis are now available in real time.

The investment implication of this development has been better investment decisions by investors, an increase in market efficiency as this data became widely available, and an increase in the sophistication of the analysis used to forecast asset prices.

One interesting fact, however, is that while the use of consensus earnings expectations at the corporate level is widespread in availability and use, the same data and usage do not exist at all at the allocation decision level. This seems ironic because, for asset owners, the allocation decision has arguably a greater significance than a stock selection decision.

 ## 8.1 THE CONSENSUS ASSET ALLOCATION DATASET

Similar to corporate analysts, most investment banks generally also have a strategy or allocation team which performs the analogous investment research in sectors, markets, regions, currencies and asset classes. However, unlike their corporate analyst colleagues who have converged on a single data item (corporate earnings) as the basic focus of their analysis, the output of strategists is not standardized in style and content. Some choose to be specific enough to publish model portfolios with a variety of objectives, which in effect forces them to have a view on each market segment; others choose to simply qualitatively advocate their most convincing opinions. The raw data for allocation views is therefore more disparate in structure.

This does not, however, detract from the fact that if one were able to gather the views of the industry's strategists and allocators, then one would be in possession of a dataset that to date has not been exploited for the purpose of taking comprehensive allocation decisions. In fact, one could argue that the lack of availability of this dataset could be of immense investment value to a portfolio manager or asset owner allocator, who undertakes the effort to assemble the data to help him in allocation decisions.

Furthermore, given the variety of dimensions of allocations, and the variety of methodologies that are in existence today, one could argue that the efficacy of the choice of allocation method itself could be rationalized with the use of this data. The possibilities are actually limitless.

8.2 USING CONSENSUS DATA FOR ALLOCATION DECISIONS

Similar to the use of consensus corporate earnings data, consensus asset allocation data can be used in multiple ways and in multiple dimensions. While some surveys of investors exist today, where the input is both optional and unverifiable for its accuracy, there is no structured database service which captures expectations and forecast of investment bank strategists. It seems logical to hypothesize that just as corporate analysts' earnings expectations have been useful predictors of stock prices, asset class expectations of strategists may have a similar forecasting ability. We discuss below the basic investment decisions where investment decisions can be improved through the use of consensus allocation data.

8.2.1 Basic Allocation Decisions

Strategic asset allocation decisions are generally based on long run return expectations, which change infrequently and by small amounts, thus providing little predictive information for advantage. However, tactical allocation decisions can be influenced significantly by participant short-term return expectations. This information can be useful in improving tactical allocation investment decisions.

There are five basic dimensions along which tactical allocation decision making can be improved using such a dataset. These include:

1. Global asset class allocation.
2. Equity regional allocation.
3. Equity country allocation within a region.
4. Sector allocation – within a country, region or globally.
5. Fixed income grade allocation.

Knowledge of consensus expectations of asset classes can help an investor decide his positioning relative to consensus expectations. Whether one chooses a trend or contrarian position is left to the decision maker. Figures 8.1.1–8.5 and Tables 8.1–8.5 depict an illustrative dataset to display the potential additional input such a dataset can provide to the investment decision maker.

8.2.2 Creating Tactical Allocation Changes

It is important to note the changes that happen to the consensus allocation stances over time, in every allocation decision set. This change can be a pre-cursor to how investors

Figure 8.1   Illustrative consensus data for global asset class allocation decisions

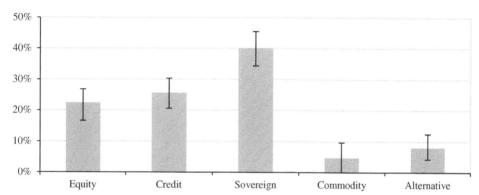

Table 8.1   Illustrative consensus data for global asset class allocation decisions

Asset Class	Consensus	High	Low
Equity	22.4%	26.8%	16.6%
Credit	25.7%	30.4%	20.6%
Sovereign	40.1%	45.5%	34.4%
Commodity	4.8%	9.7%	0.0%
Alternative	8.0%	12.4%	4.3%

Figure 8.2   Illustrative consensus data for equity regional allocation decisions

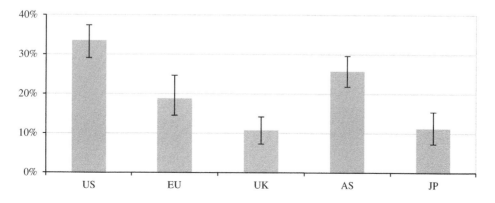

Table 8.2   Illustrative consensus data for equity regional allocation decisions

Region	Consensus	High	Low
US	32.3%	36.3%	27.5%
EU	19.0%	23.0%	13.7%
UK	11.8%	15.8%	6.9%
AS	25.7%	30.7%	20.6%
JP	11.2%	15.5%	6.9%

Figure 8.3   Illustrative consensus data for Asia equity country allocation decision

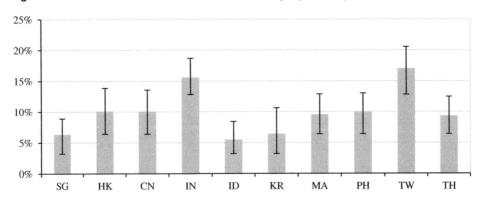

Table 8.3   Illustrative consensus data for Asia equity country allocation decision

Country	Consensus	High	Low
SG	7.2%	11.1%	2.9%
HK	10.6%	14.1%	5.8%
CN	9.1%	13.6%	5.8%
IN	14.9%	17.3%	11.7%
ID	8.1%	11.8%	2.9%
KR	7.0%	11.1%	2.9%
MA	9.4%	13.3%	5.8%
PH	8.6%	12.7%	5.8%
TW	16.1%	20.9%	11.7%
TH	9.1%	13.1%	5.8%

Figure 8.4   Illustrative consensus data for sector allocation decisions

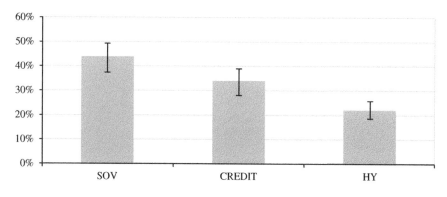

Table 8.4   Illustrative consensus data for sector allocation decisions

Sector	Consensus	High	Low
ENGR	5.5%	8.9%	2.4%
MAT	7.4%	10.3%	4.8%
IND	7.3%	9.4%	4.8%
COND	16.9%	19.0%	14.5%
CONS	4.5%	7.0%	2.4%
HEA	4.7%	7.4%	2.4%
FIN	17.0%	20.2%	14.5%
IT	16.8%	19.2%	14.5%
TEL	12.2%	15.1%	9.7%
UTL	7.5%	10.4%	4.8%

Figure 8.5   Global fixed income allocation

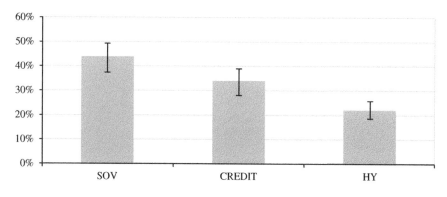

Table 8.5 Illustrative consensus data for fixed income grade allocation decisions

Fix Inc Grade	Consensus	High	Low
SOV	42.9%	47.3%	38.2%
CREDIT	32.5%	34.5%	28.7%
HY	24.6%	30.0%	19.1%

may move in the coming period. Such changes can be evaluated over multiple periods, such as one month and three months, to estimate the effectiveness of the signal. Figure 8.6 illustrates this dataset.

8.2.3 Conviction Level in Allocation Stances

Apart from the choice of which asset buckets are to be overweight or underweight, there is still the additional question of the level of activeness for each allocation silo. This

Figure 8.6 1-month change in consensus estimates and 1-month performance of various allocation categories, for use in tactical allocation decisions

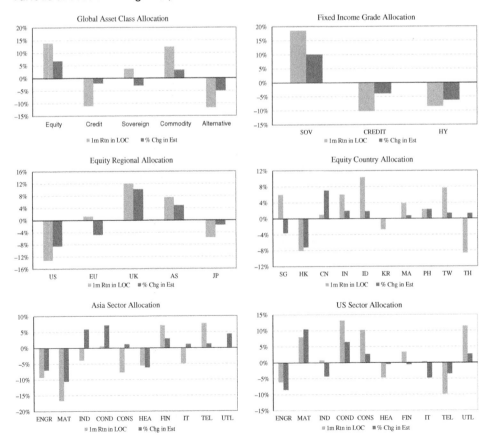

Figure 8.7 Illustrative tie-series variance of consensus estimates for use in determining active bet size in allocation decisions

determination of the level of conviction in an active stance or conversely the risk in each stance can be improved by the availability of consensus data.

Figure 8.7 illustrates the time series of the variance in estimates for various allocation decisions. A higher variance can imply greater dispersion of views for that allocation decision, leading to a greater risk. A lower variance implies greater consensus among market participants for asset returns. Again, while the data displays the view of various participants, it does not necessarily impose whether the allocation decision maker should take a higher active bet in higher dispersion decisions (where possibility of excess return by being different can be higher), or take a higher active bet on lower variance decisions (where the likelihood of being incorrect can be smaller, but also the expected excess return is likely to be lower).

8.2.4 Currency Hedge Ratio Decisions

Currency exposure decisions can be managed independently of the asset decisions for any portfolio. The decision of a hedge ratio for each currency exposure in a portfolio is

Figure 8.8 Illustrative 3-month and 12-month change in currency exchange rate consensus expectations for use in determining currency hedge ratios

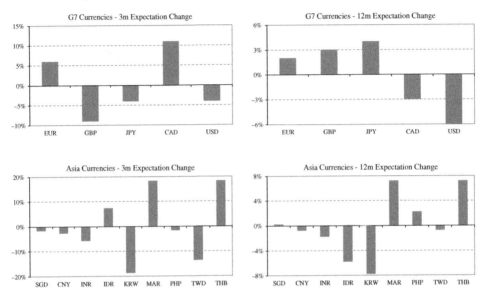

an allocation decision based on expectations of exchange rate and volatility. The use of knowledge of expectations of exchange rates by various currency forecasters can improve this decision. Figure 8.8 illustrates the consensus change in expectations of various currency exchange rates on two horizons. This is further illustrated for a G7 and an Asian currency basket. Figure 8.9 displays the overlay of the actual exchange rate over the expected exchange rate.

Figure 8.9 Illustrative actual versus consensus estimate exchange rate for a currency pair

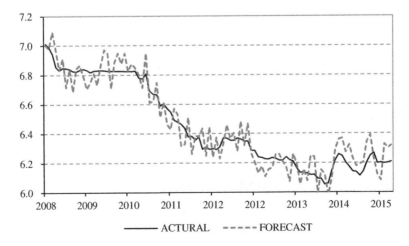

8.2.5 Separating the Poor Forecasters from the Accurate Ones

With a short history of the allocation stances of various strategists and allocators, one can track the performance of their recommendations versus what actually transpired. This can therefore lead to the conclusion of which forecasters are more accurate in their predictions, which can be used to hone the estimate for an allocator. Table 8.6 illustrates information ratios and hit ratios of various investment bank forecasters, as an illustration. These can be used to condition their future estimates to arrive at a smart consensus estimate.

8.2.6 Contrasting the Variety of Allocation Methodologies

Apart from the traditional return-based fundamental and systematic allocation investment processes that aim to forecast expected return on asset buckets, various other methodologies are often used to allocate assets. These include risk budgeting, risk parity, equal weighting and 60/40, to name a few. While the relative efficiency of each of these methods is debatable, what is clear is that they tend to work at different points of time in the market cycle. A comparison of these methodologies over the recent past would allow a researcher to compare the consensus fundamental expectations with the other methodologies to decide which methodology may be appropriate at the present time.

Figure 8.10 illustrates the advocated allocation for the equity bond allocation decision as proposed by various allocation methodologies. It further illustrates the performance of each of these allocation methodologies over time.

This analysis would be of specific use in multi-strategy allocation processes, as is proposed in Chapter 5, where there is an additional allocation decision of the level of risk or assets to be allocated to various allocation processes.

Table 8.6   Hit ratio and information ratio of estimates made by various investment bank strategists, for use in creating "smart" allocation estimates

	HR	IR	HR	IR
Investment Bank 1	33.3%	0.37	45.3%	0.45
Investment Bank 2	56.0%	0.54	76.0%	0.65
Investment Bank 3	45.5%	0.54	47.5%	0.33
Investment Bank 4	71.1%	0.68	78.1%	0.85
Investment Bank 5	60.2%	0.65	52.2%	0.69
Investment Bank 6	83.0%	0.87	88.0%	0.86
Investment Bank 7	34.4%	0.37	25.4%	0.45
Investment Bank 8	66.0%	0.70	75.0%	0.56
Investment Bank 9	23.2%	0.26	24.2%	0.31
Investment Bank 10	52.2%	0.59	38.2%	0.39

Figure 8.10 Comparison of the efficiency of 60/40, risk parity and consensus estimate allocation methodologies – (a) current advocated allocation weights, (b) 12-month rolling performance

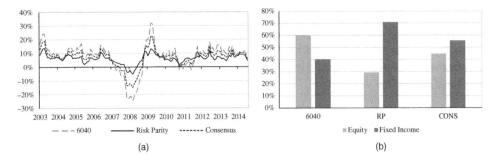

This chapter has elaborated on the use of a new dataset of allocation forecasts, made by investment bank strategists but not collated and analyzed in the same way as corporate analyst expectations. It is proposed that both as a business opportunity and as an investment opportunity, creation of such a dataset would be of value in allocation decisions.

CHAPTER NINE

Optimization for
Multi-Asset Portfolios

Mean variance methods of allocation and portfolio construction make three basic assumptions to arrive at an optimal portfolio. Firstly, they assume that asset returns are distributed normally, and hence do not build in any asymmetry. Second, they believe risk to be defined in terms of the volatility of returns. Finally, they believe that the most efficient portfolio is one that maximizes return per unit of risk and cater for only the risk aversion of the asset owner, but without any direct reference to the return requirement.

We include the behavioral aspects of an investor's risk aversion and return requirement in formulating the allocation for a multi-asset fund. We attempt to develop a portfolio construction methodology for a multi-asset fund to cater for this "real" risk and "real" return, with a minimal set of assumptions. While the developed framework is for the allocation to active strategies, the process is equally applicable to the standard allocation problem to asset classes in total return space.

 ## 9.1 EVOLUTION OF THE MEAN VARIANCE FRAMEWORK

Markowitz's mean variance framework (1952) is a single period static portfolio-planning model, which illustrates that for a utility maximizing investor, the efficient frontier specifies optimal portfolios, which maximize the expected return for a given level of risk. Hanoch and Levy (1969) have shown that with the assumption of Gaussian normal distributions, the mean variance framework is valid for any investor's utility function.

Several researchers have proposed alternative portfolio planning models, which extend the mean variance formulation with different risk parameters and utility functions. Examples of asymmetric risk measures that have been used are expected downside risk, semi-variance, worst-case scenarios and Value at Risk. Kunno (1988) used a piecewise linear approximation function in a portfolio optimization framework. Bawa (1975) and Fishburn (1977) introduced the use of lower partial moments (LPM) as a generic representation of risk within which both symmetric and asymmetric measures of risk could be encapsulated. Harlow (1991) investigates portfolio allocation in the context of downside risk.

While mean variance analysis is widely accepted, our motivation to research alternative approaches to the portfolio allocation problem arises for three main reasons:

1. **The Distributional Assumption**

    Most multi-asset funds have at their disposal a range of active products or strategies that employ a variety of investment processes in an attempt to outperform a given benchmark. These relate to underlying factors in a nontrivial way and there is rarely a reason to assume any particular shape for a strategy's active return distribution. Some strategies have return profiles that are skewed, as for example an event driven strategy thought to outperform only in the presence of certain events. Other strategies have elements of option replication, as for instance a strategy dynamically replicating a sold put. Others simply react asymmetrically to changes in the market. It is often difficult to assess these characteristics a priori and in fact this is typically with the very nature of an active strategy. While seeking to expand boundaries of market efficiency, dependencies on factors and events can be difficult to predict.

    This non-constructive view on distributions puts additional emphasis on the specification of risk measures and basic preferences. In a world with normally distributed returns, mean and variance are sufficient to describe the entire distribution of a portfolio, typically implying that a precise specification of preferences is not needed – in general, a manager prefers lower variance for a given mean. With a greater variety of distributional characteristics, however, the assumption of normality becomes too severe, and more attention to preferences is required.

2. **The Reference Return**

    All asset owners inherently begin with a target return requirement over a specified investment horizon. Typically, for a fund manager this target constitutes an exogenously given reference point against which the performance of the fund is defined. It is as such an entity of fundamental importance for the allocation process. The fund's required return determines a minimum risk that the portfolio must take to achieve this objective. Owners who announce a target that is high say that they seek a high return, but in doing so, by the nature of markets, they at the same time communicate a high tolerance to risk. Conversely, owners setting a low target communicate a preference for not wanting to take a high risk. The implication of this is that to a significant degree the target will determine the space of strategies that can be of interest to the fund manager, and furthermore, for a given set of strategies it will constitute the basic parameter determining the level of risk that the manager can be allowed to take. When formulating the optimal allocation decision of a fund manager, it is essential that the target be taken into the analysis.

3. **Multi-Dimensional Risk**

    As the basic objective of the fund is to achieve a target return at the end of the investment horizon, the greatest risk is the possibility of not being able to achieve the desired end of horizon return. In addition, we believe that within the investment horizon, while investors continuously seek the maximum available return for a given risk level, they articulate risk within the portfolio as threshold constraints, which are a function of the expected duration of the risks. We divide these risks into shocks (event risk), medium- or short-term risks (regime risk) and long-term risks (macro risk). We believe that this multi-dimensional nature of investor risk preference needs to be specifically incorporated in the allocation decision.

These three reasons make our situation notably different from that in classical portfolio allocation theory. While it can be debated whether mean-variance is a reasonable approximation for an investor of basic assets, we argue that the position for a fund manager is inherently different. There is a need to build the asset allocation framework from basic principles.

We open with our motivation to appropriate measures for evaluating portfolio performance, and develop a utility-based framework for the unconstrained allocation problem. We then start by deriving the optimal unconstrained allocation. Using this as a reference allocation, we study the impact of the constraints, select a set of constraints, and then present results for the optimal constrained portfolio. The following notation is used:

$\Omega(X;L)$	Omega of the stochastic variable X relative to the target L.
$R(X;L)$	Adjusted Sharpe ratio of the stochastic variable X relative to the target L.
$\mathrm{lpm}(X;L)$	Lower partial moment of the stochastic variable X relative to threshold L.
X	Scalar stochastic variable, typically the active return of a strategy.

9.2 PORTFOLIO ALLOCATION AND MEASURES OF PERFORMANCE

To evaluate a given allocation, we seek a performance measure that links to our notion of risk and return. We find that the Omega measure by Keating and Shadwick (2002), ties closely to our analysis. Their motivation for a new performance measure was similar to ours – the Sharpe ratio measures risk as standard deviation, while ideally a risk measure should assign higher weights to downside risks. We adopt here a formulation of Omega that differs slightly from the original.[1] For a stochastic variable X the Omega relative to the threshold L is defined as

$$\Omega(X;L) = \frac{E[X-L]}{E[\max(L-X,0)]}$$

---

[1] The definition differs from Keating and Shadwick's original by a constant term. Their definition of Omega equals the ratio $E[\max(X-L,0)]/E[\max(L-X,0)]$. It is straightforward to show that this equals $\Omega(X;L)+1$. Our notation is along the lines of Kaplan and Knowles (2004).

If X is a return, we can interpret the quantity as expected excess return per unit of risk, where excess return is return relative to the threshold L, and where risk is defined as the expected shortfall relative to the same threshold. The return X can be either the fund's total return, or the active return relative to a benchmark.

To facilitate a comparison with the classical framework, we adopt a related performance measure based on standard deviation as the unit of risk. The natural counterpart to the Omega in a mean-variance setting is the ratio

$$R(X;L) = \frac{E[X-L]}{\text{std}(X)} \tag{9.1}$$

This coincides with the Sharpe ratio in the special case that X is the total return and L is the risk free rate. If X is the active return of a strategy and $L = 0$, the measure is known as the *Information Ratio*. Because of its resemblance with the Sharpe ratio we refer to R as the *Adjusted Sharpe Ratio*.[2]

9.3 A UTILITY-BASED APPROACH

To incorporate our three motivations, we proceed to develop the analytical framework. For expositional purposes we leave out the constraints for now. We deliberately avoid making any distributional assumptions.

Basing our approach in conventional expected utility theory, we open by making a case for a utility function that is non-quadratic. The resulting expected utility makes use of the expected shortfall, which effectively takes the role of a risk measure. We then present an associated efficient frontier and illustrate how Omega is related. Finally, we discuss the optimal allocation, the manager's risk tolerance and the Omega measure.

9.4 THE FUND MANAGER'S OBJECTIVES

To a fund manager, the basic variable of interest is the fund's performance relative to the target. Without modeling explicitly underlying preferences, a simple way to incorporate the fund target is to assume a utility function with a kink at the point of the target. A typical example is given in Figure 9.1. We use the following notation:

$u(x)$ Utility function over a given outcome x.
$U(X)$ Utility function over a stochastic outcome X.
λ Parameter of risk aversion.

---

[2] The notation is non-standard. The term Adjusted Sharpe Ratio has been used to mean different things elsewhere in the literature.

The kinked shape resembles the value function frequently adopted in the behavioral literature. The location of the kink is usually referred to as the reference point. At this point the marginal utility is different for losses than for gains. One should be careful, however, of taking the analogy too far. In behavioral finance the reference point is typically an individual specific unit – it can be initial endowments or the result of an initial framing or anchoring. In the present case the reference point is an explicit number imposed on the fund manager exogenously (from the asset owners). The target does work as an anchor for the manager, but in contrast to much of work in the behavioral field, it anchors in a very material sense. Meeting the target is the fund manager's job.

As the most important aspect of this utility function is the kink, it can be motivated to assume a function that is linear on both sides of the target, implying that the utility function can be written as[3]

$$u(x) = x - L - \lambda \max(L - x, 0)$$

with L equal to the target, and $\lambda \geq 0$ a parameter measuring the sharpness of the kink. With the utility function given we can calculate the expected utility, which we assume is in the manager's interest. The utility of an active return distribution X is then

$$U(X) = E[X - L] - \lambda \mathrm{lpm}(X; L), \tag{9.2}$$

where we use the notation for the lower partial moment with respect to the threshold L

$$\mathrm{lpm}(X; L) = E[\max(L - X, 0)].$$

Figure 9.1 A kinked utility function

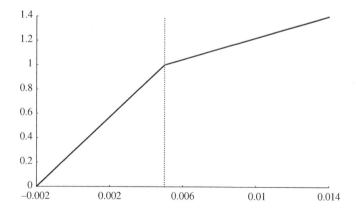

---

[3] In accordance with standard utility theory we allow for multiplication and addition of a scalar.

With this specification two measures suffice to describe the fund manager's preference of the distribution, the expected active return and the expected shortfall. The
parameter λ is the rate of substitution between the two. For the fund manager to consider
an increase in portfolio expected shortfall of Δlpm , the expected active return has to be
at least λ × Δlpm higher.

9.5 THE EFFICIENT FRONTIER

As expected active return and expected shortfall are sufficient determinants of the manager's utility, the set-up naturally lends itself to a risk–reward analysis where we take
the expected shortfall as the risk, and the expected return as the reward. In Figure 9.2
we plot the efficient frontier in the lower partial moment sense for a threshold 0.003,
corresponding to an active return of 3.6% per year.

We also depict the portfolio corresponding to the maximum Omega with respect
to the same threshold, and refer to it as *the Omega allocation*. This is the allocation that
maximizes the slope of the line originating at the level of the target on the *y*-axis, and
passing through some allocation in the opportunity set. It is clear that the maximizing
line must tangent the opportunity set. Although this resembles the CAPM capital market
line, there is a distinction in that along the line only the Omega allocation is actually
investable. The drawing of the line is merely a way to graphically represent the location
of the Omega allocation in risk–return space.

Figure 9.2   Efficient frontier with threshold equal to 0.003: expected active return on
the *y*-axis, lower partial moment on the *x*-axis

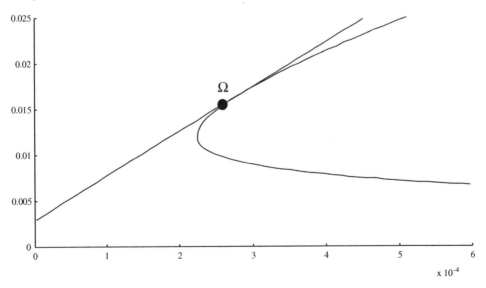

9.6 OPTIMAL PORTFOLIO CHOICE

With the utility function and the efficient frontier, we are now ready to locate the optimal allocation. Returning to the utility function (9.2), if we fix a level of expected utility U_0, it is clear that a fund manager is indifferent between any active return distributions that satisfy

$$E[X - L] = U_0 + \lambda \mathrm{pm}(X;L).$$

Mean-expected shortfall pairs that satisfy this relation define indifference curves, and we see that for a given U_0 the mean is linear in the lower partial moment with slope equal to λ. Higher levels of expected utility are associated with higher intercepts, and any two indifference curves are parallel. Figure 9.3 plots indifference curves corresponding to different values of U_0. Each panel in the figure corresponds to a different value of λ.

The figure also plots the efficient frontier of the previous section. A fund manager seeking to maximize expected utility will seek the point in the allocation opportunity set corresponding to the highest attainable indifference curve. In the figures this allocation is marked with an "x." The figures also mark the Omega allocation.

In Figure 9.3(a), λ is relatively low, meaning that the fund manager has a relatively high tolerance to risk. Compared to the Omega, the manager's choice is an allocation higher up on the frontier. Tracing the indifference curve corresponding to the x-portfolio back to the y-axis, we see that the fund manager is indifferent between the allocation x

Figure 9.3 Efficient frontiers with threshold equal to 0.003: indifference curves corresponding to different values of λ. (a) $\lambda = 35.5$ (b) $\lambda = 71$ (c) $\lambda = 47.1$ (d) $\lambda = \infty$. Other settings as in Figure 9.2

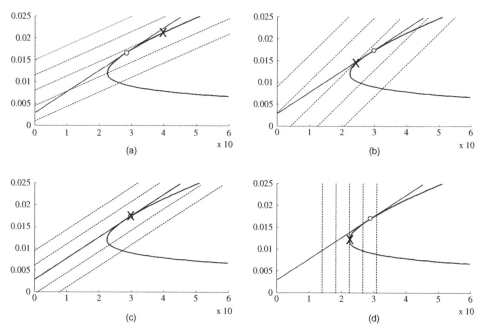

and a portfolio that generates an annual active return of 8.4% for certain, i.e., without risk. Although this is not in the opportunity set, it provides a convenient way to compare points in the risk–return space. Each allocation has a certainty equivalent in the indifference curve's intercept with the y-axis.

In Figure 9.3(b), the value of λ is higher, which means that the fund manager is more risk averse. The optimal allocation is further down on the efficient frontier and its certainty equivalent is negative, -3.6%. In Figure 9.3(c) the value of λ coincides with Omega. In this case the certainty equivalent coincides with the target.

An important special case is the limiting optimal allocation as the fund manager's risk aversion parameter λ approaches infinity. In this instance the manager will always prefer lower risk, and indifference curves are vertical. The optimal allocation is that for which risk is minimized as illustrated with the star portfolio in Figure 9.3(d). The minimum risk portfolio is sometimes known as the safety first allocation.

Depending on the manager's risk tolerance different optimal allocations obtain. Whereas one manager may argue that the safety first allocation is preferable because it minimizes the expected shortfall, another may find that the increase in expected return when moving to a point higher up on the frontier outweighs the cost of additional risk exposure. Among efficient frontier allocations – with expected return above the safety first allocation – we cannot say that one is better than the other unless we have additional information about the manager's attitude to risk.

 ## 9.7 INCORPORATING THE CONSTRAINTS

With the general framework developed we now turn to the constraints. As the constraints restrict the allocation permutations possible, they decrease the opportunity set. In particular, if constraints are binding along the efficient frontier, this is being pushed rightward in risk–reward space, saying that each level of expected active return is associated with a minimal risk level that is higher than in the unconstrained case.

We stress, however, that this narrowing of the opportunity set does not represent an impediment to the fund manager's prospects of an optimal allocation. Rather, it is the expected implication of a proper description of the manager's true opportunity set – the set of allocations that are feasible in a practical setting. An immediate example is the nonnegativity constraint on allocation weights. Active strategies are typically constructed to add value, and a fund manager would never short a strategy. In the subsections below we discuss other facets of the strategy allocation with similar reasoning.

The constraints represent our notion of a behavioral component in the allocation decision, and they should be regarded as controls that a fund manager would naturally take into consideration. Whereas in practice these usually go into a subjective decision process, we attempt here to formalize them in a manner that allows us to incorporate them in a numerical optimization. Furthermore, as part of the active manager's function is to forecast various factors, he may have specific preferences on variables, which are not directly incorporated in the active strategies. Our proposed framework caters for this facet by incorporating them in the set of constraints.

Although we emphasize the inclusion of the constraints, we refrain from formally building them into the general framework, as the exact formulation of the constraints is subject to individual preference. We believe, however, that as formulated they give a fair representation of managerial preferences that are not captured by the single-dimensional expected utility framework of the preceding section.

An alternative interpretation of the constraints follows from a strictly statistical argument. As we cannot calculate either expected returns or expected shortfalls with arbitrary precision due to limited availability of data, there is a need for stabilizing the results of the optimization. One way to do this is to impose constraints on the problem. When a constraint becomes binding, the number of free parameters in the problem effectively reduces, whereby the degrees of freedom reduces and the significance of the estimators increases. The identification of an appropriate set of constraints, that represents properties that the data is expected to satisfy, will bring additional information into the optimization.

 ## 9.8 TAIL RISK CONSTRAINT

While we believe that the primary risk that an asset owner or fund manager articulates is at the end of the investment horizon, within the horizon period there is always a threshold at which the asset owner or fund manager will lose confidence and abandon the strategy. We incorporate the fund manager's threshold for maximum intra-horizon loss as a tail risk constraint in our formulation.

In line with the idea of downside risk, we formulate tail risk in terms of expected shortfall, which we constrain to keep it below a certain level. The constraint thus takes the form

$$E[\max(L - \mathbf{w}'\mathbf{X}, 0)] \leq \gamma$$

where $\gamma > 0$ is the level of the constraint. $\mathbf{w}$ represents the vector of weights, which always sums to unity, and $\mathbf{X}$ is a vector of stochastic variables, typically active returns.

As this intends to capture the tail of the distribution, the threshold level L will in applications be set significantly higher than that used in the objective function. To save notation we do not indicate the difference here. We become precise, however, when we present the exact formulation of the problem later in the chapter.

 ## 9.9 EVENT RISK

While many practitioners and economists attempt to predict the occurrence of a stress event, we believe that most asset owners have a primary objective of protecting their portfolio, in case a stress event happens, without actually trying to predict the event itself. We use the classification proposed by the Bank for International Settlements (BIS, 2001) to categorize stress events, and propose that this is incorporated as part of investor risk behavior. These event categories are: Commodities; Credit; Emerging Markets; Equities; Exchange Rates; and Interest Rates. Those events are chosen where market prices changed at least 10% within 30 days of the event.

Constraining the loss attributable to a given event suggests a constraint of the form

$$E[\mathbf{w}'\mathbf{X}|\{event\ v\}] \geq \gamma,$$

for some constant γ. However, since these events by their very nature are rare, the expectation of them can be difficult to estimate. One event gives rise to only one observation per strategy, with obvious implications for estimation errors. This may not be too severe as long as we are dealing with major events such as the October 1987 stock market crash, but in less dramatic instances dependencies can be difficult to infer statistically. A solution in this case is to collect events into groups, so that for instance all events relating to credit form one group.

9.10 MACRO RISK

Long-term determinants of asset prices in general have a relationship with the macroeconomic climate or business cycle. Investors would like to be able to generate the target return in any macroeconomic environment. We propose to constrain the loss that would happen in their presence.

If β is a vector of strategy betas with respect to a macroeconomic variable, then the fund's beta with respect to the variable is $\mathbf{w}'\beta$. A natural formulation of the constraint is therefore

$$|\mathbf{w}'\beta| \leq \gamma$$

for some $\lambda > 0$. Note that we have taken the absolute value of the exposure as we seek to constrain the magnitude regardless of the sign.

We suggest using the following macroeconomic variables: GDP Growth; Consumer Price Index; 10-Year Bond; Term Spread; Credit Spread; and Oil Price. We do not address here the question of how the betas should be estimated. Although important, this is a nontrivial exercise that would take us away from the current focus.

9.11 REGIME RISK

Just as macro environments can dictate asset returns over a medium- or long-term horizon, style or factor returns can dictate asset returns over the short-term horizon. We refer to this phenomenon as market regimes. A regime analysis is performed to detect whether the performance of a strategy depends significantly on a prevalent market regime. An asset owner would naturally want to achieve the target return irrespective of the prevalence of any market regime, and hence the risk in this context needs to be constrained. The choice of variables for this analysis is motivated by the availability of liquid instruments to hedge exposures. We propose these to be: Market Movement; Earnings-to-Price; Book-to-Price; EPS Growth; Value-Growth; Global Market Beta; Momentum; Size; Earnings Quality; Volatility; Credit Spread; Term Structure; and Slope of Yield Curve.

We restrict our definition of a regime to two states: the factor making an up-move and the factor making a down-move. It is, of course, possible to partition the state space more finely, so that there are more than two states for each factor.

Formulating the regime risk, we impose a lower bound on the conditional Omega of the fund when in a particular regime. For a regime r, the conditional Omega is given by

$$\Omega\big(\mathbf{w}'\mathbf{X}|\{regime\ r\};L\big)=\frac{E\big[\mathbf{w}'\mathbf{X}-L|\{regime\ r\}\big]}{E\big[\max(L-\mathbf{w}'\mathbf{X},0)|\{regime\ r\}\big]}. \tag{9.3}$$

We encounter here an estimation problem. The regime comprises only a subset of the data and if we were to estimate the conditional Omega over only those periods for which we have data for all strategies simultaneously, then the number of observations could be small. To deal with this difficulty, we note that for positive weights summing to unity we have the Jensen inequality

$$\max(L-\mathbf{w}'\mathbf{X},0)\le\mathbf{w}'\max(L-\mathbf{X},0).$$

Making use of this, moving weight vectors outside the expectations in (9.3) yields

$$\Omega\big(\mathbf{w}'\mathbf{X}|\{regime\ r\};L\big)\ge\frac{\mathbf{w}'E\big[\mathbf{X}-L|\{regime\ r\}\big]}{\mathbf{w}'E\big[\max(L-\mathbf{X},0)|\{regime\ r\}\big]}. \tag{9.4}$$

Here the expectations on the right hand side can be measured for each strategy individually, and since the right hand side underestimates Omega we can formulate the regime risk constraint as

$$\frac{\mathbf{w}'E\big[\mathbf{X}-L|\{regime\ r\}\big]}{\mathbf{w}'E\big[\max(L-\mathbf{X},0)|\{regime\ r\}\big]}\ge\gamma. \tag{9.5}$$

The level of the constraint γ may differ from those used above and the level of the threshold L need not be the same.

9.12 CORRELATION RISK

The final facet of risk, which we believe is relevant for the asset owner, is correlation risk. Even though most investors realize that there is always a possibility of losing money in any non-risk free investment, in general they do not like to lose money in all their investments at the same time.

To incorporate this dimension of risk, we formulate a measure of the overall correlation in the portfolio. Denoting the correlation matrix of active returns by Γ, a natural candidate is $\mathbf{w}'\Gamma\mathbf{w}$, which is a number between zero and one for all allocation weight vectors $\mathbf{w}$. In the special case where the strategies are perfectly correlated this measure equals the upper bound one regardless of $\mathbf{w}$. For an opposite extreme, if strategies are independent, the correlation matrix equals the identity matrix. In this case, an equally weighted portfolio will take the measure toward zero as the number of strategies grows.

The overall correlation resembles the tracking error variance, which is more standard. There is a vital difference, however, in that the overall correlation disregards the strategies' individual tracking errors.

Since we want the overall correlation to be low, we form the correlation constraint according to

$$\mathbf{w}'\Gamma\mathbf{w} \leq \gamma,$$

with $\gamma > 0$ being the level of the constraint.

9.13 FORMULATION OF THE OPTIMIZATION PROBLEM

We are now ready to formulate the optimization problem for a portfolio with six assets. We have used simulated results of six strategies (P1 to P6) as assets. The equations for maximizing Omega are as follows:

Objective fn, Omega $\quad$ $\max_{w} \Omega(\mathbf{w}'\mathbf{X}, L)$

subject to

Tail risk $\quad$ $E\left[\max\left(L_T - \mathbf{w}'\mathbf{X}, 0\right)\right] \leq \gamma_T$,

Event risk $\quad$ $E\left[\mathbf{w}'\mathbf{X}\,\middle|\,\{event\ v\}\right] \leq \gamma_{V,v}$ $\quad\quad$ all events v,

Macro risk $\quad$ $\left|\mathbf{w}'\beta_{M,m}\right| \leq \gamma_{M,m}$, $\quad\quad$ all variables m,

Regime risk $\quad$ $\Omega\left[\max\left(L_R - \mathbf{w}'\mathbf{X}, 0\right)\middle|\{regime\ r\}\right] \geq \gamma_{R,r}$ $\quad$ all regimes r,

Correlation risk $\quad$ $\mathbf{w}'\Gamma\mathbf{w} \leq \gamma_C$,

Weight bounds $\quad$ $\mathbf{w}^L \leq \mathbf{w} \leq \mathbf{w}^U$

For the computation of the measures involved we use the sample counterparts. In case of the regime risk, the Omega is the sample counterpart of the measure in equation (9.3). In the last constraint, the vectors $\mathbf{w}^L$ and $\mathbf{w}^U$ represent minimal and maximal allocation weights. When we subsequently refer to the unconstrained optimization problem, we always include the weight bounds constraint with a lower bound of 5% and an upper bound of 40% for each strategy.

When calculating expected shortfall frontiers we replace the objective function with

Objective function, LPM $\min_w E\big[\max(L - \mathbf{w}'\mathbf{X}, 0)\big]$

and we add the constraint

Expected value $E\big[\mathbf{w}'\mathbf{X} - L\big] = \mu,$

where μ is the expected active return in excess of the target.

Applying this framework in an unconstrained problem provides us with the Omega allocation as a reference. We can then take the reference allocation and study the impact of the constraints and, selecting one set of constraints, examine the constrained problem.

The multi-strategy framework in our empirical analysis holds six active strategies,[4] each of which is based on a specific philosophy.

 ## 9.14 THE UNCONSTRAINED ALLOCATION

As an initial point of reference we start with the unconstrained problem. For the calculations we use $L = 0.0015$ corresponding to an alpha target of 0.15% per month or approximately 1.8% per year. The choice is motivated by the nature of the data – it is a level of L that allows us to illustrate how the framework may be applied.

To highlight the characteristics of expected shortfall in relation to variance, we compare optimization results with the mean-variance framework. We begin with the Omega and the Adjusted Sharpe (Equation (9.1)) optimal allocations, and then move on with the corresponding efficient frontiers. As the optimizations are performed using historical data, the optimal Omega and the optimal Adjusted Sharpe are both associated with historical time series of active returns for the total fund. The corresponding empirical active return distributions are given in Figure 9.4. While the general shape of the distributions is similar, there are differences worth noting.

Figure 9.4 Fund active return distributions in the unconstrained Omega and MV frameworks

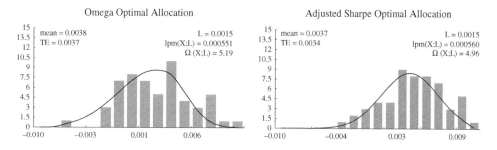

---

[4] With active strategy we refer to a strategy run against a benchmark.

In spite of the higher standard deviation, the optimal Omega allocation exhibits a lower value for the expected shortfall, while the mean is higher. This illustrates our main point. Using expected shortfall as a risk measure constrains the downside while relaxing constraints on the upside. Allowing for a higher variation on the upside opens for a higher mean.

Turning to the efficient frontiers, we are interested in both the expected shortfall frontier, and the variance frontier. The former is plotted in Figure 9.5(a). In the figure are also the expected shortfalls corresponding to the variance efficient allocations. By construction, in expected shortfall space these are located to the right of the expected shortfall frontier.

In Figure 9.5(a) the solid straight line locates the Omega allocation at the tangency with the expected shortfall frontier, marked with an "o." At this level of mean active return, 4.6% per year, the lower partial moments of the two frontiers are 0.055% and 0.059% respectively. The adjusted Sharpe optimal allocation is marked with an "x." It obtains at a yearly mean active return of 4.4% and expected shortfall of 0.056%. The minimal possible expected shortfall for the same expected active return is 0.053%.

The mirror image of Figure 9.5(a) is Figure 9.5(b), which depicts the efficient allocations in mean-variance space, although the figure gives the x-axis in terms of standard deviation. The two frontiers of the previous figure have now switched places – the variance frontier is located to the left, which simply says that expected shortfall efficient allocations need not be variance efficient.

The Adjusted Sharpe optimal allocation obtains at the tangency of the line with the variance frontier, marked with an "x." The mean active return is 0.37%, corresponding to frontier yearly standard deviations of 1.19% and 1.23%, respectively. The Omega allocation is marked with an "o." Its mean active return, 4.6%, corresponds to a standard deviation of 1.30%, which is just slightly higher than the variance frontier's 1.28%.

Figure 9.5 Optimal Omega portfolio(o): (a) depicts the frontiers with lower partial moment for monthly returns along the x-axis, (b) with the standard deviation along the x-axis

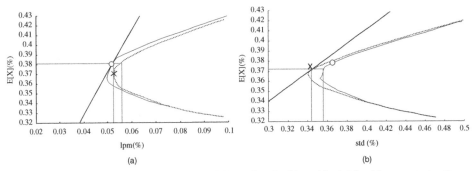

(a)   (b)

Notes: Expected shortfall frontier (solid line), Variance frontier (dotted line). Monthly expected active return in percent along y-axis.

Figure 9.6 plots strategy allocation weights for the two frontiers. The difference between expected shortfall and variance lies primarily with the allocations to strategies P1, P4 and P5, where Strategy P1 has a higher preference under expected shortfall.

9.15 APPLYING THE CONSTRAINTS

With the unconstrained Omega as reference allocation we are now ready to investigate the impact of the constraints. We go through each constraint type separately, and within each type we vary only one variable at the time, always using the unconstrained allocation as reference.

The variables are:

γ_T Tail risk constraint level, with a tail risk threshold of L_T.

$\gamma_{V,v}$ Event risk constraint level.

$\gamma_{M,m}$ Macro risk constraint level, with β_m as the vector of strategy betas with respect to the macroeconomic variable m.

$\gamma_{R,r}$ Regime risk constraint level, with a regime risk threshold of L_R

γ_C Correlation risk constraint level, Γ as the correlation matrix of active returns.

L Threshold used in the objective function, with w^L and w^U being the vector of lower bounds and upper bounds on weights.

The following constraints are applied in turn:

a. Tail Risk Constraint

As tail risk refers to a loss of some magnitude, we find it justifiable to set the threshold level significantly higher in magnitude than what is used in the objective function. For our application we use $L_T = -0.0065$. Although individual strategies have losses that exceed 0.0065, for the unconstrained allocation the maximal drawdown is 0.0053, so the measure of the tail risk is always zero. The optimal allocation is therefore unaffected by changes in the level of the constraint (Figure 9.6).

While this means that we cannot investigate the sensitivity with respect to the constraint, it does not mean that we can disregard the constraint. If other constraints are taken into account, different allocations obtain, and these could potentially be in violation of the tail constraint. Further, the availability of this constraint enables the asset owner to specify a maximum loss threshold that he is not willing to violate, which is of fundamental importance.

b. Event Risk Constraint

Figure 9.7 depicts the loss in Omega, with the tightening of the event risk constraint. The x-axis measures the level of the constraint. As the constraint becomes successively more binding, Omega deteriorates. A first point to notice is that the highest sensitivity is with respect to equities, which appears plausible, as the fund under study is an equity fund. Credit and Emerging Market events are also important, while events with less immediate relation to equities have less impact.

Figure 9.6 Strategy allocation weights

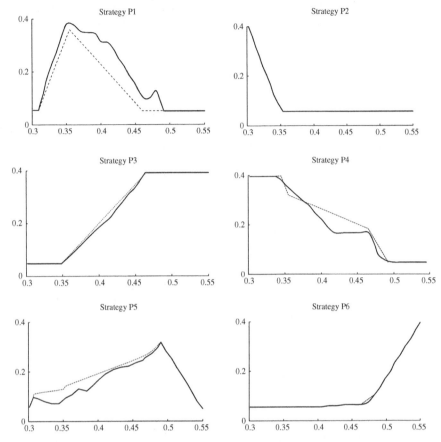

Notes: Expected shortfall efficient weights (solid line). Variance efficient weights (dotted line). The *x*-axis measures expected active return per month in percent, the *y*-axis the allocation weight.

Figure 9.7 Impact on fund Omega of tightening the event risk constraint by category

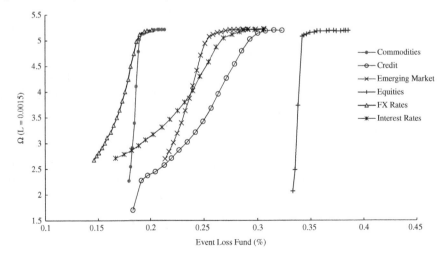

Second, we see that the fall in Omega can proceed with different speeds as the constraint is tightened. If a strategy with importance for the total Omega of the fund is associated with a particular type of event risk, then the Omega will fall more quickly as the allocation to this strategy is reduced.

For each event, there is a bound to how tight the constraint can be set while still yielding a feasible allocation. As we approach this bound, we move towards the allocation with 40% in each of the two strategies with the least exposures to the event, with the remaining 20% split between the remaining strategies. Allocation weight graphs are shown in Figure 9.8 for each event.

Figure 9.8 Sensitivity of optimal portfolio weights to the six event risk constraints

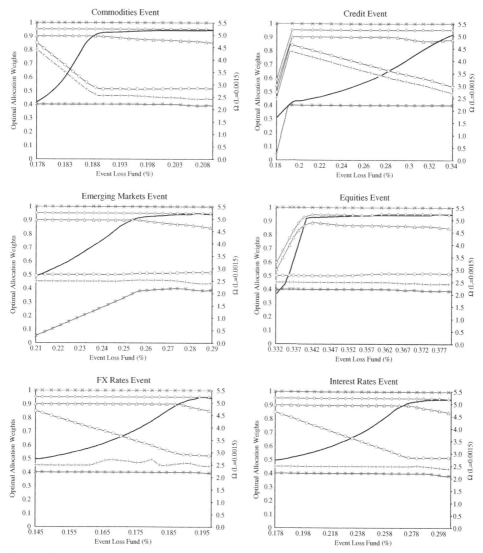

Notes: Allocation weights of the strategies cumulative (sum to one), thin lines with markers, left axis. Omega thick solid, right axis.

It is noteworthy that the event risk measure is negative for all of the strategies and all of the events. If event risk is priced in the market, this suggests that the strategies extract the associated risk premium. Furthermore, this comes in spite of a less than perfect correlation between the strategies. Although not formally tested, it supports the view that the constraint does indeed bring additional information into the problem.

c. **Macro Risk Constraint**

The decline in Omega with successive tightening of the constraint for each macroeconomic variable is depicted in Figure 9.9. Because we are interested in the absolute value of the fund's beta, the *x*-axis measures only non-negative values, even though the corresponding beta may be negative.

The greatest sensitivities are found for interest rates and credit spreads, each of which is associated with a negative beta, suggesting that overall the strategies take on both a term premium and a credit premium (Figure 9.10). The third most important is inflation, whose beta is positive. When inflation is high, strategies tend to perform better. The placement of the lines is worth noting. Each line is plotted over the range of minimal feasible beta to unconstrained beta in absolute terms. For a given macroeconomic variable, the betas of the strategies tend to be similar in both magnitude and sign. Also, the sign is in accordance with the market price of risk for the underlying variable. Again, although not formally tested, it supports the view that the constraints bring additional information into the problem.

Figure 9.9   Impact on fund Omega of tightening the macro risk constraints

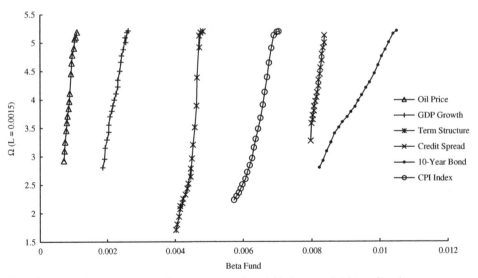

Note: For comparison purposes each macroeconomic variable is normalized to unit variance.

Figure 9.10 Sensitivity of optimal portfolio weights to the six macro risk constraints

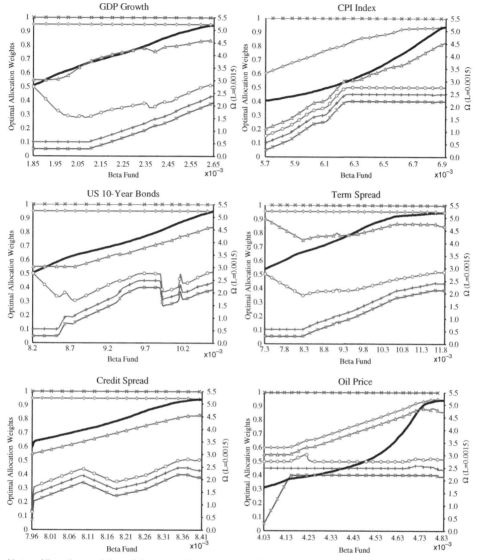

Notes: Allocation weights of the strategies cumulative (sum to one), thin lines with markers, left axis. Omega thick solid, right axis.

d. Regime Risk Constraint

For regime risk analysis, numerous variables can be potentially investigated. For the constraints analysis we have selected Volatility, Value minus Growth and Market Movement. The choice is motivated by fund manager preference, and by the generation of significant differences in conditional Omega between the two regimes (Figure 9.11).

Figure 9.11 Impact on fund Omega of tightening the regime risk constraints

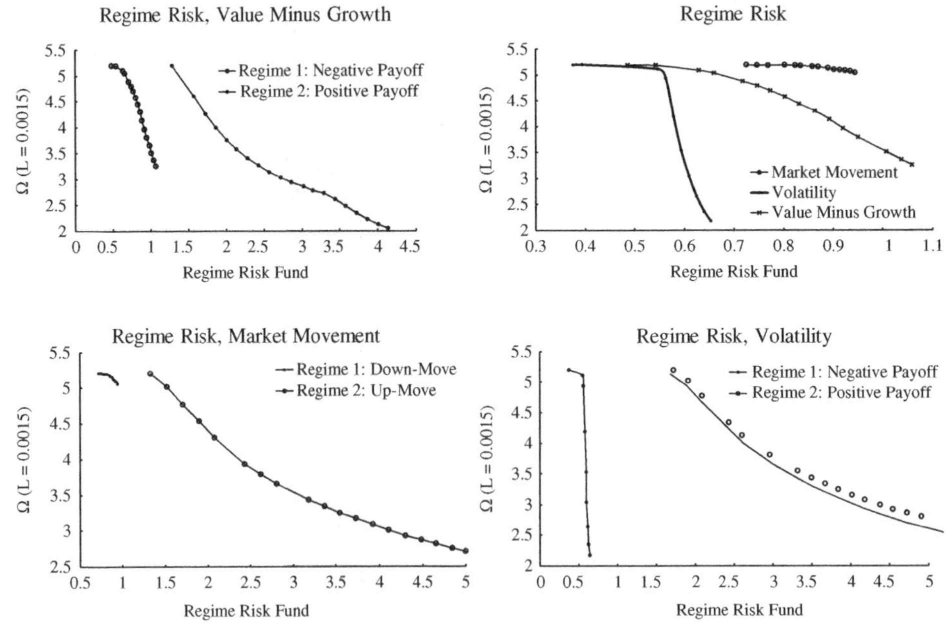

For a given variable and a given regime, the constraint is a lower bound on the conditional Omega in the sense of the measure in equation (9.5). Results in terms of optimal fund Omega are depicted in Figure 9.9 with the x-axis measuring the level of the lower bound. For each line in the figure the constraint varies between the conditional Omega of the unconstrained allocation, forming the lower bound, and the maximal feasible conditional Omega, forming the upper bound. Adherent allocation weight graphs are shown in Figure 9.12.

For each variable, at the unconstrained allocation there are two Omegas, corresponding to the two regimes. Even though these together cover the complete set of observations, the conditional Omegas are generally both lower than the unconstrained. For example, in the case of market movement the conditional Omegas are 0.55 and 1.56 respectively; significantly lower than the unconditional 5.24. This is primarily due to the use of the inequality (9.4), by which there is a tendency to underestimate the true conditional Omega.

e. Correlation Risk Constraint

The correlation risk constraint does not cause unexpected changes in the allocation. The allocation moves first into the direction of the optimal allocation obtained in the MV framework. Figure 9.13 shows that after an upper bound of approximately 0.245 much steeper changes follow in Omega, because the allocation is getting close to the minimum correlation portfolio. How the corresponding portfolio weights change during this trade off can be found in Figure 9.14.

Figure 9.12 Sensitivity of optimal portfolio weights to the regime risk constraints

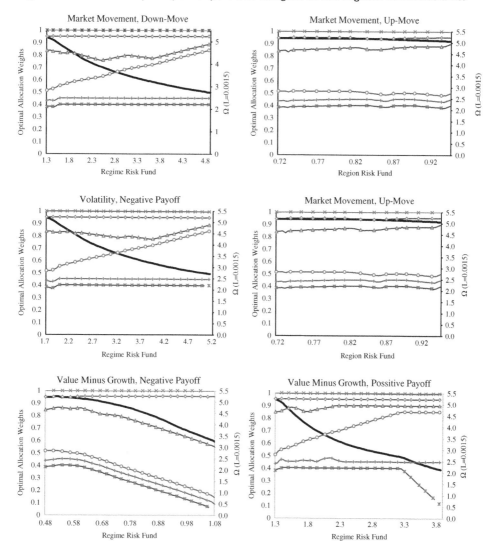

Notes: Allocation weights of the strategies cumulative (sum to one), thin lines with markers, left axis. Omega thick solid, right axis.

9.16 THE PREFERRED PORTFOLIO

In order to construct a preferred allocation, taking all of the above constraints into consideration, a practical approach is to create a final allocation that does not diverge in any particular dimension of risk. However, a difficulty is that as formulated, the constraints are non-standard, which makes it difficult to form a prior on what is a reasonable level of constriction. Investigating the marginal impact on the efficient frontier as

Figure 9.13 Impact on fund Omega of tightening the correlation risk constraints

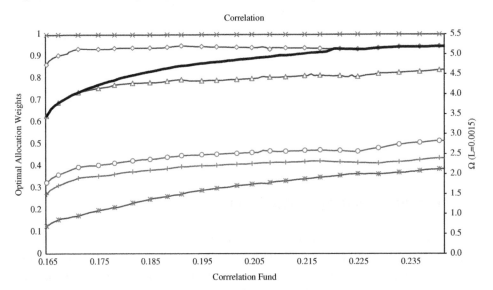

the constraint is made successively more binding, helps in finding an appropriate set of constraint levels.

We restrict the analysis here to three types of risk: event, macro, and regime risk. The tail risk remains zero for all relevant portfolios and the correlation risk reduces as the other constraints are tightened. Also, for each constraint type we select one constraint level to be the same for all the partial constraints, so that for example all event risks are set to be below one and the same value of $\gamma_{V,v}$.

Figure 9.14 Sensitivity of optimal portfolio weights to the correlation risk constraint

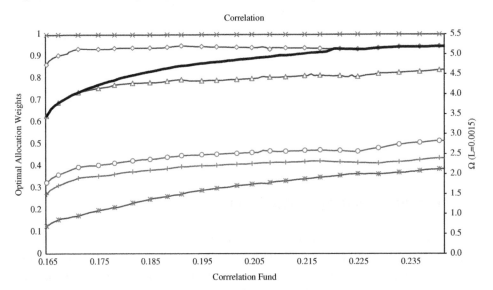

Notes: Allocation weights of the strategies cumulative (sum to one), thin lines with markers, left axis. Omega thick solid, right axis.

Figure 9.15 depicts sequences of constrained efficient frontiers, corresponding to the event, macro and regime risks respectively. For event risk, Figure 9.15(a), the frontier is primarily compressed from the upside and the downside as the constraint is tightened. The lowest attainable mean active return increases, so that for $\gamma_V = 0.35$ the minimal expected active return equals 4.4% per year.

In Figure 9.15(b) the macro risk constraint is made binding. This time the frontier is compressed from the southwest. The impact of the regime constraint, in Figure 9.15(c), is similar to that of the event constraint. The frontier shrinks from above and below.

The difference in impact between event risk and macro risk can be found with Strategies P3 and P5. While these have the smallest sensitivities to changes in the US 10-year bond yield, they are also the ones with the greatest sensitivities to equity event risk. This implies that when the event and macro constraints are made tighter, portfolio allocations move in opposite directions.

Comparing the event and regime risk constraints, a similar story is revealed when we look at Strategies P4 and P6. These have the highest conditional Omegas in the high volatility regime, implying they are valuable for keeping the conditional Omega high. At the same time, they have relatively high betas with respect to the US 10-year bond yield.

Figure 9.15 Expected shortfall frontiers as constraints are made more binding; Numbers in graphs indicate constraint limits: (a) Event risk constraint, (b) Macro risk constraint, (c) Regime risk constraint

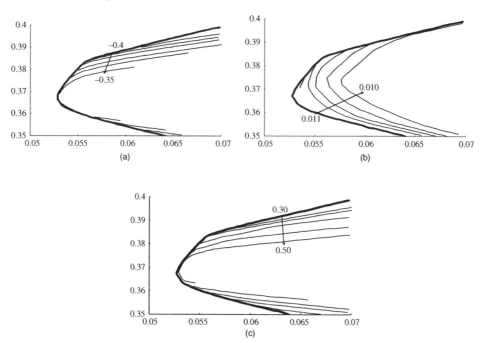

Notes: Unconstrained frontier (thick solid). Constrained frontiers (thin solid).

Table 9.1   Constraint settings for constrained optimization

γ_T	$\gamma_{V,v}$	$\gamma_{M,m}$	$\gamma_{R,r}$	γ_C
not binding	−0.38	0.01046	0.46	not binding

Figure 9.16   Historical distributions of (a) active returns of the total fund in the preferred portfolio and (b) the unconstrained Omega

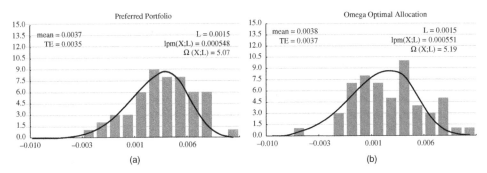

(a)   (b)

Therefore, as event and regime constraints are tightened, portfolio allocations tend to move in opposite directions.

Taking all the constraints into consideration, we find it justified to set the monthly mean active return between 4.4 and 4.6%. With a certain degree of subjectivity, we arrive at constraints as given in Table 9.1.

Maximizing Omega subject to these constraints defines our preferred portfolio. The associated time series of portfolio active returns has an empirical distribution as given in Figure 9.16(a). Its unconstrained counterpart from Figure 9.4 is repeated in Figure 9.16(b). The distributions have approximately the same lower partial moment, but the constrained allocation's expected active return is lower. The figure does not however give the active return distributions along the other dimensions of risk.

Concluding the analysis, we finally revisit the efficient frontier. Figure 9.17 locates the preferred portfolio in relation to the unconstrained expected shortfall and unconstrained variance frontiers. The preferred portfolio lies between the two.

 9.17 CONCLUSIONS

Conventional methods of asset allocation employ a mean variance framework for allocating assets across asset classes. As it is reasonable to assume a symmetrical normal distribution of returns, the methods aim to achieve an optimal portfolio in a risk–reward framework, which can also be related to conventional utility theory.

Figure 9.17 Similar to Figure 9.3(a) except that the preferred portfolio is marked with a solid dot

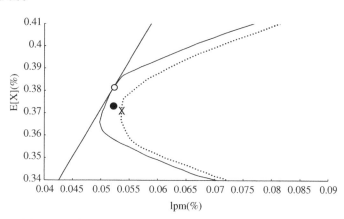

Notes: Lower partial moment for the monthly returns in percent along the *x*-axis and monthly expected active return in percent along the *y*-axis

However, in the context of multiple active strategies such as multi-asset funds, the above assumptions become too severe. Three main differences arise in this context. First, it is the basic intention of active strategies to achieve positively skewed return distributions, which therefore cannot be assumed to be normal. Second, there is a very specific target return requirement, which needs to be accounted for in the selection and allocation to strategies. Finally, one of the basic objectives of a multi-strategy architecture is to achieve strategy diversification, and hence have the capability to achieve excess return in any macro environment, any market environment and be relatively insulated during stress events. We believe this needs to be specifically incorporated in a strategy allocation process. Here we propose a methodology for allocation in a multi-asset framework, which incorporates all the above facets into a unified allocation methodology.

We demonstrate that in an unconstrained setting, an Omega optimal allocation to strategies results in a portfolio with a higher Omega and a higher mean return than an allocation based upon conventional optimal Sharpe allocation. While taking into account all moments of the strategy return distribution, the allocation also specifically accounts for the fund manager's return target. Further, by applying constraints that are meaningful in a practical setting, we illustrate how to obtain a preferred allocation, which accounts for this real risk. We believe that the resulting preferred allocation more accurately reflects the preferences of an asset owner whose objective is to maximize his probability of obtaining a target return while seeking to minimize downside risk and risk from macro and regime factors and stress events.

While we have demonstrated the application of the methodology in a multi-strategy equity fund, the framework is applicable, and perhaps more relevant in a situation where the constituent strategies are more disparate in nature. A second application of the framework is also feasible at the level of allocation to asset classes.

Two extensions of this framework can be considered. As the allocation process is an active decision, if the fund manager has the ability to forecast any of the macro, regime or stress variables, he will be able to incorporate these specifically in the allocation process. Secondly, if the above framework were applied in total return space, including both active and passive strategies across asset classes, the resulting solution could have possibilities for the debate surrounding the formulation of a policy portfolio for asset owners, and that of active vs. passive strategies.

CHAPTER TEN

Managing Tail Risk in Multi-Asset Portfolios

O
ne of the most prominent problems in multi-asset portfolio management is the management of tail risk, which arises at each step in the investment process. This chapter tackles the tail risk that can arise when allocating assets or risk into buckets, and while selecting securities within each investment strategy.

Conventional literature often uses the end-of-horizon asset return distribution to measure tail risk. In practice, however, the governance structure of all asset owners and asset managers forces the review of performance periodically within the investment horizon. Thus, we propose that tail risk should not be measured using only an end-of-horizon estimation but should be a composite of two drawdown risks:

- *End-of-horizon risk* – the probability of the target returns not being met at the end of the investment horizon.
- *Intra-horizon risk* – the probability of breaching a given maximum drawdown threshold at any time within the investment horizon.

Using such a composite represents portfolio risk more accurately and is more likely to lead to a portfolio that does not suffer unexpected outcomes, as compared with using only an end-of-horizon risk estimation.

We first discuss the basic practical setting of how assets are managed. With this as motivation we propose a new risk measure, which we believe captures the true risk in managing portfolios, incorporating both end-of-horizon and intra-horizon risk. We then present an extension of the standard model, where it is assumed that the mean return is not known with certainty. Although this has an aspect of uncertainty, partnered with a long and extensive history in the literature, its implications for risk in a dynamic context appear to be limited. Finally, we study the related subject of stop losses and how they can be used to improve performance when model parameters are not known with certainty.

10.1 PORTFOLIO MANAGEMENT – THE PRACTICAL SETTING

Consider the case of an active equity portfolio manager investing in securities of, say, the S&P 500 index, with the objective of beating the stock benchmark. In order to achieve this aim, he uses his judgment combined with various fundamental or quantitative techniques to arrive at those stocks which he believes are likely to have a higher target price after a certain time period. He constructs a portfolio of these stocks, with the aim of achieving his target return objective for the fund, while seeking never to have a large enough loss at any time, where his client (the asset owner) would lose faith in the investment process and withdraw the assets.

In essence, two external parameters are given to the portfolio manager – a return target and a maximum drawdown threshold that the client is prepared to tolerate, the breaching of which would impose a stop-loss decision. The risk that the portfolio manager takes is that the stop-loss is breached intra-horizon or that the return target is not met at the end of the horizon.

Parameters inherent in the setting are the stock universe and the long-term Sharpe ratio of the manager.

The controls which are in the hands of the portfolio manager are the number of stocks he selects in the portfolio, their volatilities and correlations, and the investment horizon over which the manager makes a price forecast for each stock.

Conceptually, uncertainty in all of these controls as well as the inherent parameters represents sources of risk in the final portfolio. While this is a very standard situation in asset management, in practice portfolio managers seldom use the investment horizon as a parameter, nor do they specifically incorporate the management of intra-horizon risk in their portfolio management process.

10.2 ASSET ALLOCATION – THE PRACTICAL SETTING

The setting for the asset allocation decision is similar to that for the security selection decision, where the assets are asset classes rather than individual securities. Here again, a return target is usually specified along with an intra-horizon drawdown threshold. However, when constructing the allocation these constraints are often not fully incorporated. Instead, a common approach is to make an assessment of what long-run Sharpe ratio is attainable using the main asset classes. The risk exposure is then calibrated to align the portfolio's expected return with the specified target return. This is an approach which completely ignores intra-horizon risk. The portfolio might achieve its target return in expectation, but does so at a certain risk of breaching the intra-horizon drawdown threshold. In case this occurs, the portfolio is terminated with the immediate consequence that the return target is not achieved. If intra-horizon risk was incorporated into the initial allocation decision, it could lead to a different allocation where termination may be avoided. In fact, a more appropriate allocation design could be to ask what expected return is feasible subject to a constraint that the probability of breach does not exceed some pre-specified value.

We therefore seek to develop a model which incorporates both end-of-horizon and intra-horizon risk, and where we are able to define the control parameters to meet the requirements of the asset owner. Specifically, given a target return and a maximal loss acceptance intra-horizon for both the asset allocation and stock selection decision, we seek to decide:

1. The investment horizon that would be permissible in each of the investment decisions.
2. The skill level required by the portfolio manager or asset allocator, which would enable him to meet the target return without breaching the intra-horizon threshold.
3. The stop-loss policy which would be consistent with the investment process being deployed.
4. The relative skill in different segments of the portfolio (or portfolio managers), given that the stock universes are different.

Another factor which is a determinant of tail risk is the amount of leverage used. We assume, however, an unleveraged portfolio, and further assume that the manager responsible for investment decisions has positive skill, though this can vary over time. Finally, tail risk can also be a function of an exogenous shock, creating event risk. The management of this risk in portfolios is discussed in Chapter 9 and we omit this also from our discussion here.

As a starting point, we first define a risk measure, which incorporates both intra and end-of-horizon risk.

10.3 CREATING A REAL RISK MEASURE: END-OF-HORIZON VS. INTRA-HORIZON RISK

In either of our previously defined settings, a straightforward definition of risk is the probability that either condition is violated, which effectively comes to formulate risk as a function of two variables, end-of-horizon performance and intra-horizon loss.

Setting our focus on these two sources of risk, we introduce the two variables X_t and Y_t defined as

$$X_t = \log(P_t / P_0), \; Y_t = \min_{0 \leq s \leq t} \log(P_s / P_0), \tag{10.1}$$

where P_t is the value of the portfolio at time t. Here X_t is simply a normalization of the portfolio, where expressing it as the logarithm of the portfolio somewhat simplifies the exposition. The variable Y_t represents our notion of intra-horizon loss – the minimal value that X_t assumes intra-horizon. With regards to intra-horizon risk we thus focus on loss since inception. While the literature on intra-horizon risk pays significant attention to peak to trough maximum drawdown and variants thereof, in our setting we believe loss since inception is more relevant.

With the two risk variables developed, Definition 10.1 gives a formal definition of the risk measure. Note that this makes no use of volatility. Volatility is a means by which risk can be controlled, and often the investment manager is also subjected to a constraint that volatility does not exceed a certain level. However, the risk that is under the investment manager's responsibility is that of breaching the intra-horizon or end-of-horizon threshold.

Definition 10.1

For a portfolio P_t and an investment horizon $0 \le t \le T$, let X_t and Y_t be as in (10.1). Also, let x be the end-of-horizon target return and let y be the intra-horizon drawdown threshold, both expressed with reference to the logarithm of P_t / P_0. The *tail risk* of P_t is denoted ψ and is given by

$$\psi(x, y) = \mathbb{P}(X_T \le x \text{ or } Y_T \le y).$$

A convenient representation of ψ is obtained by breaking it up into two components corresponding to intra-horizon and end-of-horizon risk. Intra-horizon risk is the probability of breaching y at some point before T regardless of end-of-horizon performance, and it is given by $\psi(y, y)$. End-of-horizon risk is the risk of being below x at the end of the horizon while not breaching y at any point prior to that. This results in a decomposition of the risk measure according to

$$\psi(x, y) = \psi_{IH}(y) + \psi_{EH}(x, y), \tag{10.2}$$

where

$$\psi_{IH}(y) = \psi(y, y), \ \psi_{EH}(x, y) = \psi(x, y) - \psi(y, y).$$

In the special case that only intra-horizon risk matters, (10.2) can be applied with $x = y$ since this ensures $\psi_{EH} = 0$. In the opposite extreme case that risk is only a function of end-of horizon performance, (10.2) can be applied letting $y \to -\infty$. The risk decomposition is illustrated in Figure 10.1, where the straight dotted line represents the portfolio's target performance. The solid line portfolio path exemplifies an intra-horizon breach, while the circled line is an example of end-of-horizon shortfall.

Figure 10.1 Illustration of the risk decomposition in intra-horizon and end-of-horizon risk

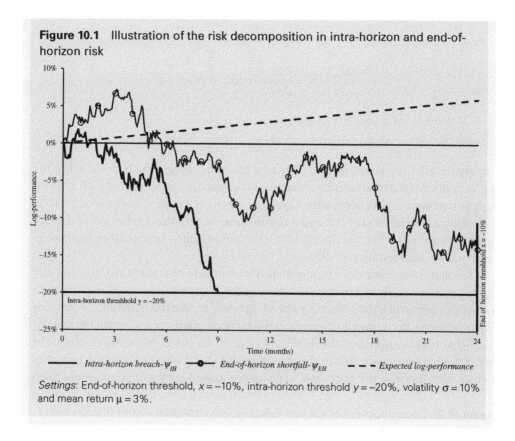

Settings: End-of-horizon threshold, $x = -10\%$, intra-horizon threshold $y = -20\%$, volatility $\sigma = 10\%$ and mean return $\mu = 3\%$.

To examine how ψ behaves under standard assumptions about asset prices we derive explicitly a formula in the case that the portfolio follows a geometric Brownian motion with drift. Suppose therefore that the portfolio evolves according to

$$dP_t = \mu P_t dt + \sigma P_t dW_t, \tag{10.3}$$

with the initial portfolio value $P_0 = 1$. Here W_t is a standard Brownian motion starting at zero, the drift term μ is the annualized expected return over the investment horizon and σ the annualized volatility.

Theorem 10.1

Suppose that the portfolio P_t evolves according to (10.3). Fix an investment horizon $0 \leq t \leq T$ and let X_t and Y_t be as in (10.1). Then, for any x, y with $y \leq 0$ and $x \geq y$ the tail risk ψ is given by

$$\psi\,(x,\,y) = \mathcal{N}\,(d_1) + \exp\left(\frac{2y\mu_{\log}}{\sigma^2}\right)\mathcal{N}\,(d_2),$$

where

$$d_1 = \frac{x - \mu_{log}T}{\sqrt{\sigma^2 T}}, d_2 = \frac{2y}{\sqrt{\sigma^2 T}} - d_1, \mu_{log} = \mu - \sigma^2 / 2$$

and $\mathcal{N}$ denotes the standard normal distribution function.

Figure 10.2 gives an example of ψ as a function of the time horizon using the decomposition (10.2). Parameters are selected to exemplify a pension fund with a 60/40 equity-fixed income allocation, which typically results in a total volatility around 10%. Assuming a Sharpe ratio of 0.3 and a risk free rate of zero this implies a μ of 3%. We investigate an end-of-horizon threshold of −10% and an intra-horizon drawdown tolerance of 20%, thus setting $y = -20\%$.

The figure demonstrates a hump-shaped form for end-of-horizon risk ψ_{EH}. Initially the risk goes up simply as a result of volatility in the asset price process. However, due to a positive mean return the probability of ending below a given threshold diminishes over longer horizons. In contrast, intra-horizon risk increases monotonically with the time. At the 5-year horizon, although the fund shows a mere 3% risk of being below −10%, the risk of having breached −20% in the meantime is 21%.[1] As the time horizon increases further, intra-horizon risk continues to go up and end-of-horizon risk continues to go

Figure 10.2 Decomposition of the risk function into intra- and end-of-horizon risk

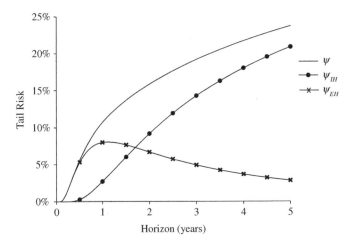

Settings: End-of-horizon threshold, $x = -10\%$, intra-horizon threshold $y = -20\%$, volatility $\sigma = 10\%$ and mean return $\mu = 3\%$

---

[1] Note that the 3% probability of being below −10% is while not having touched the intra-horizon threshold in the meantime. At the 5-year horizon the probability of being below −10% regardless of intra-horizon drawdowns is 16%, thus making the difference less striking but still significant. Note also that the difference accentuates for higher T.

down. In the current example total risk ψ levels out at around 37%, all resulting from intra-horizon risk.

The importance of intra-horizon risk addresses the issue of the investment horizon that would be permissible for investment decisions. In the presence of a tangible maximum intra-horizon drawdown threshold, it is not in the interest of the asset owner to have a long-term investment horizon, as such a stance would inordinately increase the probability intra-horizon of breaching a tolerable threshold, thus leading to closure or demise. This is in sharp contrast to the currently accepted practice followed at most pension plans and sovereign wealth funds, where a long-term investment horizon is standard procedure.

10.4 MODEL UNCERTAINTY

In a practical scenario, while an asset manager makes an assessment of the assets' expected returns and constructs an allocation or portfolio to maximize the portfolio expected return subject to certain constraints, the manager acknowledges the possibility that the assessments about the expected returns may be wrong. We therefore investigate an extension of the standard model incorporating this facet, which we find has important consequences for the risk measure that we have developed.

Parameter uncertainty is of course only one of the possible extensions of the model (10.3) which has implications for intra-horizon risk. Other directions which have been investigated in the literature include non-normal return distributions, event risk, time-varying volatility, and autocorrelation in returns. These are all extensions with implications for the tail risk. Our choice to investigate uncertainty about the mean return is not to discount the relevance of other factors, but it is something which we find has some important consequences.

Keeping the assumption that the portfolio is governed by (10.3), we assume that the drift term μ is a drawn from a distribution of drift terms which is normal according to

$$\mu \sim \mathcal{N}(\bar{\mu}, v^2). \tag{10.4}$$

Here $\bar{\mu}$ represents the manager's expectation of the portfolio return, while the presence of other possible return drivers contributes with a standard deviation v about the mean.

The model is in fact well-established, dating back to the Black and Litterman (1992) framework for portfolio allocation. We believe, however, that its implications for intra-horizon risk have not been well investigated. The literature on asset returns and parameter uncertainty also extends well beyond Black and Litterman and it already appeared as a subject of investigation in Zellner and Chetty (1965). Following a large amount of related research, Avramov and Zhou (2010) provided a literature overview of parameter uncertainty in the context of portfolio analysis.

Of particular interest to the asset allocation problem is Pástor and Stambaugh's (2012) investigation of the statistical properties of stock market returns over various horizons from the point of view of an investor having imperfect knowledge of the mean return. Their paper reverses some previous findings that stock market volatility tends to decrease with the investment horizon. Instead, they find that uncertainty about the mean return causes the return distribution to broaden faster than the square root of time over longer investment horizons. The mechanism driving their finding is the same as in the model presented here, even though our model is more reduced.

An important implication of the above set-up is that the standard deviation about the log-price at a future date t is given by

$$\sqrt{\sigma^2 t + v^2 t^2}.$$

This shows that while the risk contribution of regular price volatility σ grows with the square root of time, the impact of parameter uncertainty v is linear in time. Thus, regular price volatility remains the primary contributor to risk in the short run, but for longer horizons parameter uncertainty takes over and dominates.

The difference in time dependency points to an interesting difference when comparing with one period models, since this easily misses a relevant aspect of parameter uncertainty. If the investment horizon is fixed at, say, one year, then in the above model the expected change in the log-stock price is normal with mean $\bar{\mu}$ and variance $\sigma^2 + v^2$. This implies that when it comes to the assessment of risk it matters little whether the uncertainty is the result of regular price volatility or parameter uncertainty. However, in a multi-period setting the difference is important since regular price risk propagates with the square root of time while risk related to parameter uncertainty grows linearly with time.

The observation in turn has implications for optimal allocation. In the Black–Litterman model the portfolio optimization problem can be reformulated in a standard Markowitz form, only that the covariance matrix is replaced with one that is the sum of two matrices: one coming from regular price volatility and one coming from uncertainty about the mean. However, when risk is also a function of intra-horizon drawdowns this approach is no longer feasible. It matters where risk comes from.

Theorem 10.2 gives an analytical expression for the risk measure taking uncertainty about the mean return into account, thus providing a generalization of Theorem 10.1.

The dependency on parameter uncertainty is illustrated in Figures 10.1(a) and (b) where the volatility, mean return and lower threshold have all been fixed.

Theorem 10.2

Given assumptions as in Theorem 10.1, assume in addition that the mean return μ is a random variable as specified by (10.4). Then for any x, y with $y \leq 0$ and $x \geq y$ it holds that

$$\psi(x, y) = \mathcal{N}(d_1) + \exp\left(\frac{2y}{\sigma^2}\left(\bar{\mu}_{\log} + \kappa^2 y\right)\right)\mathcal{N}(d_2),$$

where

$$d_1 = \frac{x - \bar{\mu}_{\log}T}{\sqrt{\sigma^2 T + v^2 T^2}}, d_2 = \frac{2y}{\sqrt{\sigma^2 T + v^2 T^2}}\left(1 + \kappa^2 T\right) - d_1, \bar{\mu}_{\log} = \bar{\mu} - \sigma^2/2$$

$\mathcal{N}$ denotes the standard normal distribution function and $\kappa^2 = v^2/\sigma^2$.

Figure 10.3(a) gives the intra-horizon risk ψ_{IH} as a function of the investment horizon, and Figure 10.3(b) gives the total risk ψ.

Figure 10.3 (a) Intra-horizon risk $\psi_{IH}(y)$ and (b) Total risk $\psi(x, y)$

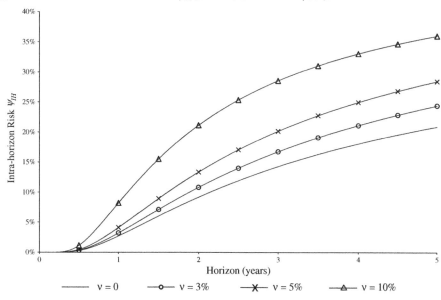

(a)

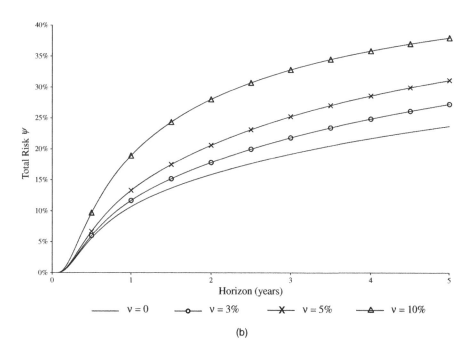

(b)

Notes: With $x = -10\%$ and $y = -20\%$ for an investment process with volatility $\sigma = 10\%$ and expected mean return $\mu = 3\%$. The different lines correspond to different uncertainty about μ as indicated.

The lines correspond to different uncertainty about the mean. The view is altered in Figures 10.4(a) and (b), where ψ_{IH} and ψ are given as functions of the uncertainty about the mean while keeping the investment horizon fixed.

Figure 10.4 (a) Intra-horizon risk $\psi_{IH}(y)$ and (b) Total risk $\psi(x, y)$

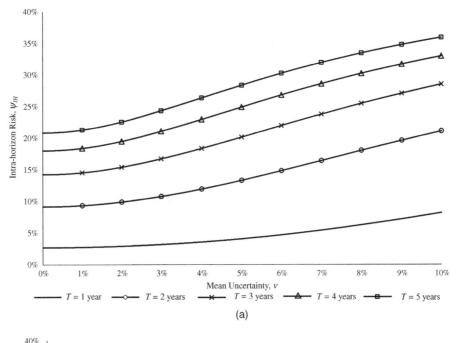

(a)

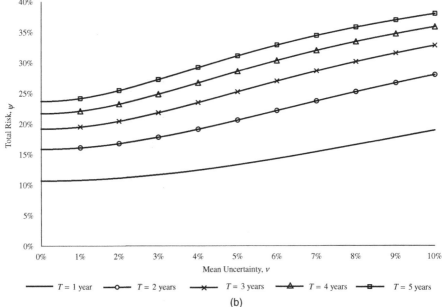

(b)

Notes: with $x = -10\%$ and $y = -20\%$ for an investment process with volatility $\sigma = 10\%$ and expected mean return $\mu = 3\%$. The different lines correspond to different time horizons as indicated.

It is evident that apart from an increase in time horizon, with a greater level of uncertainty in the mean return there is also an increase in intra-horizon and total risk. For example, at an uncertainty level of 10%, the intra-horizon risk more than triples, as the horizon goes from one to three years. Similarly, for a horizon of two years the intra-horizon risk doubles, as the uncertainty level goes from 2% to 9%.

In Figures 10.5(a) and (b) the risk levels are kept fixed and the intra-horizon threshold y is given as a function of the investment horizon. For example, Figure 10.5(a) shows that at the 3-year horizon an intra-horizon risk threshold of −15% is breached with a 30% probability. In Figure 10.5(b) note that the line corresponding to $\psi = 10\%$ approaches −∞ at an investment horizon approximately equal to nine months. This is where the probability of breaching the end-of-horizon threshold x exceeds 10%.

We note that if an asset owner specifies that he does not want more than a 10% probability of breaching a maximum intra-horizon drawdown threshold of say 15%, then he cannot have an investment horizon of more than 11 months. Having an investment horizon longer than this would mean that he has a higher risk of breaching his intra-horizon risk level. This therefore means that the mere definition of an intra-horizon risk tolerance by an asset owner automatically implies a maximum investment horizon for his investment process. This facet is rarely seen either in asset allocation or portfolio management processes.

10.5 STOP-LOSSES

When the risk is defined in terms of end-of-horizon and intra-horizon performance the question arises as to how risk exposure should optimally be managed over time. By applying a dynamic rebalancing rule, it is often possible to reduce the probability of shortfall, as studied in Grossman and Zhou (1993) or Carpenter (2000). Common to these approaches is that portfolio risk exposure is gradually reduced as performance approaches the lower threshold. In practice a common method is to apply a stop-loss, which simply cuts risk exposure before the lower bound is breached.

When assets' mean returns are not known with certainty stop-losses have the additional benefit that they can be used as a screening device for positive mean returns. If a stop-loss is breached, it is more likely to have been generated by a process with a low mean return. By consistently exiting these investments – and replacing them with others of a similar initial evaluation – the portfolio can be managed to maintain a higher mean return on average.

To study this mechanism, we propose here a simplified model where a portfolio manager is invested in only one stock at a time. Each stock purchase is subjected to a maximum holding period and a stop-loss level, and together these two parameters determine how the portfolio is managed over time. The maximum holding period is primarily determined by the investment manager's style, i.e., the method that the portfolio manager uses to estimate expected returns, and it is therefore less in the manager's control. The stop-loss on the other hand can be set at the manager's discretion to optimize performance over time.

Figure 10.5 (a) Iso-intra-horizon risk ψ_{IH} lines and (b) Iso-total risk ψ lines, for intra-horizon threshold y and horizon $(0, T)$

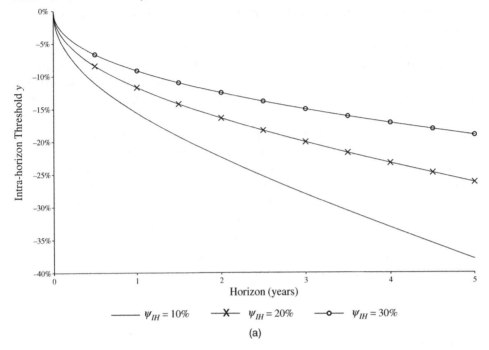

(a)

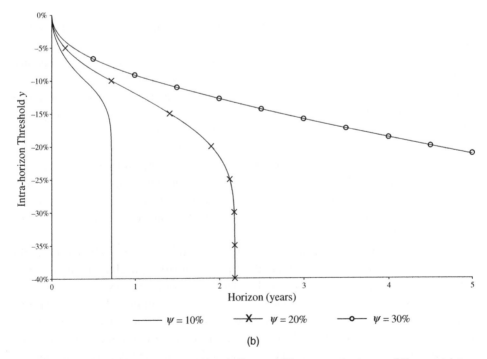

(b)

Settings: End-of-horizon threshold $x = -10\%$, volatility $\sigma = 10\%$, expected return $\mu = 3\%$, uncertainty about the mean $\nu = 5\%$.

It should be noted that a stop-loss need not be the optimal screening mechanism in the given context, and it might for instance be that a time-varying boundary actually proves more efficient for filtering out high returns. However, that aside, a stop-loss set as a maximally accepted price fall is something which is frequently applied in practice and we will stay with this convention.

We assume that each stock the manager selects to include in the portfolio follows a process as in (10.3) where – from the viewpoint of the investment manager – the mean return is uncertain as in (10.4). When a stock reaches either its maximum holding period or its prescribed stop-loss it is immediately replaced with a new stock with similar volatility and with its mean return picked from the same distribution for the mean, independent of previous stocks. Replacing the stock involves selling the old and buying the new, each of which is assumed to incur a relative transaction cost of $1 - \exp(-\delta)$ for a $\delta \geq 0$. For the new stock the investment horizon and stop-loss are reset similarly to what was initially prescribed for the first stock. The process is repeated indefinitely. An illustration is given in Figure 10.6.

In this manner the portfolio evolves similarly to the standard model (10.3) except that every time a boundary is breached the process makes a jump downward as a result of the transaction cost, after which its mean return changes. An analytical representation of the distribution function for the value of the portfolio at a given point in time

Figure 10.6 Model illustration

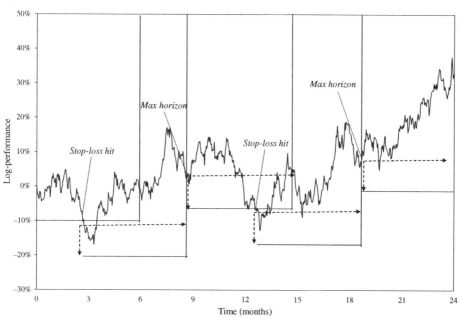

Settings: stop-loss =−20%, maximum holding period $T = 6$ months, stock volatility $\sigma = 3\%$, average mean $\bar{\mu} = 3\%$, mean uncertainty $v = 3\%$ and transaction cost $\delta = 40$ basis points.

does not appear tractable, and for the analysis we instead resort to a statistical moment $M(\mathcal{P})$ defined as

$$M(\mathcal{P}) = \rho^2 E\left[\int_0^\infty e^{-\rho t} \log P_t dt\right],$$

where we use $\mathcal{P}$ and P_t to refer to the portfolio. We similarly use $\mathcal{S}$ and S_t to refer to the stock first purchased into the portfolio and define the moment $M(\mathcal{S})$ accordingly.

For the derivation of the portfolio moment we initially assume that the mean return is known with certainty, i.e., that $v = 0$. The simplifying assumption also allows us to derive a representation of the portfolio moments from which it is possible to calculate moments for the more general case $v > 0$, at least numerically. The main result is given in Theorem 10.3.

Theorem 10.3

Suppose that $\mu = \bar{\mu}$ and $v = 0$. Then $M(\mathcal{P})$ satisfies the relation

$$(1 - \mathcal{R})\,(M(\mathcal{P}) - M(\mathcal{S})) = -2\delta\rho\mathcal{R},$$

where

$$\mathcal{R} = E[e^{-\rho(\tau \wedge T)}],$$

and $\tau = \inf\{t \geq 0 : S_t = \exp(y)\}$. The above applies the conventions $\tau \wedge T = \min(\tau, T)$ and $\inf\{\varnothing\} = \infty$.

Applying the theorem requires calculating $M(\mathcal{S})$ and $\mathcal{R}$, which involves the use of the normal distribution function, allowing for a straightforward implementation. Suppose that $\mu = \bar{\mu}$ and $v = 0$.

   i. The moment for the stock is given by

$$M(\mathcal{S}) = \mu_{\log}.$$

  ii. The quantity $\mathcal{R}$ can be written as

$$\mathcal{R} = \mathcal{Y} + e^{-\rho^T} X,$$

   where

$$\mathcal{Y} = E\left[e^{-\rho\tau}; \tau \leq T\right], X = \mathbb{P}\,(\tau > T).$$

 iii. The quantities $\mathcal{Y}$ and X are given by

$$\mathcal{Y} = \exp(ab)\,(\exp(-ac))\,\mathcal{N}\,(a-c) + \exp(ac)\,\mathcal{N}\,(a+c)),$$
$$X = \mathcal{N}\,(b-a) - \exp(2ab)\,\mathcal{N}\,(b+a),$$

where

$$a = \frac{y}{\sqrt{\sigma^2 T}}, b = \frac{\mu_{\log} T}{\sqrt{\sigma^2 T}}, c = \frac{\mu_{\log,\rho} T}{\sqrt{\sigma^2 T}},$$

$$\mu_{\log} = \mu - \frac{1}{2}\sigma^2, \mu_{(\log,\rho)} = \sqrt{(\mu_{\log}^2 + 2\sigma^2\rho)}.$$

In Theorem 10.3, for the special case that $\delta = 0$ it is readily verified that setting $M(\mathcal{P}) = M(\mathcal{S})$ satisfies the relation. This affirms the intuitive reasoning that when the mean return is known with certainty stop losses are inconsequential and do not improve portfolio performance. Moreover, if transaction costs are positive and $\mathcal{R}$ is strictly between zero and one, then it must hold that $M(\mathcal{P}) < M(\mathcal{S})$, which says that performance deteriorates as a result of transaction costs.

The idea of Theorem 10.3 is that when the mean return is uncertain, all the relations hold in expectation, where the expectation is taken over the possible values of μ. We then have

$$E_\mu[(1 - \mathcal{R})(M(\mathcal{P}) - M(\mathcal{S}))] = -2\delta\rho E_\mu[\mathcal{R}],$$

where subscript "μ" denotes that the expectation is taken over the possible values of μ. This gives the portfolio moment as

$$M(\mathcal{P}) = \frac{E_\mu[(1 - \mathcal{R})(M(\mathcal{S})] - 2\delta\rho E_\mu[\mathcal{R}]}{E_\mu[1 - \mathcal{R}]}.$$

Calculating the expectations involves some nontrivial integrals and in the application we apply a numerical integration routine.

A numerical example is presented in Figure 10.7, which gives the expected log-return as a function of the stop-loss level. The different lines correspond to different transaction costs. It is clear from the figure that when the stop-loss is set too tight the expected performance deteriorates rapidly. However, appropriately managed stop-losses always improve expected performance. For higher transaction costs, the optimal stop-loss is located further away from zero but it is still beneficial in terms of expected performance.

Figure 10.8 gives the expected performance as a function of the uncertainty about the mean. As uncertainty about the mean increases the stop-loss becomes more efficient for screening processes with a higher mean return, which explains the positive relationship seen in the figure. In Figure 10.9 expected performance is given as a function of the investment horizon. A longer investment horizon implies less frequent rebalancing and consequently lower transaction costs, again resulting in a positive relationship.

Figure 10.7 Expected log-performance $M(\mathcal{P})$ as function of the stop-loss level y for different transaction costs

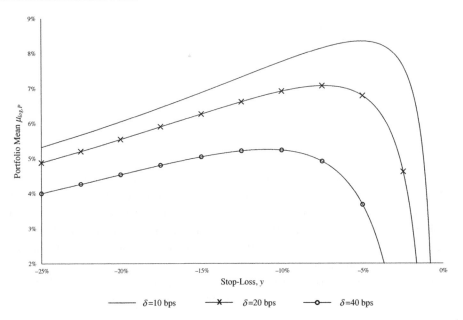

Notes: Avg mean $\bar{\mu} = 10\%$, volatility $\sigma = 30\%$, mean uncertainty $v = 15\%$, investment horizon $T = 1$ year, discount factor $\rho = 1/3$.

Figure 10.8 Expected log-performance $M(\mathcal{P})$ as function of mean uncertainty for different transaction costs

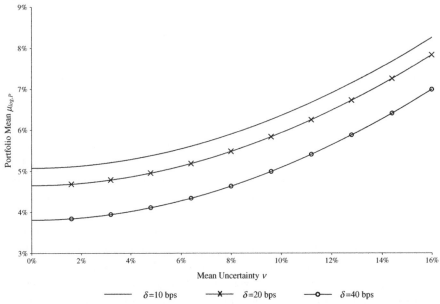

Notes: Avg mean $\bar{\mu} = 10\%$, volatility $\sigma = 30\%$, investment horizon $T = 1$ year, discount factor $\rho = 1/3$, stop-loss $y = -10\%$.

Figure 10.9 Expected log-performance $M(\mathcal{P})$ as function of investment horizon for different transaction costs

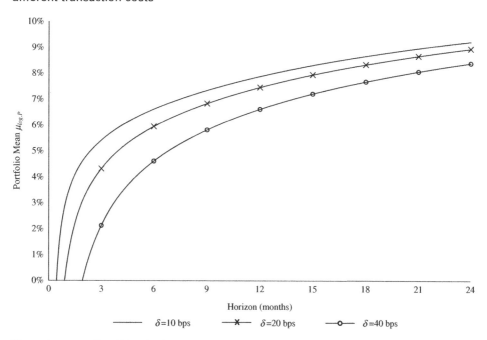

Notes: Avg mean $\bar{\mu} = 10\%$, volatility $\sigma = 30\%$, mean uncertainty $v = 15\%$, discount factor $\rho = 1/3$, stop-loss $y = -10\%$.

Lastly, Figure 10.10 gives the optimal stop-loss for different levels of uncertainty about the mean. Note the accelerating improvement in expected performance as uncertainty about the mean goes up. When uncertainty about the mean is higher it is better to close out strategies earlier, i.e., apply a tighter stop-loss.

We can now demonstrate with an example how stop-losses might be applied in a portfolio management setting. Table 10.1 shows six hypothetical assets corresponding to a long, medium and short investment horizon, and with high and low uncertainties about the mean return. The assets can be securities in a portfolio, strategies within a multi-strategy architecture or asset classes in a multi-asset allocation investment problem. All of these situations have assets with an expected return, an expected volatility and an investment time horizon. The optimal stop-loss corresponding to different transaction costs is given to the right in the table. For the long-term investment strategies, note how higher mean uncertainty implies a tighter stop-loss. Comparing the long and medium-term uncertain strategies we also see that the long-term strategy applies a tighter stop-loss. This results as the potential benefit of throwing out a bad strategy is more limited for the medium-term strategy, since the position will be exited sooner.

Figure 10.10 Optimal stop-loss and associated expected log-performance $M(\mathcal{P})$ as functions of mean uncertainty

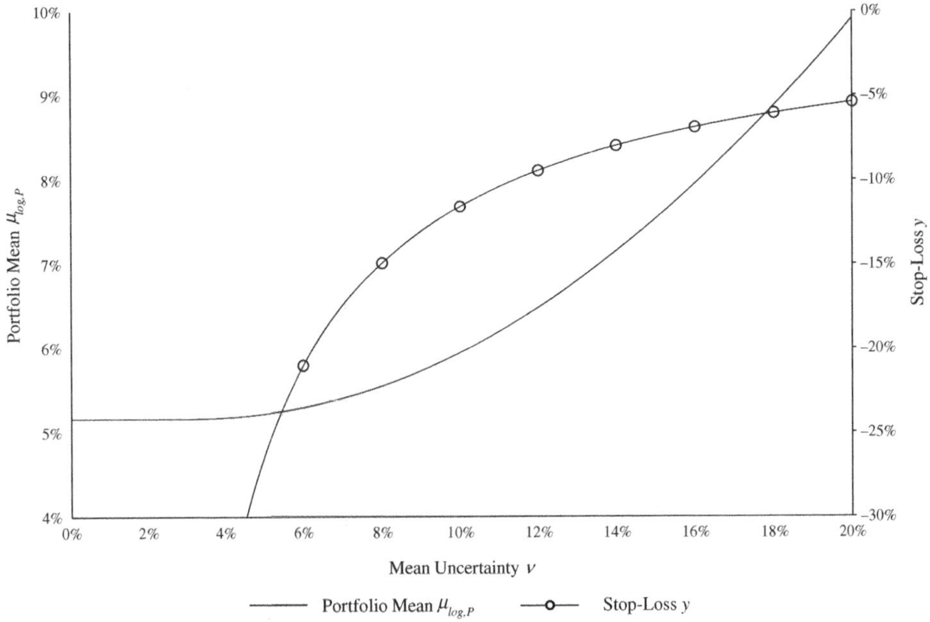

Notes: Avg mean $\bar{\mu} = 10\%$, volatility $\sigma = 30\%$, investment horizon $T = 1$ year, discount factor $\rho = 1/3$, transaction cost $\delta = 20$ bp.

10.6 IMPLEMENTING TAIL RISK MANAGEMENT

We have re-examined the risk inherent in some typical settings within asset management. Focus has been on the asset allocation decision at one end of the investment management process and on individual stock selection strategies at the other. The asset allocation decision is of interest as this decision is taken with low breadth, and the drawdown caused by asset class movements is the primary cause of asset liability funding gaps at asset owners. In both cases an investment mandate is issued together with an end-of-horizon return requirement and an intra-horizon drawdown tolerance. In this chapter we propose specific tools which can help manage the tail risk of a multi-asset portfolio.

1. **A Multi-Strategy Allocation Process**

Constructing a multi-asset portfolio with a constraint of tail risk aversion is challenging because (1) the individual asset classes have poor tail risk characteristics, and (2) diversification between asset classes is minimal. A better portfolio can be achieved using a multi-strategy framework for the allocation process, whereby different methods of asset and risk allocation coexist as independent strategies within the same portfolio. This framework creates strategy diversification, allows allocation to be done at multiple investment horizons and helps to manage tail risk of the portfolio.

Table 10.1 Optimal stop-losses for six assets as characterized by the triple $(T, \bar{\mu}, \nu)$ under different transaction costs. Optimal stop-loss y^*.

Asset type				y^*			μ^*_{log}			μ_{log}		
Horizon – Level of certainty	T	$\bar{\mu}$	ν	10bps	20bps	40bps	10bps	20bps	40bps	10bps	20bps	40bps
Long-Term – Certain	18 months	20%	15%	-3.90%	-5.70%	-8.30%	18.80%	18.30%	17.50%	15.40%	15.30%	15.10%
Long-Term – Uncertain	18 months	20%	30%	-1.90%	-2.70%	-3.90%	29.40%	28.40%	27.00%	15.60%	15.50%	15.30%
Medium-Term – Certain	6 months	10%	10%	-9.80%	-14.70%	-23.00%	5.60%	5.10%	4.10%	5.10%	4.80%	4.00%
Medium-Term – Uncertain	6 months	20%	30%	-2.70%	-3.90%	-5.70%	23.50%	22.00%	19.90%	15.10%	14.80%	14.00%
Short-Term – Certain	1 month	5%	3%	none	none	none	-1.90%	-4.20%	-9.00%	-1.90%	-4.20%	-9.00%
Short-Term – Uncertain	1 month	5%	30%	-5.40%	-8.30%	-13.40%	-0.50%	-3.60%	-8.80%	-1.90%	-4.20%	-9.00%

Settings: Volatility $\sigma = 30\%$, discount factor $\delta = 1/3$. Varying transaction costs of 10, 20 and 40 bps.

2. **Using a Composite Risk Measure**

   Conventional tail risk measures, which use only the end-of-horizon return distribution, fail to capture the real risk that an asset owner has of intra-horizon drawdown. We have proposed a new risk measure defined as the probability that an investment strategy falls short of either its end-of-horizon performance target or its maximally accepted drawdown intra-horizon. This tail risk measure, which is a composite of intra-horizon and end-of-horizon risk, should lead to a portfolio with fewer unexpected outcomes.

3. **Using Investment Horizon to Manage Tail Risk**

   We demonstrate that end-of-horizon risk decreases as investment horizon increases. This finding substantiates conventional logic as to why one should have a long investment horizon: you are more likely to reach your desired investment objective in the long run. At the same time, intra-horizon risk increases quite dramatically as investment horizon increases. That is, if an investor chooses a longer horizon as advocated, the investor is more likely to breach the tolerance for maximum drawdown at some point during the investment horizon. If an investor truly did not want to observe mark-to-market returns periodically, or was unable to observe them (as with illiquid investments), then a long-term investment horizon would indeed make sense. In practice, however, because performance reviews are possible at any time, it might not be appropriate for all asset owners to have a long-term investment horizon. Instead, a portfolio's optimal investment horizon should be determined based on the asset owner's tolerance threshold for intra-horizon risk.

4. **Incorporating Return Uncertainty in Tail Risk Management**

   The basic result of tail risk increasing as return uncertainty increases is an expected one. However, we then use this framework to construct a portfolio that explicitly incorporates the asset owner's intra-horizon risk aversion. Specifically, the portfolio manager can choose the combination of investment horizon and uncertainty of expected return (skill) for each asset so as to stay within intra-horizon risk limits. It then follows that for a given maximum intra-horizon risk threshold, long-term fundamental managers need to be much more certain of their skill compared with short-term traders.

5. **Defining Optimal Stop-Loss Levels**

   Given a maximum drawdown threshold for a portfolio, can customized stop-loss levels be defined for each asset based on its individual characteristics? If the stop-loss is set too tight, increased transaction costs will negatively affect portfolio return, and if set too loose, large drawdowns may occur. Our parameterized model is used to determine the impact of implementing varying stop-loss levels on different portfolio assets. Results show that stop-loss levels need to be tighter when mean uncertainty increases, investment horizons are longer and transaction costs are lower. This finding then leads to a framework that can be applied to determine optimal stop losses at the asset level and to a framework that can be aligned with the asset owner's tolerance threshold for intra-horizon drawdown. This approach can be used for stocks in a stock portfolio, asset classes in a multi-asset portfolio or strategies in a fund of managers.

A better and more aligned portfolio is created if intra-horizon risk is incorporated into the portfolio construction process, the investment horizon of each asset in the portfolio is chosen, and customized stop-loss levels are implemented at the asset level.

10.7 NOTATION AND VARIABLES

x, X_t	Logarithm of the stock price S_t at time t.
y, Y_t	Running minimum of X_t up until time t: $\inf\{X_s: 0 < s \le t\}$. Also the stop-loss applied by the portfolio manager.
δ	Logarithm of one-way transaction cost.
φ	The probability density function for a standard normal variable.
κ^2	Auxiliary variable defined as v^2 / σ^2.
μ	Drift term for the stock price.
$\bar{\mu}$	Expected value of μ when μ is a random variable.
μ_{log}	Auxiliary variable defined as $\mu - \sigma^2 / 2$.
$\mu_{log,\rho}$	Auxiliary variable defined as $\sqrt{\mu_{log}^2 + 2\sigma^2 \rho}$.
v	Standard deviation of μ when μ is a random variable.
ρ	Time discount rate for calculation of $M(\mathcal{P})$ and $M(\mathcal{S})$.
σ	Volatility term for the logarithm of the stock price.
τ	The stopping time $\inf\{t > 0 : x_t = y\}$.
$\psi(x, y)$	Risk function for end-of-horizon threshold x and intra-horizon threshold y.
$M(\mathcal{P})$	The first moment of the log-value of the portfolio.
$M(\mathcal{S})$	The first moment of the log-value of the stock first purchased into the portfolio.
$\mathcal{N}$	The probability distribution function for a standard normal variable.
$\mathbb{P}$	Probability.
$\mathcal{P}, P_t$	The portfolio manager's portfolio and the value of the portfolio at time t.
$\mathcal{R}$	The expectation $E[e^{-\rho(\tau \wedge T)}]$.
$\mathcal{S}, S_t$	The stock first purchased into the portfolio and the value of a stock at time t.
T	Risk time horizon for ψ. Also the portfolio manager's maximum holding period for a stock.
W_t	Standard Brownian motion with initial condition $W_0 = 0$.
X	The expectation $E[1; \tau > T] = \mathbb{P}(\tau > T)$.
Y	The expectation $E\left[\exp(-\rho\tau); \tau \le T\right]$.

CHAPTER ELEVEN

Multi-Asset Investing in Emerging Markets

I nvestment in emerging market equities is generally made by an asset owner taking a strategic or tactical view of the region, followed by investment with a passive or an active equity manager using a market capitalization weighted benchmark such as the MSCI Global Emerging Markets Index. Investment in emerging market debt is often first divided between hard currency and local currency, and then similarly given to active and passive fixed income managers using a market capitalization weighted fixed income benchmark. This process, used by global investors, is the result of the globalizing of financial markets and portfolios over the last few decades to incorporate more diverse geographies. However, the resultant framework seems less than optimal from an economic or investment standpoint today for a variety of reasons, which we discuss below.

In this chapter, we seek to arrive at an improved framework for investing in emerging markets (EM), if one had the ability to redesign the investment process for a more efficient investment solution. We do not, however, seek to present an investment process for the forecasting of asset prices. We begin with a set of observations, which we believe should be significant determinants of any emerging market investment solution.

11.1 OBSERVATION 1: SUB-OPTIMAL GEOGRAPHIC CATEGORIZATION OF EMERGING MARKETS

Historically, asset owners have invested the bulk of their assets in their home market, as their liabilities were predominantly in local currencies and access to foreign markets was operationally difficult. As economies and financial markets globalized, and global investing became easier, investors sought to benefit from portfolio diversification by increasing global investments, thereby decreasing home (or regional) bias. A further economic rationale for portfolio globalization was the belief that faster economic growth rates internationally would manifest into superior corporate earnings, eventually translating to higher equity market returns.

Index providers supported the globalization of portfolios by creating indices to represent regions, as they became important to investors. MSCI launched the EAFE Index (Europe, Australia, Far East) in 1986 as the benchmark for US investors investing in global developed market equities. This was followed in 1988 by the launch of the Global Emerging Markets (GEM) Index with 10 constituent countries, totaling 0.73% of global market capitalization, which helped create GEM as a separate asset class within equities. In 2007, MSCI and other index providers augmented the index set with the launch of a Frontier Markets Index covering financial markets considered to be less developed than emerging. While sequential index creation was consistent with the business rationale of sufficient investor demand, the categorization of some markets as developed, and others as emerging or frontier, progressively seems less optimal from an investment and economic standpoint today. Europe and Japan have become stand-alone allocation buckets in most investor portfolios, having their independent indices. And for the remainder of global equity markets, multiple overlapping indices have proliferated such as Asia ex-Japan, Asia Pacific ex-Japan, BRIC and Horizon, without a specific investment rationale as to what categorization would be optimal for a global investor.

A similar trend is evident in emerging market fixed income. As companies in EM began sourcing debt from global investors, an emerging market hard currency debt market was created, represented by index providers such as HSBC, Barclays (originally Lehman Brothers) and JP Morgan. As the local currency bond market in most countries continues to be dominated by local financial institutions, and regulations sometimes inhibit investment by foreign investors, this has become represented by another segregated set of local market bond indices by the same index providers.

Today, the segmentation created by market benchmarks, which guide investments into emerging market assets both in equity and debt, seems to be investment inefficient. Figures 11.1 and 11.2 illustrate the fragmented structure of GEM equity and Asian fixed income universes.

11.2 OBSERVATION 2: INAPPROPRIATE SECTOR CLASSIFICATION FOR EMERGING MARKETS

The long history of developed markets has led to a large number of companies across industry segments being listed in capital markets. This has meant that sector classification across 10 sectors such as GICS (Figure 11.3) still results in a broad population within each sector. EM, however, do not have this breadth as of now for a 10-sector

Figure 11.1   Country composition of EM Equities Index (including developed Asia)

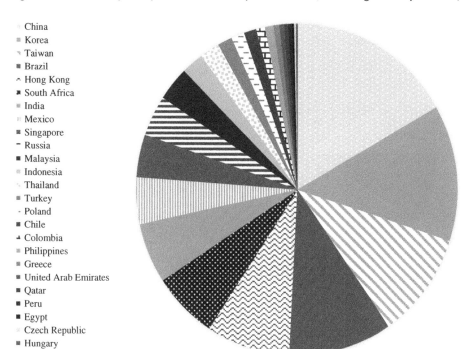

- China
- Korea
- Taiwan
- Brazil
- Hong Kong
- South Africa
- India
- Mexico
- Singapore
- Russia
- Malaysia
- Indonesia
- Thailand
- Turkey
- Poland
- Chile
- Colombia
- Philippines
- Greece
- United Arab Emirates
- Qatar
- Peru
- Egypt
- Czech Republic
- Hungary

Data Source: MSCI

Figure 11.2   Country composition of Emerging Asia bond indices: (a) HSBC Asia Local Currency Bond Index (ALBI); (b) JP Morgan Asia Hard Currency Bond Index (JACI)

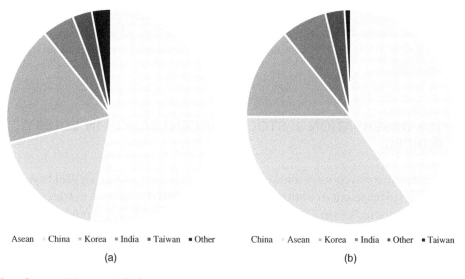

Asean   China   Korea   India   Taiwan   Other   China   Asean   Korea   India   Other   Taiwan

(a)   (b)

Data Source: JP Morgan, HSBC

Figure 11.3   Sector composition of Global Emerging Markets Index, Jan 2015

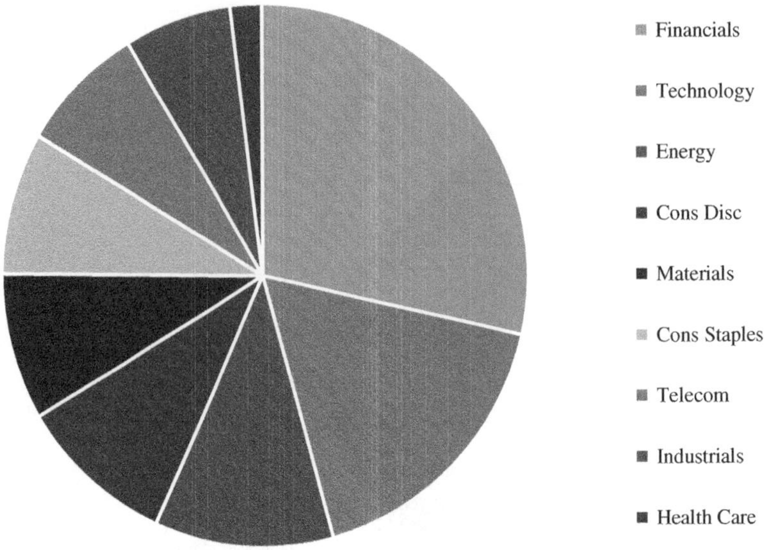

- Financials
- Technology
- Energy
- Cons Disc
- Materials
- Cons Staples
- Telecom
- Industrials
- Health Care

Data Source: MSCI

classification to be appropriate. Given that EM comprise of multiple countries, each with its own business cycle, this classification creates a country-sector matrix with more than 100 potential buckets for asset allocation. This becomes extremely difficult to manage. Furthermore, with a 10-sector classification, as of January 2015, just two sectors (Financials and Technology) accounted for 47% of the total index, with the remaining 53% spread across the remaining eight sectors. This disparity is also sub-optimal for allocation purposes. A more balanced sector classification, where each sector is broadly populated, would be more appropriate from an investment standpoint.

11.3 OBSERVATION 3: STOCK CONCENTRATION IN EQUITY INDICES

A basic objective of a country market benchmark is to serve as a diversified basket of investments to represent a country. Unlike developed market indices, market capitalization weighted indices in EM become dominated by a handful of companies, which dominate the risk and return characteristics for the index. Figure 11.4 illustrates the extent of this concentration effect in international markets compared to the US. Hence, the use of a market cap-weighted benchmark in EM amplifies the problem of misallocation of capital.

Figure 11.4   Percentage weight of top 10 stocks in country equity benchmarks

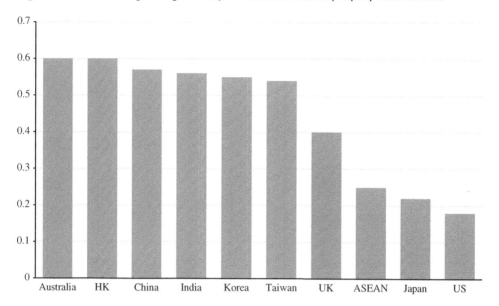

Data Source: MSCI

 11.4 OBSERVATION 4: THE POTENTIAL FOR ACTIVE MANAGEMENT

Whether the allocation to an asset class should be managed actively or passively should be based on the confidence that active management can generate excess returns. A high dispersion of securities within the asset class creates the opportunity for a skilled active manager to be able to generate excess return, whereas a low dispersion of securities is likely to lead to lower alpha generated, for a given level of skill. Figure 11.5 shows the dispersion of equities in EM relative to developed markets in a variety of segments. It is clear that the dispersion of returns in EM, at the country, sector and security level, is greater than it is in developed markets. This implies that there is greater opportunity for investors in EM to outperform with successful geographic, sector or stock selection, compared to their developed market counterparts. As such, if an investor with constraints of cost and active risk was forced to choose, he should probably decide to be active in EM and passive in developed markets, rather than the other way around.

 11.5 OBSERVATION 5: PERFORMANCE OF ACTIVE MANAGERS

Given the higher potential for active return in EM, one would expect active managers in EM to be comparatively more successful than their developed market counterparts

Figure 11.5 Analysis of dispersion within developed and emerging market equity indices

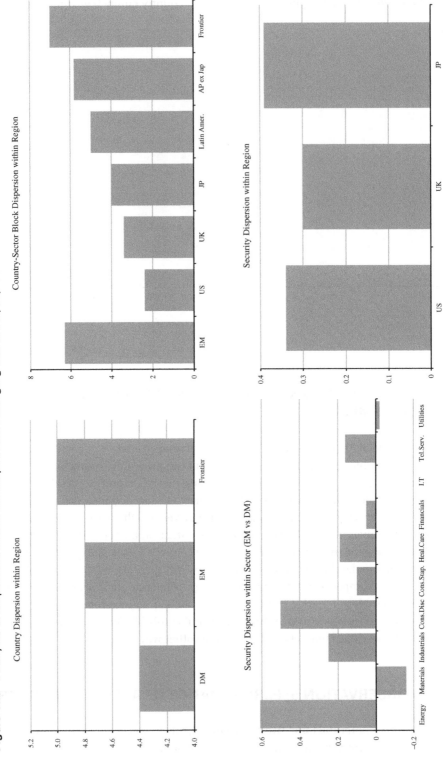

Data Source: Bloomberg, Standard & Poor's MSCI

Figure 11.6 Distribution of active emerging market manager returns, trailing 3 years: (a) Total 5-year trailing annualized return of managers, grouped by manager selection skill; (b) Cumulative distribution of active manager annualized active returns

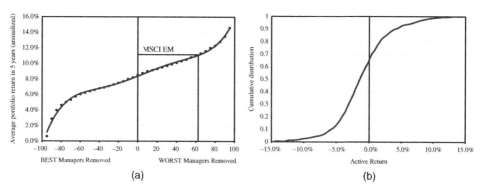

(a)　　　　　　　　　　　　　　　　　　　(b)

Source: Gupta (2014), Morningstar

in generating excess return. Actual historic performance numbers, however, lead to the opposite conclusion. Whereas approximately 50% of developed market active managers outperform their benchmarks on average, Figure 11.6(b) shows that on a 3-year trailing basis, only about 25% of emerging market active managers outperform. Further, Figure 11.7 shows that only about 8% of the emerging market managers are able to generate consistent outperformance consecutively for three years.

Finally, worse still, Figure 11.7 shows that when an EM active manager manages to reach the top quartile, he is most likely to fall to the bottom quartile in the subsequent period. In summary, EM active managers have a distinctly poorer track record than developed market active managers.

Figure 11.7 Sequential performance of active managers in emerging markets – Cumulative distribution of active manager annualized active returns

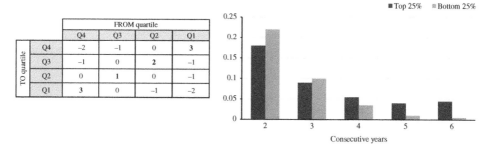

Data Source: Morningstar

11.6 OBSERVATION 6: OVER-DEPENDENCE ON A SINGLE INVESTMENT DECISION

While one would like to believe that EM portfolios are invested across a range of diversified variables, in reality they are over-dependent on a single investment decision in most cases – the level of equity market risk in the portfolio. Figure 11.8 displays the total return of 13 of the largest and most prominent Asian multi-asset funds for the calendar years 2012 and 2013. It is noticeable that all of the funds have a positive performance in 2012 when the equity market rallied, and all of them have a negative performance in 2013, when the equity market fell. This can be rationalized by the fact that as market timing is not possible on a sustainable basis, the biggest determinant of the risk and return of the portfolio becomes this single equity-bond allocation decision. If such a "balanced" strategy simply rises and falls with the equity market, it does not sync with the belief of asset owners that the portfolio is diversified and will perform equally well across market cycles. There appears to be a need for a better investment solution.

11.7 SUMMARY OF OBSERVATIONS

A few conclusions can be reached from the preceding observations:

- The historic segregation of EM financial assets, by conventional benchmarks, results in an inefficient allocation and risk management structure. While the concept of

Figure 11.8   Total return for 2012 and 2013 for 13 large Asian multi-asset funds

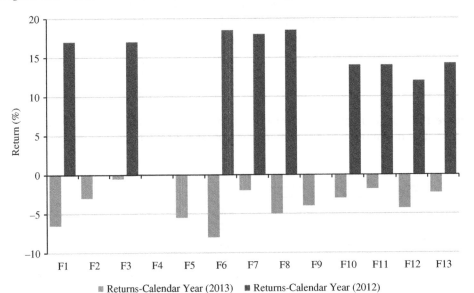

■ Returns-Calendar Year (2013)   ■ Returns-Calendar Year (2012)

Data Source: eVestment

segregation between developed and EM is itself a debatable issue, within an EM universe there needs to be greater thought on structural links between and within the EM asset classes.

▨ Skill in asset allocation is of paramount importance in EM in order to generate performance. This can be facilitated by redesigning the allocation framework to be more effective. Consideration should be given to incorporating a risk premium structure which creates mutually exclusive allocation buckets, creating an economic segmentation more relevant for EM, and designing an investment framework which integrates top-down macroeconomics with bottom-up corporate fundamentals, while diversifying the impact of a single equity-bond allocation decision.

▨ Active managers in EM have far lower skill than developed market managers, despite ample opportunity being available. There is, therefore, a need for reevaluating the structure of EM portfolios, including benchmark construction and the process to implement asset forecasts.

▨ Finally, the higher risk in EM, which results in higher intra-horizon drawdowns, requires a skilled tail risk management process for any investment process in EM to be successful.

 ## 11.8 PITFALLS IN EMERGING MARKET INVESTMENT FRAMEWORKS

A crucial aspect of investing is being able to separate skill from luck in every part of the investment process. Critical examination of existing philosophies in EM leads to several conclusions:

a. Benchmark Gaming

The diverse set of countries in EM represented by a market cap-weighted benchmark is a structure accepted to be inefficient. This has facilitated creativity in product construction by simply choosing a subset of countries that are in vogue as the universe, having the broad market cap EM index as a benchmark, and selling either the exposure or the outperformance as skill. This has resulted in a plethora of products such as BRICs, Asia ex Japan, Asia Pacific ex-Japan, Frontier Markets, Horizon Markets, ASEAN, Greater China, Asia small cap, Asia hi-div, etc.

b. Risk Parity Allocation

Much has been written about the merits or otherwise of risk parity as an allocation methodology. We don't discuss this specific subject here, save to comment that risk parity is a methodology for benchmark weight design similar to equal weighting or fundamental indexation. It is not an active management skill, nor should it be represented or charged as an actively managed product.

c. Smart Beta in EM

There is plenty of literature on the value or otherwise of smart beta strategies, which is beyond the scope of this chapter. It is a fact, however, that manufacturers have found it more difficult to produce smart beta strategies in EM. We note that

evaluation of any smart beta EM strategy needs to focus on the fact that, by definition, smart beta strategies need to be transparent (i.e., the manager cannot use an
undisclosed proprietary methodology which cannot be openly replicated) and need
to be priced as a beta strategy and not an alpha strategy.

d. Currency Management

Balance sheets of corporate issuers in EM are denominated in local EM currencies, and investment in any EM asset, except hard currency debt, has embedded direct currency risk for an investor. As such if asset price forecasts are done in
local currency (as is mostly the case), any investment strategy which either does not
hedge, or actively forecast currency values, is flawed by design.

e. Use of Index Futures

Managers in developed markets ubiquitously use listed index futures to manage
their equity exposure. However, EM managers historically have not been active users
of index futures because of a lack of liquidity or lack of experience and skill. Today,
however, almost all EM markets have liquid readily available index futures, and their
lack of use by active EM managers should be questioned.

11.9 AN IMPROVED FRAMEWORK FOR EMERGING MARKET INVESTMENTS

We propose here three specific improvements in the traditional EM investment framework, which mitigate some of the shortcomings discussed above:

a. A Composite Investment Universe

We believe an investment universe that integrates emerging equity, emerging
hard currency debt, and emerging local currency debt would be far superior in its
characteristics than trying to manage these independently. For the GEM and Frontier
equity market universes we rationalize the segmentation into seven global groups,
as portrayed in Figure 11.9(a). For Asia, we rationalize the segmentation into five
geographic groups, as portrayed in Figure 11.9(b). We propose that this creates a
more balanced and manageable bucket structure for forecasting and allocation.

For Asian debt, we propose combining the local and hard currency debt universes, and classifying the combination into the same geographic groups as the
equity universe. Figure 11.10 depicts the rationalized segmentation.

Finally, we propose integrating the equity and fixed income universes to create a holistic EM universe, allowing a more balanced allocation structure which
is synchronized between all three asset classes. These weights are displayed in
Figure 11.10.

b. An Integrated Top-down and Bottom-up Allocation Process

One of the challenges of creating a portfolio has always been to design an
investment process which can seamlessly dovetail top-down allocation decisions
and bottom-up security selection decisions. As current investment frameworks segregate the investment process into multiple independent components (such as asset

Figure 11.9 Reclassifying the geographic segmentation of Equities: (a) GEM equity;
(b) Asia equity

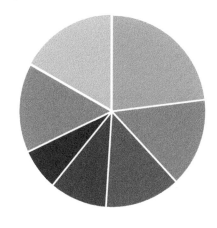

Region	%Wt
China	23%
Korea	15%
Taiwan	13%
Asean	10%
India	7%
Latam	15%
E Eur	17%

▪ China   ▪ Korea   ▪ Taiwan   ▪ Asean   ▪ India   ▪ Latam   ▪ E Eur

(a)

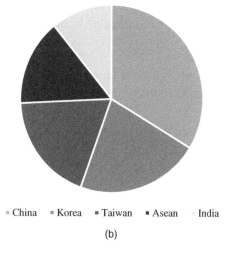

Region	%Wt
China	34%
Korea	22%
Taiwan	19%
Asean	15%
India	11%

▪ China   ▪ Korea   ▪ Taiwan   ▪ Asean   ▪ India

(b)

Data Source: MSCI

class allocation, geographic and sector allocation and security selection), the output
of each stage often does not synchronize with the others, leading to a mismatch and
consequent compromise between them. Furthermore, as previously highlighted, the
sequential nature of these steps creates overdependence on the single decision of
the level of equity and credit risk in a portfolio. We propose a bottom-up economic
segmentation structure for securities, which matches the top-down framework
based on economic cycles. Figure 11.11 (left) depicts the top-down economic cycle

Figure 11.10 Reclassifying the geographic segmentation of emerging equities and debt – combined Asian local and hard currency debt

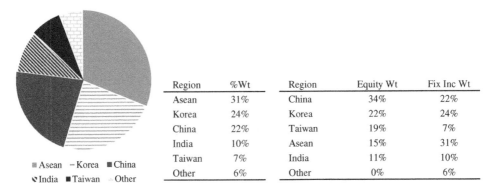

Region	%Wt
Asean	31%
Korea	24%
China	22%
India	10%
Taiwan	7%
Other	6%

Region	Equity Wt	Fix Inc Wt
China	34%	22%
Korea	22%	24%
Taiwan	19%	7%
Asean	15%	31%
India	11%	10%
Other	0%	6%

Legend: ▦ Asean – Korea ■ China ❧ India ■ Taiwan ─ Other

Data Source: MSCI

and Figure 11.11 (right) the synchronized bottom-up security categorization for Asian equities. As the economic cycle of a country would affect both its debt and equity markets, the equity-bond decision is taken independently at the level of each country, rather than at an overall portfolio level as is conventionally done now. This therefore diversifies the risk of dependence on a singular decision. A similar exercise could be done for GEM.

c. Redefining Style Premiums in EM

In Chapter 3 we discussed a rationalization of the evolution of investment style in financial markets. Developed market equities have coalesced on the definition of

Figure 11.11 Synchronized top-down (left) and bottom-up (right) segmentation of Asian equities

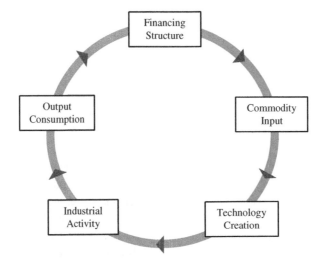

Data Source: Bloomberg, MSCI

Figure 11.12 Redefined premiums appropriate for global emerging equity markets

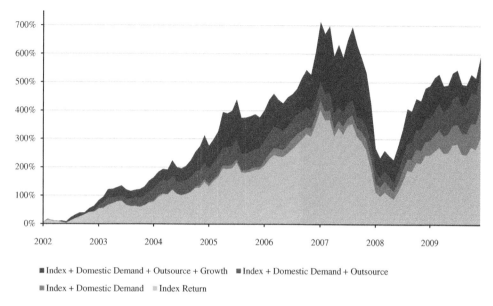

■ Index + Domestic Demand + Outsource + Growth   ■ Index + Domestic Demand + Outsource
■ Index + Domestic Demand   ▨ Index Return

Data Source: Bloomberg, MSCI

investment style by classifying factors such as value, size and momentum as systematic factors. It has since been assumed that this definition of style should also be valid for EM. We don't believe this should be the case. We propose that style in EM should be defined along the same dimensions as the basic reasons why any investor traditionally invests in EM – for exposure to higher economic growth, greater domestic demand and low cost outsourcing. This redefinition would create a better alignment both for passive exposure products and active EM products.

An empirical test of this methodology can be conducted to verify if these style premiums exist in EM. We classify each GEM stock on the basis of its exposure to each of these variables, and construct portfolios with exposure to one, two or three of these EM styles. Figure 11.12 displays the results, and empirically confirms the value addition above a market capitalization weighted MSCI EM benchmark, by using this definition of EM style.

This definition of style allows EM product design to be aligned with the investment objectives of a global investor; investment in various EM strategies coincides with economic rationale.

We have seen that emerging markets have a fragmented structure, where benchmarks have been constructed inadequately, investment frameworks are disjointed and active managers fare poorly. We have proposed three improvements, which align with the concept of multi-asset investing: an integrated investment universe; an integrated investment approach; and the redefinition of style.

CHAPTER TWELVE

The Importance of Asset Allocation in Asian Equities

A ctive portfolio managers managing Asian equity portfolios largely market the value of their strategies by claiming that they are able to pick the right stocks within the Asian universe. This claim is further justified by the fact that the Asian equity investment landscape – unlike European and US equity markets – is varied in nature across various countries, investment information is unreliable and has a smaller history, and, supposedly, one really needs to know the individual companies to be able to make good investment decisions. As the majority of active asset managers in Asia underperform on a 3-year investment horizon, we hypothesize the skill that is really required to manage an Asian equity portfolio successfully is that of asset allocation, and that the focus of stock selection by active managers in Asia is misplaced.

In general, the active return of any active investment process can be divided into an allocation component (across countries, sectors and styles) and a security selection component (while remaining neutral to allocation buckets). Active managers use these two processes with differing degrees of emphasis; we seek to distinguish them explicitly, in order to segregate the proportion of portfolio return coming from each skill, irrespective of what the manager himself may claim.

12.1 IMPACT OF BREADTH ON PORTFOLIO EXCESS RETURN

Asset allocation and security selection can be performed largely independently of each other; however, they differ in terms of breadth of assets available and return dispersion of assets which can be exploited by active management. In order to compare their value to the portfolio, we need to account for these differences.

Figure 12.1 Variation in information ratio with a change in breadth, with $IC = 5\%$. var (IC) = 0 (grey); var (IC) = 0.01 (black)

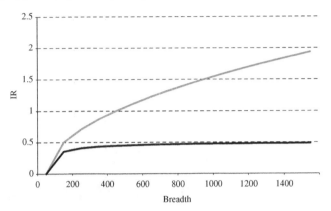

Data Source: MSCI

The relationship between ex-ante information ratio (IR), and breadth (B) can be written as

$$IR = \frac{IC}{\sqrt{\dfrac{1}{B} + \sigma_{IC}^2}} \tag{12.1}$$

where IC is the information coefficient and σ_{IC} is the variance of IC. Ye (2008) gives the derivation of this equation.

If investment skill is assumed to be constant, then $\sigma_{IC} = 0$, and equation (12.1) reduces to the fundamental law of active management proposed by Grinold and Kahn (1999). However, in reality no strategy has constant skill, as skill is in general time-varying. The variability of skill puts a cap on the IR that can be achieved, even if breadth is higher. This is depicted in Figure 12.1.

In our example, given the level and precision of the skill, the maximum IR is 0.5. Even as breadth increases, the marginal benefit in IR diminishes, even in the absence of the trading costs. It can therefore be said that it does not pay to increase the breadth if the precision of the skill is low.

 12.2 IMPACT OF VARYING CROSS-SECTIONAL DISPERSION ON PORTFOLIO EXCESS RETURN

We can derive the relationship between the cross-sectional dispersion of assets D and the time-series variance and covariance. If R_p denotes portfolio excess return and TE is performance tracking error to the benchmark, then

$$IR = R_p/TE$$

and

$$R_p = \frac{IC}{\sqrt{\frac{1}{B} + \sigma_{IC}^2}} TE.$$ (12.2)

Ex-ante portfolio volatility can be expressed as

$$TE = \overline{\Delta w}' V \overline{\Delta w}$$ (12.3)

where $\overline{\Delta w}$ is the N×1 vector of stock active weight in the portfolio, $\overline{\Delta w}'$ is the transpose of $\overline{\Delta w}$, and V is a N×N covariance matrix of stock returns. For stock active weight $\sum \Delta w_i = 0$.

As a special case, assuming all stocks have the same volatility σ and the correlation between any pair of stocks is identical (ρ), we get

$$TE = \sigma \sqrt{(1-\rho) \sum_i \Delta w_i^2}$$

Substituting TE in equation (12.2), we get

$$R_p = \frac{IC}{\sqrt{\frac{1}{B} + \sigma_{IC}^2}} \sigma \sqrt{(1-\rho)A}$$ (12.4)

where $A = \sqrt{\sum_i \Delta w_i^2}$ is the activeness of the portfolio.

Thus in a scenario where all stocks are perfectly correlated, active return will be zero.

The cross-sectional dispersion is an instance of a joint distribution characterized by an expected returns N×1 vector $\overline{\mu}$ and a covariance matrix V. One can perform a joint draw and measure the average cross-sectional variation as the standard deviation across returns for a particular joint draw.

If X~N(μ,V) follows multivariate Gaussian, which can be expressed as $X = \mu + CY$, where Y~N(0,1) is a standard Gaussian and C is the lower-triangular Choleski matrix of V. The consistent estimator of the variance $v = \frac{1}{n-1} \sum_i (x_i - \overline{x})^2$, where $\overline{X} = \frac{1}{n} \sum_i x_i$, in terms of Y and C. The expected value of v is then

$$(n-1)E(v) = \sum_i \mu_i^2 - \frac{1}{n} \sum_{i,j} \mu_i \mu_j + \sum_i c_i c_i' - \frac{1}{n} \sum_{i,j} c_i' c_j$$

where c_i is the ith row of the Choleski matrix.

The dispersion, D, is defined as the square root of the variance v, and can be simplified as

$$D^2 = E(v) = \frac{1}{N-1} trace(\mu\mu' + V) - \frac{1}{N(N-1)} i'(\mu\mu' + V)i$$ (12.5)

where i is a N×1 unit vector.

Figure 12.2 Cross-sectional dispersion of assets with varying asset volatility and different correlation between asset pairs

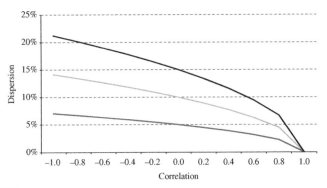

Data Source: MSCI

Figure 12.2 shows that the cross-sectional dispersion increases with stock volatility but decreases with correlations. To illustrate this point, we can examine a special case where the expected return of all stocks is the same. Then we get:

$$D^2 = \frac{1}{N-1}trace(V) - \frac{1}{N(N-1)}i'Vi \tag{12.6}$$

If all stocks have the same volatility σ and the correlations between any pair of stocks are also identical (ρ), the dispersion can be simplified as:

$$D = \sigma\sqrt{1-\rho} \tag{12.7}$$

The portfolio active return R_P can then be derived as:

$$R_p = \frac{IC}{\sqrt{\dfrac{1}{B}+\sigma_{IC}^2}}DA \tag{12.8}$$

12.3 THE RELATIVE IMPORTANCE OF ASSET ALLOCATION AND STOCK SELECTION

Let R_{ss} represent the excess return generated by a particular investment team with a skill represented by IC_{ss}, if they were to perform only stock selection (without allocation decisions). However, if this team is used for allocation decisions instead, they would face a different market structure, which would result in a different opportunity set and hence generate a different excess return. Let IC_{aa} represent the team's skill in asset allocation, and R_{aa} represent the excess return only from an asset allocation decision. Using equation

(12.8), for the same level of activeness with either asset allocation or stock selection, we get

$$\frac{R_{aa}}{R_{ss}} = \frac{IC_{aa}}{IC_{ss}} \frac{D_{aa}}{D_{ss}} \sqrt{\frac{B_{aa}}{B_{ss}}} \sqrt{\frac{1 + \sigma_{IC}^2 B_{ss}}{1 + \sigma_{IC}^2 B_{aa}}} \tag{12.9}$$

where B_{aa} and B_{ss} represent the breadth of the investment processes. The breadth is equivalent to the degrees of freedom, which for an unconstrained portfolio would be equal to the number of assets minus 1. Equation (12.9) thus delineates the return that can be harnessed from each of the two independent investment processes, as a function of the differences in the opportunity set of the two decisions and the skill of each investment decision process.

12.4 COMPARING THE US AND ASIAN EQUITY INVESTMENT UNIVERSE

To illustrate the relative importance of the asset allocation decision versus the stock selection decision, we compare the investment processes in the US equity and Asian equity universe. The MSCI Asia Pacific ex Japan Index is used as the benchmark for Asian equities, and the S&P 500 for US equities, and each defines the universe of securities for the stock selection definition. We categorize all stocks in the benchmark based on their country and sector classification, and exclude all stocks with an average daily trading value less than US$1 mn, to ensure a minimum liquidity for each stock.

In Asia, the assets relevant for the allocation decision are the country-sector blocks, on which an active allocation decision can be made. As of May 2014, there were 99 such asset blocks. The security selection decision is represented by the ability to pick any stock in the universe of securities, at any chosen weight, such that the block weights of the resulting portfolio match that of the benchmark. For the US, the only allocation dimension is sectors. We assume here, for simplicity, that the portfolio is small enough to allow for desired active bets at the stock and the block level, without undesired tracking error deviation created by liquidity. In addition, we ignore transaction costs in this basic study, as much will depend on portfolio turnover of the active investment processes used.

If we have N_{ss} stocks in the investment universe which are categorized into N_{aa} blocks, then $(N_{aa} - 1)$ would be the degrees of freedom for the asset allocation decision, and $(N_{ss} - N_{aa})$ would be the degrees of freedom for the stock selection decision. Figure 12.3 depicts the time series of the ratio of breadth of the stock selection decision to the asset allocation decision, which is calculated as

$$\frac{B_{ss}}{B_{aa}} = \frac{N_{ss} - N_{aa}}{N_{aa} - 1}. \tag{12.10}$$

The ratio could be overstated for long-only portfolios when negative active bets are constrained by the asset's benchmark weight, when activeness is increased, and when

Figure 12.3   Ratio of breadth of the stock selection decision to the asset allocation decision

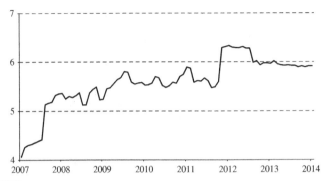

Data Source: MSCI

the skew in the distribution of stock sizes is higher. Figure 12.4 depicts how the breadth ratio drops, as we tighten the constraint on the minimum liquidity required for a stock. It can be seen that in Asia (Figure 12.4(a)), there is a steep decline in the breadth ratio as liquidity constraint is tightened. Large funds in Asia would therefore find a decreased breadth advantage in stock selection, as they are forced to invest in only more liquid stocks. In the US equity market, however, as evidenced by Figure 12.4(b), the breadth ratio is relatively constant as liquidity is tightened, indicating that larger funds are not necessarily disadvantaged compared to smaller funds.

Cross-sectional dispersion of the blocks in the asset allocation decision and stocks (block neutral) in the stock selection decision are both time-varying, and impact the portfolio return.

Figure 12.5 shows the variation in the dispersion of the benchmark as divided into the allocation and stock selection components for the Asian (Figure 12.5(a)) and the US equity universe (Figure 12.5(b)). It is apparent that in Asia, approximately 70% of

Figure 12.4   Breadth of the stock selection (grey) and asset allocation (dashed) decisions with change in minimum stock liquidity, Breadth ratio (rhs in black), for (a) Asian equities, (b) US equities

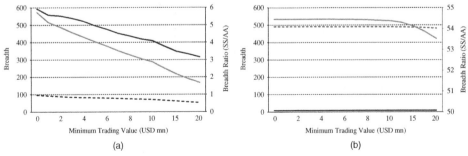

Note: Data as of Dec 2013.

Data Source: MSCI, Standard & Poor's

Figure 12.5 Percentage of dispersion from the asset allocation decision (dark grey) and the stock selection decision (light grey) for (a) Asian equity, (b) US equity

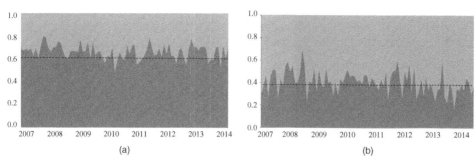

(a)   (b)

Note: Dotted line indicates period average.

Data Source: MSCI, Standard & Poor's

the dispersion is from asset allocation, whereas in the US this is only about 40%. It can therefore be said dispersion would advocate that asset allocation should play a much more important role in Asia relative to stock selection, as compared to managing a US equity portfolio.

From (12.9) and (12.10), we get

$$\frac{R_{aa}}{R_{ss}} = \frac{IC_{aa}}{IC_{ss}}\frac{D_{aa}}{D_{ss}}\sqrt{\frac{N_{aa}-1}{N_{ss}-N_{aa}}}\sqrt{\frac{1+\sigma_{IC}^{2}\left(N_{ss}-N_{aa}\right)}{1+\sigma_{IC}^{2}\left(N_{aa}-1\right)}}. \qquad (12.11)$$

Assuming a typical skill variation σ_{IC} to be 10%, we can deduce the return ratio over time, for different ratios of investment skill, to be as depicted in Figure 12.6.

Figure 12.6 Ratio of returns of asset allocation over stock selection at different levels of IC ratio, over time: 0. 5 (black); 1.0 (dashed); 1.5 (grey)

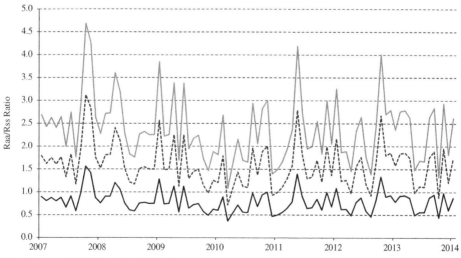

Data Source: MSCI, Standard & Poor's

Figure 12.7 Ratio of returns from asset allocation at different levels of IC ratio for (a) Asian equity, (b) US equities

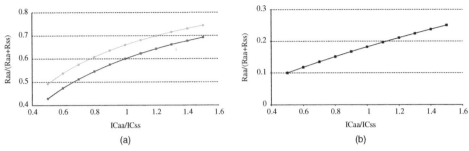

(a)

(b)

Notes: Min daily trading $1mn (black), $20mn (grey).

Data Source: MSCI, Standard & Poor's

Obviously, as the investment skill of asset allocation increases relative to security selection, the return from asset allocation also is higher. It is, however, noticeable that when the skill of both processes is the same, i.e., when the IC ratio is equal to 1, the return ratio of asset allocation to security selection is almost always above 1. This indicates the greater significance of asset allocation at all points in time.

We can compare the overall impact of breadth and dispersion on the asset allocation and stock selection decisions, by comparing the return contribution of both processes, if skill were the same. This can be done when the minimum liquidity constraint is set at US$1 million (to be relevant for small portfolios) and set at US$20 million (to be relevant for large portfolios). Figure 12.7 shows the variation of the proportion of return from asset allocation for different skill ratios, for the two cases of Asian equity and US equity.

It can be seen that if there were equal skill in asset allocation and stock selection (the case of the IC ratio being equal to 1), then in Asia approximately 66% of the return would from asset allocation. In a US equity portfolio, however, only about 18% of the return would come from asset allocation. This stark difference between the two markets is a point to be noted.

 12.5 CONCLUSIONS

The Asian equity investment landscape has two definitive dimensions of allocations (country and sector), unlike the US and European landscape, which is largely one-dimensional (sector). Further, the market depth in terms of number of investable stocks is deeper in US and Europe than it is in Asia. Both these factors make Asian equities a much richer space for asset allocation than stock selection conceptually. However, this is at odds with the fact that most Asian equity managers emphasize security selection as their primary skill, and not asset allocation.

We find empirically from Figure 12.7, that if one's skill in asset allocation and security selection were the same, them approximately 60% of the portfolio return of an active Asian equity portfolio would come from asset allocation, after accounting for market differences. Put another way, in order for the return from security selection to be equal or more than that of asset allocation for a small portfolio, the skill of the manager in security selection would have to be about 50% more than in asset allocation for an Asian portfolio.

By contrast, for a US equity portfolio, we find that that if one's skill in asset allocation and security selection were the same, then only about 18% of the portfolio return would come from asset allocation, and the remaining 82% would come from stock selection.

We further consider the case for a larger portfolio. By tightening the liquidity constraint to have only stocks with a average daily trading volume of US$20 mn, we are implying that if the fund size was US$400 mn, then it could still take a 5% active position in a stock, while only requiring one day's trading volume to accumulate the required position from the market. This is still considerable, as it is widely accepted that above a 20% of ADV requirement, there is significant market impact. We find that for larger funds, it makes even more sense to focus on asset allocation rather than security selection. When one's skill is the same in both processes, approximately 67% of the return comes from allocation. Furthermore, for the return from security selection to be more than from asset allocation for a larger portfolio, the skill in security selection would have to be almost double that in asset allocation.

It therefore seems that active Asian equity strategies should consider a much greater emphasis on asset allocation as part of the investment process, rather than purely on security selection, which is in sharp contrast to what is required for managing an active portfolio in US equities.

CHAPTER THIRTEEN

Implementing a Multi-Asset Strategy – Active or Passive

We have so far examined the allocation, portfolio construction and risk management processes for multi-asset strategies. A subsequent decision for the creation of the multi-asset portfolio is the choices offered in the implementation of investment decisions. There are two broad parameters on which decisions need to be taken in this regard:

a. The choice of active or passive strategies; and
b. The incorporation of asset owner specific constraints.

Moreover, asset owners have varying risk profiles and have different investment sizes. This demands that the implementation process be flexible to accommodate varying levels of risk, and be implementable over a range of asset sizes.

13.1 INVESTMENT DETERMINANTS FOR THE ACTIVE–PASSIVE DECISION

The debate of whether the assets should be implemented in active strategies or passive investments has largely focused on two factors – the cost of active management versus the low cost of indexing, and the performance of active managers. We propose that seven variables should determine the ratio of active versus passive managers in any implementation:

1. **Active Manager/Strategy Skill**
   The return achieved by the eventual active investment is a result of the combination of the IR of the manager selection process, and the IR of the strategy itself.

Figure 13.1 Distribution of 3-year excess return of over 6000 active managers

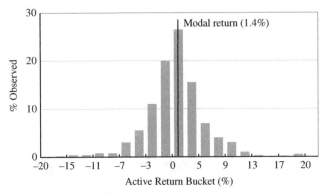

Data Source: Morningstar

Figure 13.1 shows the distribution of 3-year active return for over 6000 managers, as an example. While the modal excess return of active managers is +1.4% during the sample period, there is a distribution of superior and poor managers. The individual experience of any investor will therefore vary greatly based upon the actual manager selected.

Figure 13.2 depicts the excess return the asset owner would achieve as a function of his manager selection skill. The right side of the graph shows that as the selection skill increases (represented by the worst managers being removed progressively from the manager universe), the excess return achieved is higher. If the asset owner was able to have the skill to select from the top quartile of active managers, he would have achieved a 3-year excess return of about +4.5%. Conversely, the left

Figure 13.2 Active manager excess return based on skill of asset owner manager selection process

Note: Period Apr 2004–Mar 2009.

Data Source: Morningstar

side of the graph depicts a situation where the manager selection was progressively poor (represented by the best managers being removed from the manager universe). If the investor, in the worst case, was only able to select managers in the bottom quartile, he would have achieved an excess return of −7.0%.

If we overlay a passive investment on the same graph (being an investment by definition having a zero excess return), it aligns with 20% of poor managers being removed from the universe. That is, if the investor has the skill to select an active strategy in the top 75% of the manager universe, then it is a better decision to be active, rather than passive. Further, the better an investor is in active manager selection, the greater should be the allocation to active management versus passive indexation.

2. The Ability to Short

The ability to use shorts in a portfolio or within a strategy has a significant impact on the risk and return characteristics of the active portfolio. Figure 13.3(a) shows the distribution of monthly returns of a passive investment in the S&P 500 index, i.e., a long-only investment with no shorting. Figure 13.3(b) shows the distribution of monthly returns of the HFR Equity Market Neutral index (which we use to represent the active component of manager portfolios). The graphs are purposely made with matching scales, to illustrate the difference in return distribution of the two kinds of strategies.

It is evident that the strategy which does not have the ability to short is susceptible to higher volatility and larger drawdowns, whereas a strategy which has the ability to systematically hedge market risk using shorts can reduce volatility and drawdowns to a large extent. As such the ability to short can significantly determine the risk and return characteristics of an active strategy.

3. Investment Universe

The investment universe of an active strategy can impact its ability to generate excess return at different points of time. For example, the average active strategy in US Equity Large Cap stocks may not be as successful as the average active strategy in Mid Cap European stocks in certain periods, either because of the difference in

Figure 13.3 Distribution of monthly returns: (a) S&P 500; (b) HFR equity market neutral strategies

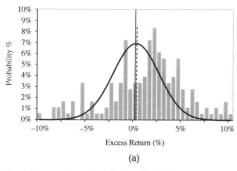
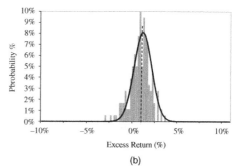

Data Source: Standard & Poor's, HFR

Figure 13.4 Average 3-year relative excess return by strategy category

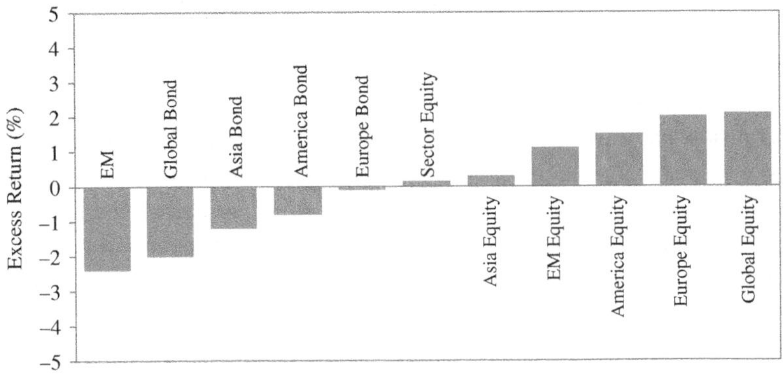

Data Source: Morningstar

skill of active managers for each area, or the difference in the opportunity set. Figure 13.4 displays the average 3-year excess return of active strategies in various equity universes for an illustrative period. While the actual results for each strategy category will vary depending upon the test period, the figure illustrates that the average excess return varies by category at any given time. Investors should therefore consider being active in areas where the average active manager is expected to be better, and passive where the average active manager excess return is likely to be poor.

4. Market Conditions

All active strategies tend to be biased towards the market regimes where they are likely to fare better and regimes where they are likely to be poor. There will be certain market environments that will favor active strategies and others that will not. While this may be difficult to generalize, as the investment process of each active manager is different, we can try and distinguish broadly between the extreme conditions of market factors, which either favor or act against active strategies. In Chapter 14 we will discuss a risk analysis process, from which we can conclude the regime biases of active strategies. Active management returns vary greatly in market regimes based on variables such as market direction, market volatility and value-growth. This result is significant in that it can help an investor decide when he strategically wants to have active management, and when passive indexation may be appropriate.

5. Investment Horizon

The investment horizon over which the strategy will be evaluated is a critical factor in determining the active–passive decision, as the risk and return characteristics of the investment can change dramatically based on the period considered. A behavioral bias present in the evaluation of investments is that asset owners tend to give a much longer evaluation horizon to a passive investment than to an active strategy. While a passive strategy is often thought of for three to five years and any interim evaluation is considered unnecessary, an active strategy is generally evaluated quarterly for its risk return characteristics. Rationally, however, there should be a common yardstick

Figure 13.5 3-year annualized rolling return of the S&P 500 index

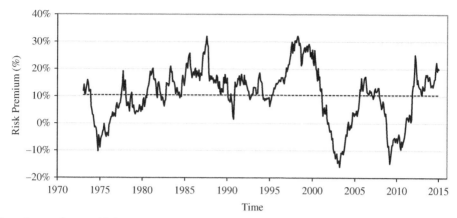

Data Source: Standard & Poor's

for the evaluation of any strategy, active or passive, especially when one is comparing strategies.

Figure 13.5 shows the 3-year rolling return of the S&P 500 index, which would represent the actual return achieved by a passive investment for a 3-year investment horizon, depending upon when the investment decision was implemented.

We can conclude that from a return perspective, just as the actual return achieved in an active strategy is not certain, the return from a passive investment is also uncertain. A common horizon framework is therefore essential in arriving at the active or passive implementation decision.

6. **Allocation Rebalancing Frequency**

Allocation processes which by nature do not require frequent rebalancing can tolerate investment in active funds and alternative funds, where there is often a considerable lead time between redeeming the investment and receiving the funds. However, allocation methods which require frequent rebalancing will find implementation in active funds difficult. For frequently rebalancing allocations, therefore, a portion of investments in passive indexation through futures is most time and cost effective. Active manager implementation is only possible where the allocated capital or risk is unlikely to change as a result of the allocation process.

7. **Asset Size**

Finally, the size of the assets under consideration can also change the structure followed for implementation. Implementation for an asset size above US$50mn (approximately), would benefit greatly from the multi-strategy allocation structure discussed in Chapter 5. The size here is sufficient to allow allocation to a variety of allocation processes. Each allocation method would then dictate the possibility of allocating to active or passive strategies based on the investment parameters discussed above. However, for a size below this amount, a multi-allocation process is generally unfeasible. In this scenario, as a single allocation process is implemented, there is greater room to allow for the active–passive decision.

13.2 ASSET OWNER CONSTRAINTS IMPACTING THE ACTIVE–PASSIVE DECISION

Apart from the basic risk and return parameters which determine the final client investment solution, every client has unique requirements which can influence the active–passive decision. These can include:

a. Liquidity requirement.
b. Expense ratio caps.
c. A cap on the allocation to absolute return/alternative/hedge fund products.
d. Home bias preferences.
e. A preference to use direct securities, rather than funds both from a cost and control standpoint.
f. A preference not to use leverage and shorting of securities/futures if possible.

These parameters act as constraints in determining the proportion of assets that should be implemented in active management versus passive management. We discuss the impact of these parameters in creating the final investment solution, in Chapter 16.

Much debate exists in the investment community on the value (or lack thereof) of active management. Most research in this area focuses on the excess return generated by active managers and the fees they charge for this effort. We propose here that the determinant of the active–passive implementation is more specific to the allocation process and the asset owner itself, rather than active managers. There will always be good and poor active managers. The active–passive debate thus needs to evolve from the absolute value of active management to the proportion of active versus passive management that is appropriate for any asset owner.

CHAPTER FOURTEEN

An Exposure-Based Risk Diagnostics Framework

Traditionally, risk management has always been characterized as an activity that is downstream of portfolio investment decisions, an activity that is less important than the active portfolio decision role of a portfolio manager, and done by running a portfolio through a standard risk system to produce a report. This positioning of risk within investment organizations led to a lower compensation structure for risk management staff compared to portfolio managers and thus attracted only a secondary quality of talent to the function. Post-global financial crisis, while the importance of risk management has been re-established, the process of analyzing and managing portfolio risk is largely unchanged.

In reality, risk and return are two sides of the same coin. One cannot generate return without taking risk, and active investment decisions are actually decisions on where to take risk in a portfolio. Return is simply an outcome of this risk allocation decision. Risk management as an activity is thus placed pari passu to the return management function (i.e., portfolio management), for the investment process to be effective. Just as portfolio managers are deputed to decide where to take risk to achieve their target return, an evolved risk management function needs to be deputed to adjudicate on the return implications of taking these risks.

14.1 SHORTCOMINGS OF A TRADITIONAL RISK ANALYSIS APPROACH

Active managers have generally measured their risk based on a single parameter – the volatility or tracking error of the portfolio. Decomposition of the tracking error has informed them of the source of risk (such as a risk report), and that has always been generally used as a gauge to confirm that the portfolio is within the range set by the asset owner. There are many shortcomings of this approach:

1. Unlike return numbers, which are a hard fact about which there can be little debate, risk is by definition the science of measuring something that is not known. As such, the use of a single methodology, no matter how efficient it may be, cannot capture the various dimensions of risk that can exist. Risk is multi-dimensional, and the fallacy of measuring it with a single risk model or approach has led to its inefficient measurement and management.
2. Behavioral science has documented the accepted fact that risk is not symmetric in nature. All individuals have a different reaction to variability on the positive side of an expectation distribution, compared to the negative side of the same distribution. However, all parameters that are in use today for portfolio risk measurement are symmetric.
3. Financial theory in general uses a normal distribution to model asset returns. In practice, negative tail events which are supposed to happen very infrequently, as believed to be the case by the normal distribution, in practice happen much more often. The world has fat tails which need to be accounted for in risk analysis.
4. All risk analysis today uses a defined period to calculate risk parameters, which results in an estimation of risk at the end of the investment horizon. This, however, assumes that the investor is indifferent to the path taken by the asset return, which in practice is not true. Institutions that are governed by individuals, at the end of the day behave like individuals, and are averse to intra-horizon drawdowns. The current formulation of risk parameters does not account for this facet.
5. Most asset managers depict their investment process in a sequential linear manner, where there is seldom a feedback loop after risk analysis has been done, to impact the investment process itself. The portfolio may well be modified by some managers after risk analysis is done, but the process is not. As such, risk analysis fails to make any significant impact in improving the investment decision process – in reality, its main objective.

14.2 EVALUATING INTENDED AND UNINTENDED RISK

One of the crucial aspects of evaluating an investment strategy is to try and assess if the returns were generated by luck or by skill. This is a critical fact to decide if future returns of the strategy are likely to be as successful as they may have been in the past. Gupta and Straatman (2006) propose that one needs to decompose portfolio risk into intended and unintended risk, as illustrated in Figure 14.1.

Portfolio risk can arise as a result of a defined intention by the investment process, or as an unintended residual of the portfolio construction process. Thus, exposures can be both taken or hedged by intention, whereas risk factors can be intended by the investment process, but can only be constrained in the portfolio construction process, and not

Figure 14.1   Distinguishing skill from luck in investment decisions

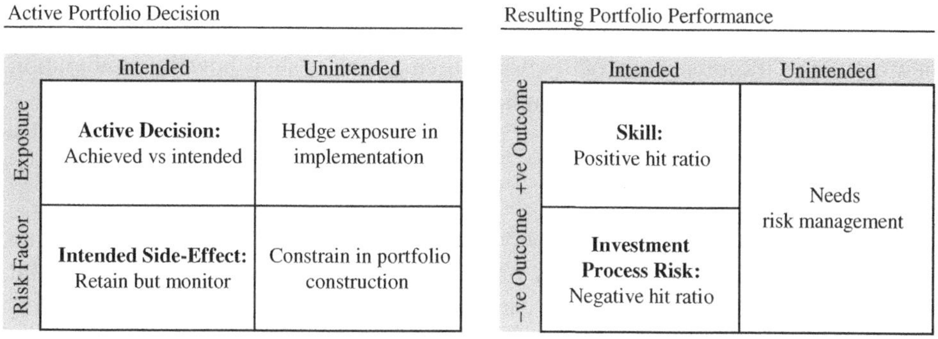

Active Portfolio Decision

	Intended	Unintended
Exposure	**Active Decision:** Achieved vs intended	Hedge exposure in implementation
Risk Factor	**Intended Side-Effect:** Retain but monitor	Constrain in portfolio construction

Resulting Portfolio Performance

	Intended	Unintended
+ve Outcome	**Skill:** Positive hit ratio	Needs risk management
–ve Outcome	**Investment Process Risk:** Negative hit ratio	

hedged. A composite of the intended and unintended risks which do not result in a positive active return, then comprise the set of investment process risk or "the probability of being wrong." This composite is the focus for risk management from the perspective of an active asset manager.

Vendor-developed generic risk models would find it difficult to decompose portfolio risk into intended and unintended, and as such investment process-based risk decomposition is integral to managing portfolio risk.

14.3 A MULTI-DIMENSIONAL RISK ARCHITECTURE

In Chapter 3 we discussed the transition of a traditional asset demarcated organization to an exposure-based organization. This process requires transitioning the concept of using a single dimension for measurement of risk, to measuring risk in a multi-dimensional manner. While commercially available risk models can measure market risk, they can never measure risk as a mirror to the active investment decision. As such, a true risk management function requires an internal process to be able to attribute risk to actual investment decisions, rather than to components of market risk. A multi-dimensional risk analysis framework would be able to analyze the risk of a portfolio along these multiple dimensions of exposures or risk factors (or various logical collections of the same).

Apart from evaluating risk from various perspectives, one must also choose appropriate parameters which are better at articulating the "real risk" present in an investment. Several measures are available which account for the asymmetric nature of risk and don't need the assumption of a normal distribution. These are definitive improvements. However, in order to capture the risk generated by the path taken by the asset, one must be able to account for the intra-horizon risk of an investment. In Chapter 10 we have elaborated on a revised risk measure which seeks to be a composite of end-of-horizon and intra-horizon risk.

While an exhaustive discussion covering all the different types of risk analysis is not possible here, we illustrate below some of the various types of analysis that are useful for portfolio evaluation. While none of these analysis techniques in isolation are anything new or unique, the importance of discussing them here is to show how the combination of all these techniques can lead to significant conclusions.

14.3.1 Skill Analysis

Evaluating the skill of an active strategy is a basic first step. This can include analysis such as historical drawdown analysis; return distribution analysis; rolling portfolio hit ratios and rolling information ratios; variation in portfolio active share; and cross-sectional hit ratios. Figure 14.2 shows the example of a skill analysis report can be created for any strategy.

Figure 14.2 Example of skill analysis for a strategy

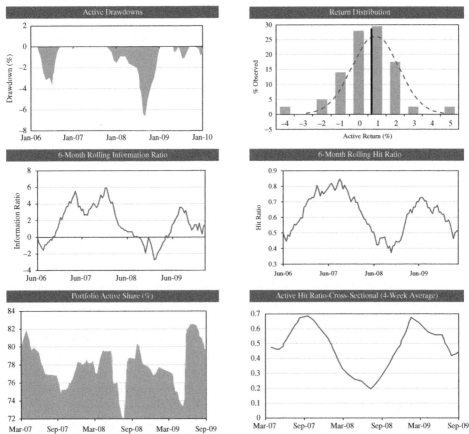

14.3.2 Investment Process Component Analysis

Attributing the return of a portfolio to the various parts of the investment process is important to understand the sources of risk and return that arise from each component of the
investment process. This synchronization of the attribution to investment process components is essential to enable a direct feedback loop to improve the investment process. As a
generic example, we illustrate in Figure 14.3 the decomposition of a portfolio into its various strategy sleeves (this is done when there is more than one investment decision maker
for the portfolio, each with a specific part of the investable universe), into allocation and
selection returns (if both are distinct in the investment process) and on the basis of risk
allocation and capital allocation.

14.3.3 Regime Risk Analysis

All active strategies generally have biases of the market regimes they perform well in, and
those where they are likely to perform poorly. An understanding of the inherent biases
of every of strategy can allow modification of the risk allocated to each strategy, so as to
favor strategies which are likely to perform in the current market regime.

We characterize market regimes using six basic variables across asset classes. Based
on this, we can conduct market regime analysis for any strategy to understand their
bias. We illustrate the regime analysis for a pure equity strategy in Figure 14.4 using
four of these regimes that are relevant – equity market direction, size, value-growth
and volatility.

Figure 14.3 Decomposition of portfolio risk based on investment process
components

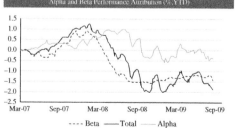

Figure 14.4 Active management regime analysis based on various factors:
(a) Market movement, (b) Volatility, (c) Value-growth, (d) Large cap–small cap

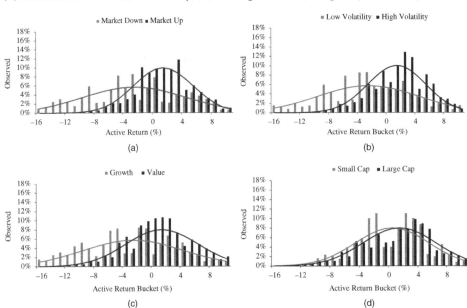

14.3.4 Style and Factor Risk Analysis

There are obviously a limitless number of styles and factors that can impact portfolio risk and return. We, however, use bottom-up variables to analyze this category of risk. Apart from simple point in time differences between portfolio factor exposures relative to the benchmark, the time series changes in this exposure can often be more significant to analyze the active bets in process by the portfolio manager. Furthermore, the impact of the combination of some of these variables can show the relationships between portfolio exposure changes over time to signify the move of a portfolio away from one aspect and towards another. Figure 14.5 shows an illustration of a point in time and time series analysis for style and factor risk analysis.

14.3.5 Macro Risk Analysis

Researchers have often included macro variables in the construction of multi-factor risk models; however, this can often give inconclusive or deceptive results, as it is significantly dependent on the variables chosen. We instead propose to use a broad range of macro variables, by categorizing them into categories of broad economy, foreign exchange related, interest rate related, credit related and commodity related. Figure 14.6 illustrates such an analysis, which analyses the portfolio at the security level for each macro variable, to arrive at the aggregate portfolio exposure.

Figure 14.5 Example of style and factor risk skill analysis for a strategy

	Value					
	PE	PE FY1	PE FY2	Div.Yield (%)	Div.Yield FY1(%)	MSCI Value(%)
PF	23.94	15.78	13.04	1.60	1.69	25.31
BM	23.59	15.78	12.97	2.39	2.44	56.44
ACT(%)	1	0	1	–33	–31	–56

	Probability Risk			
	ROE(%)	Volatility	ADV (20 days,%)	Liquid Position (%)
PF	11.90	3.64	0.86	4.42
BM	8.10	3.42	0.65	-
ACT(%)	47	6	31	-

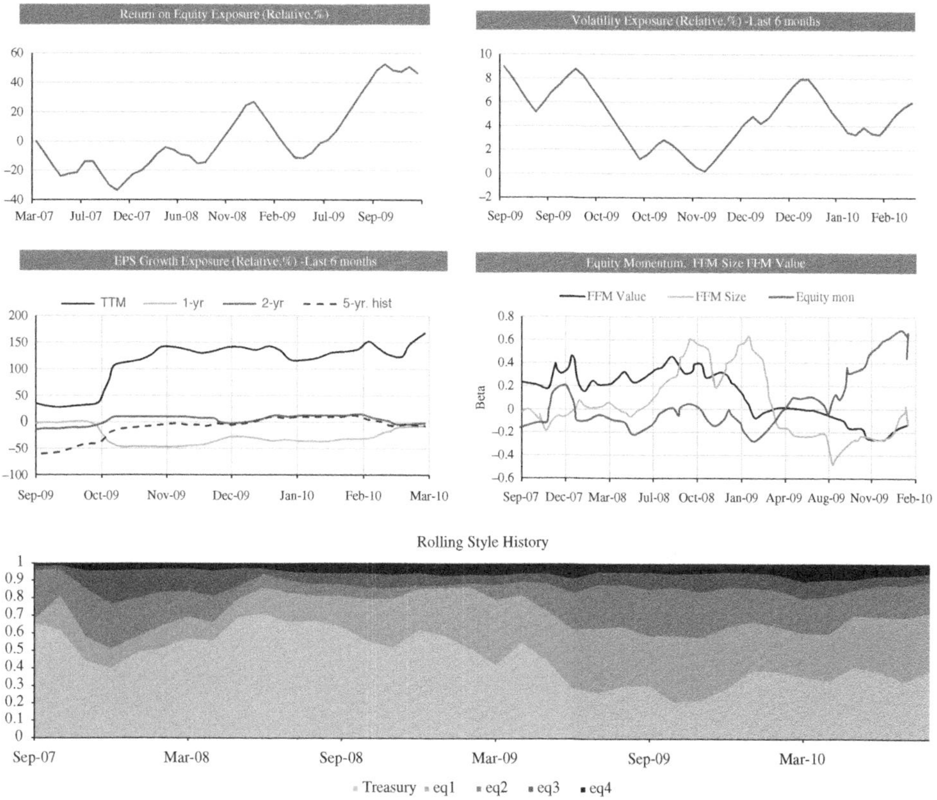
Return on Equity Exposure (Relative,%)
60
40
20
0
–20
–40
Mar-07 Jul-07 Dec-07 Jun-08 Nov-08 Feb-09 Jul-09 Sep-09
Volatility Exposure (Relative,%) -Last 6 months
10
8
6
4
2
0
–2
Sep-09 Sep-09 Oct-09 Oct-09 Nov-09 Dec-09 Dec-09 Jan-10 Feb-10
EPS Growth Exposure (Relative,%) -Last 6 months
TTM
1-yr
2-yr
5-yr. hist
200
150
100
50
0
–50
–100
Sep-09 Oct-09 Nov-09 Dec-09 Jan-10 Feb-10 Mar-10
Equity Momentum, FFM Size FFM Value
FFM Value
FFM Size
Equity mon
Beta
0.8
0.6
0.4
0.2
0
–0.2
–0.4
–0.6
Sep-07 Dec-07 Mar-08 Jul-08 Oct-08 Jan-09 Apr-09 Aug-09 Nov-09 Feb-10
Rolling Style History
1
0.9
0.8
0.7
0.6
0.5
0.4
0.3
0.2
0.1
0
Sep-07 Mar-08 Sep-08 Mar-09 Sep-09 Mar-10
Treasury
eq1
eq2
eq3
eq4

14.3.6 Stress Event Risk Analysis

While asset owners are always concerned about the impact of major events on portfolios, it is also reasonable to state that few researchers can predict stress events with any degree of certainty whatsoever. Further, no two events in the economic and financial world are ever alike. This makes event risk analysis very difficult to implement on a forward-looking basis. However, it is plausible to state that portfolio biases towards different categories of events can be assessed to a reasonable degree. As such we look at the impact of various categories of stress events in equities, bonds, interest rates, credits, commodities and FX and assess their relative impact on any portfolio. We use the classification proposed by the Bank for International Settlements to categorize stress events, and try to infer conclusions of portfolio exposure to the various categories of stress events. These results are illustrated in Figure 14.7.

Figure 14.6 Macro risk analysis for a strategy

Risk factor	Description	Unit	Value	Portfolio beta	Exposure T-stat
Economics					
Real GDP	Change in real GDP	%	3.95	0.73	3.7
Core CPI	Change in core CPI (ex.food and energy)	%	−2.11	0.58	1.2
CPI	Change in CPI (all items)	%	−0.34	0.30	2.0
Unemployment rate	Unemployment rate	%	1.68	10.51	5.9
Industrial production	Change in industrial production	%	29.98	0.04	0.7
Money supply	Change in money supply	%	23.92	−0.15	−1.5
Net export	Change in net export (normalized by GDP)	%	−26.15	−0.07	−0.2
Housing Index	Change in housing price	%	−19.42	0.13	3.6
FX					
Eff.exchange rate	Change in trade weighted exchange rate	%	−0.25	−3.39	−4.1
Exchange rate index	Change in exchange rate index	%	−1.63	0.25	1.4
USDEUR	Monthly change of USDEUR	%	1.85	0.54	0.0
HKDEUR	Monthly change of HKDEUR	%	1.88	0.16	0.0
GBPEUR	Monthly change of GBPEUR	%	−3.23	0.06	0.0
CHFEUR	Monthly change of CHFEUR	%	0.07	0.06	0.0
JPYEUR	Monthly change of JPYEUR	%	3.90	0.05	0.0
Interest rate					
Treasury bills	3 months Treasury rate		0.69	−0.70	−0.3
Mid-term Treasury	10 years or medium-term government bond yield		−3.86	2.22	0.6
Interbank 3m	3 month Interbank rate		0.01	6.08	1.6
Term spread	US Term spread		2.84	−0.16	−0.3
Credit					
TED spread	TED spread		0.12	−3.04	−4.5
Moody Aaa	Spread between Moody Aaa and US Treasury		1.67	−0.67	−0.9
Moody Baa	Spread between Moody Baa and US Treasury		2.66	−0.31	−0.8
Commodity					
Oil	Change in oil price	%	6.95	0.25	5.3
Gold	Change in gold price	%	2.10	0.11	1.1
Industrial material	Change in industrial metal price index	%	4.70	0.74	7.5
CRB	Change in CRB	%	4.00	0.82	7.3

Data Source: Bloomberg

We can conclude that active management returns vary greatly in market regimes based on market direction, market volatility and value-growth, but do not differ significantly in a market regime determined by size. This result is also significant in that it can help an asset owner incorporate a market view by decreasing allocation to active management when it is believed that market regimes do not favor active management.

14.3.7 Peer Group Comparison Analysis

A comparison of a portfolio with other participants with similar strategies can reveal areas where the portfolio in question stands out. This analysis is important in that it highlights if a particular portfolio event is unique to the portfolio being analyzed, or has impacted all peers. This is significant enough to highlight areas of expertise and concern about the portfolio. While potentially this can be across all aspects of analysis, the limitation on availability of competitor portfolio data limits this analysis to risk and return distributions. Figure 14.8 illustrates such an analysis, where the distributions show the positioning of all peers on the parameter of the graph, and the vertical line depicts the position of the portfolio being analyzed along that spectrum.

Figure 14.7 Example of Portfolio Stress Event analysis

	Start	End	Drawdown(%) PF	BM	Active
Equity					
- 1987 Black Monday and 1990s recessions					
- Recession 1990-1991	Jul-90	Sep-90	-18.13	-19.13	-0.92
- Nikkei stock price correlation in 1990 in Japan	Jan-90	Apr-90	-2.61	-2.92	-0.03
- 1991 coup attempt in Russia	Aug-91	Nov-91	-5.03	-5.07	-1.17
- IT bubble bursts					
- Tech decline 2000	Mar-00	Jun-00	-10.65	-10.48	-1.83
- Tech decline 2001	Jan-01	Mar-01	-20.74	-19.92	-2.55
- Tech decline 2002	May-02	Aug-02	-16.89	-17.19	-1.27
- Beta Stress	Apr-01	Apr-01	-2.44	-1.80	-0.77
- EURO STOXX decline in July 2001	Jul-01	Aug-01	-4.05	-3.58	-0.53
- 911 Terrorist attacks	Sep-01	Oct-01	-8.12	-7.63	-1.15
- Deta Stress	Oct-02	Oct-02	-2.30	-1.96	-0.97
- War Rally	Mar-03	Mar-03	-3.97	-4.59	-0.58
- Outbreak of SARS in 2003	Mar-03	Jun-03	-1.76	-1.57	-1.41
- 2003 high market volatility	Apr-03	May-03	-1.49	-1.36	-0.84
- Madrid Boming	Mar-04	Mar-04	-7.44	-6.74	-0.93
- Korean Rate Change	Aug-04	Aug-04	-2.21	-1.93	-0.65
- Quant crisis	Jul-07	Aug-07	-13.34	-13.26	-0.63
- Countertrend Bear Market Rally	Mar-09	May-09	-8.77	-9.59	-5.68
Bond					
- Bond correction 1994	Mar-94	Jun-94	-7.55	-6.95	-2.14
- JGB sell-off by news of JGB purchases by Trust Fund Bureau	Nov-98	Dec-98	-4.09	-5.00	-0.59
- JGB sell-off triggered by undersubscription at JGB auction in 2002	Sep-02	Dec-02	-12.54	-13.24	-0.97
- JGB Rate shock	May-03	Aug-03	-8.91	-9.10	-0.43
- US Bond market crash 2003	Jun-03	Sep-03	-8.91	-9.10	-0.43
Interest rates					
- Fed Funds 200 ptd	Jan-94	Feb-94	-4.33	-4.64	-0.22
- US Interest Rate Shock	Feb-00	Apr-00	-8.67	-8.32	-2.74
Credit					
- Japan financial crisis, collapse of Yamaichi, Sanyo and Hokkaido Takushoku Bank	Nov-97	Dec-97	-4.39	-4.52	-0.52
- Russia financial crisis					
- Collapse of Russia bond/equity market, interest rate and Ruble devaluation	May-98	Aug-98	-14.78	-15.86	-0.66
- Devaluation of Russia ruble and default of Russia treasury bills	Aug-98	Nov-98	-8.85	-8.74	-1.12
- All major stock markets rattled by Russia turmoil	Aug-98	Sep-98	-3.37	-3.68	-0.56
- Fall of LTCM	Sep-98	Oct-98	-4.73	-4.55	-1.08
- Argentine crisis					
- Restructure of Argentine's short-term debt, followed by a currency peg	Jun-01	Sep-01	-9.46	-9.44	-0.59
- Argentina 2nd debt swap, government refusal to guarantee foreign debt	Nov-01	Dec-01	-4.38	-4.09	-0.99
- Argentine Peso devaluation and free floating, and reform package	Jan-02	Apr-02	-8.78	-10.00	-2.16
- Credit Shock	Jun-02	Jul-02	-15.81	-17.05	-1.12
- US financial crisis					
- Collapse of subprime lending industry	Feb-07	Apr-07	-6.38	-6.47	-0.33
- Funds and bank losses from subprime MBS, and liquidity crisis	Jun-07	Aug-07	-13.34	-13.26	-0.63
- Bear Stearns collapse and sale to JPMorgan	Mar-08	Mar-08	-3.93	-3.26	-1.04
- Major banks report loss from involvement of subprime crisis	May-08	Jun-08	-9.16	-10.48	-0.25
- Fannie Mae /Freddie Mac Fed takeover, AIG, Merrill Lynch, Lehman crisis	Sep-08	Nov-08	-47.09	-48.64	-2.07
Commodity					
- Gulf War in 1990-91	Aug-90	Oct-90	-15.33	-16.36	-0.95
FX					
- European currency crisis in 1992 (ERM exit)	Aug-92	Oct-92	-10.91	-11.15	-1.47
- Mexican peso crisis in 1994 (Tequila Effect)					
- Mexican peso crisis - A candidate of PRI was assassinated	Mar-94	May-94	-5.65	-5.08	-1.84
- Mexican peso crisis - Secretary General of the PRI was assassinated	Sep-94	Dec-94	-10.59	-10.80	-0.77
- Devaluation of Mexican peso	Dec-94	Mar-95	-2.14	-2.28	-0.92
- Yen strenthening 1995	Feb-95	May-95	-2.17	-2.28	-0.91
- US dollar rally in July-August 1995	Jul-95	Aug-95	-8.09	-8.01	-1.09
- 1996-1997 AUD Dpreciation	Dec-96	Feb-97	-7.19	-8.11	-0.59

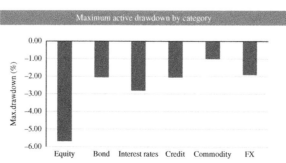

Data Source: Bloomberg, Bank for International Settlements

Figure 14.8 Peer group comparison analysis of a strategy

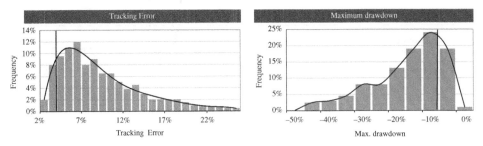

While detailing all the various kinds of risk analysis is beyond the scope of this text, the intention is to propose that the traditional approach of a single methodology-based risk analysis needs to evolve to one which has multiple dimensions. The number of dimensions can keep expanding, with the objective that one needs to create a risk process which mirrors the concepts used in the portfolio investment process.

CHAPTER FIFTEEN

Impact of Manager Compensation on Allocation Decisions

The task of portfolio managers in the management of a portfolio is to meet the return objective of clients while adhering to risk constraints. However, a traditional portfolio does not readily incorporate the behavioral biases of the portfolio manager as an individual, in arriving at portfolio decisions. A traditional manager charging a fixed fee is differently incentivized than a hedge fund manager expecting 20% of the outperformance. Compensation structure is therefore a potentially important variable for the portfolio management decision. Not only can it explain a fund's overall risk target, but it also opens the analysis to such contractual features as high-water mark provisions and stop-loss clauses.

In this chapter we adopt a well-known model of managerial compensation and apply it in the context of the compensation scheme of a typical hedge fund. We take an asset manager's view, focusing on performance measures and the implied probability distribution of returns. The underlying model is similar to Carpenter (2000), who treats the case of a manager with an option-like payout scheme. The manager adjusts risk-taking dynamically in continuous time to maximize expected utility of the compensation earned. Other applications of the same approach include Basak and Shapiro (2001) with a study of Value-at-Risk-based risk management, and Hodder and Jackwerth (2003) in the context of hedge fund management.

A central result of our model is that a hedge fund's convex payout structure, implied by the high-water mark, can give rise to return distributions quite different from the normal. In particular, for our baseline parameter values the return distribution is negatively skewed. This is in line with empirical findings on hedge fund returns, for example, Brooks and Kat (2001), McFall Lamm (2003) and Li and Kazemi (2007). Another prediction of the model is that as fund performance falls short of the high-water mark the manager is pushed into higher risk-taking. This is consistent with a finding reported in Elton, Gruber and Blake (2003), that hedge fund volatility is explained by past performance.

After defining the general contractual form and managerial constraints, we discuss the manager's optimal activeness policy. This generates a probability distribution over assets. We then turn to variations of the model and the importance of managerial skill. We analyze the impact of initial assets under management and manager age on the analysis. We also discuss how different managerial contracts found in practice can be seen as special cases of the basic set-up and examine implications for long-term fund performance.

15.1 COMPENSATION STRUCTURE

Consider a general contractual form where the compensation given to the asset manager consists of a fixed fee and a performance fee, depending on whether the manager has outperformed a set target, or high-water mark. Not meeting the high-water mark is costless, but if underperformance is severe it will be difficult to raise new funds and at some point it will in fact be impossible. To encompass all possibilities, we consider four regions for the performance of the fund:

- **Outperformance region.** If funds exceed the high-water mark, the performance fee is set as a percentage of the outperformance.
- **Underperformance region.** If funds are below the high-water mark, there is no performance fee, and as long as underperformance is moderate no additional costs apply.
- **Restructuring region.** If funds fall further below a lower threshold, the manager starts to incur a personal cost, linear in the underperformance relative to the lower threshold.
- **Default region.** If funds deteriorate even further, the manager loses his right to manage the assets.

The compensation structure is illustrated in Figure 15.1. Default is assumed to be avoided in all events. Technically, in the model this is accomplished by associating default with an infinite cost. In addition to the contractual scheme we wish to study the impact of the manager's age, or the number of years the fund has been running. Age does not emerge naturally in this set-up and including it as a parameter therefore requires some judgment. One can expect a more mature manager to have accumulated both experience and capital. Furthermore, he will be closer to retirement and may also have grown more attached to the investment technology he is pursuing. We focus on a manager of mature age being more intimately associated with fund performance overall, not only compensation earned. This is brought into the model by adding a linear segment to the compensation function in the underperformance region.

For comparison purposes it is illustrative to also consider a contract which is linear in the outperformance. Although as a contract this may be difficult to establish in practice, it forms an important benchmark as it aligns the interests of the manager with the owners. A linear contract can be thought of as a case where the manager is managing his own account.

Figure 15.1 The utility function for managerial compensation

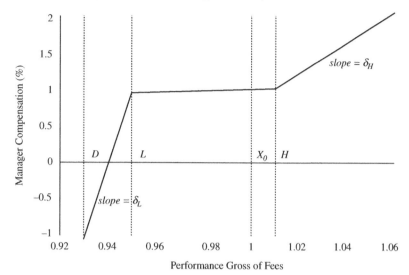

Performance Gross of Fees

For a mathematical formulation of the compensation scheme, if performance is x and the initial asset base is A_0, then the compensation to the manager is $A_0 \times C(x)$, where

$$C(x) = \begin{cases} cx + \delta_H(1-c)(x-H), & H \leq x \\ cx + a(x-H), & L \leq x < H \\ cx - \delta_L(1-c)(L-x) + a(L-H), & D \leq x < L \\ -\infty, & x < D. \end{cases}$$

Here c is the fixed fee, δ_H is the outperformance fee and H is the high-water mark. The underperformance cost is δ_L, which is triggered when assets fall below L, and D is the default point. The parameter is included as a proxy for the manager's age. The older the manager the higher is a, and we take the case $a = 0$ to be a manager with no experience.

The points D, L and H are expressed relative assets gross of the fixed fee. Their equivalents net of the fixed fee are given by $(1-c)D$ and similarly for L and H.

It can be seen that for a traditional asset manager $\delta_H = 0$, as the manager is not paid any performance fees. For a hedge fund manager δ_H is often equal to 0.2. Additionally, the risk tolerance of the asset owners determines L, which can be thought of as the evaluation level below which the asset owner becomes uncomfortable, and D the stop-loss level.

 ## 15.2 MANAGERIAL CONSTRAINTS

Given this compensation structure our main question is what risk level the manager will target. While this normally is a decision subject to a number of constraints, in our stylized framework the determinants are reduced to (1) the manager's level of skill and (2) the manager's level of risk aversion. Each is associated with a single parameter.

15.2.1 Managerial Skill

As a measure of skill, the information ratio is inarguably the most widely accepted indicator, and it is commonly adopted to measure and compare investor performance. Making use of the information ratio, a convenient way to incorporate skill is to assume that the manager has access to an investment technology under which assets under management evolve according to

$$dX_t = \lambda X_t dt + X_t dW_t,$$

where X_t is assets under management, λ is the information ratio and W_t is a standard Wiener process.

In practice, however, the manager is able to adjust the risk level that he would expose the total assets under management by using one of two methods. To reduce exposure, one option is to balance allocations between the investment technology and a risk-free asset. This reduces risk while maintaining the information ratio of the overall process. Another possibility is to keep all the holdings in the original investment technology, but to cut down the exposure of each individual holding. Again, risk is reduced without affecting the information ratio.

In this way the manager can adjust the activeness level of the overall investment strategy. We assume that this can be conducted continuously and completely at the manager's discretion. Denoting the activeness level by θ_t, assets under management will then evolve as

$$dX_t = \theta_t \left(\lambda X_t dt + X_t dW_t \right).$$

Since the volatility of the original investment technology has been fixed to one (or 100%), θ_t also becomes the instantaneous tracking error of the fund.

15.2.2 Managerial Risk Preferences

While the manager's skill is neatly compressed in the information ratio, risk aversion is less immediate. To incorporate risk preferences, we make use of a utility function, where we assume that the manager is concerned with the expected utility of the compensation received,

$$E \left[U \left(C \left(X_T \right) \right) \right].$$

We take the utility function to be of constant relative risk aversion type so that

$$U(x) = \frac{1}{1-\gamma} x^{1-\gamma}.$$

If the manager were managing his own account, this would be a version of the Merton (1971) model, in which case the optimal activeness policy is constant. That is,

Figure 15.2   Optimal activeness level as function of performance

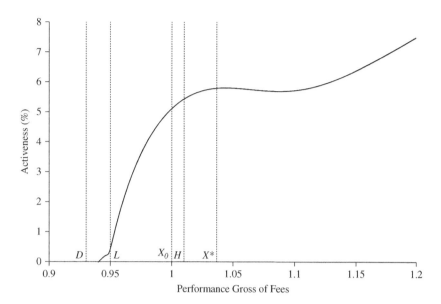

θ_t is the same for all t and X_t. As we shall see, when the compensation structure is non-linear results will be different.

 15.3 OPTIMAL ACTIVENESS

We now have the tools to deduce the activeness policy of a manager acting to maximize his expected utility. Figure 15.2 gives the activeness policy as a function of performance for a contract with one year to expiry for a manager with an information ratio of 1.5. We see that optimal activeness tends to zero somewhere around $X_t = 0{:}94$. More exactly, activeness tends to zero at the point where the manager's total compensation equals zero. This follows since utility tends to $-\infty$ as compensation approaches zero.

We use the following parameters to model our scenario:

(*i*) Contract Specifications

Initial assets	X_0	1
Fixed fee	c	0.01
High-water mark	H	1
Excess performance compensation	δ_H	0.2
Restructuring threshold	L	0.95
Investigation marginal cost	δ_L	1
Termination threshold	D	0.93
Initial assets under management	A_0	100
Age parameter	a	0

(*ii*) Investment Process

      Information ratio λ 1.5

(*iii*) Managerial Utility

      Risk aversion coefficient γ 4

As the contract approaches expiry, the manager's position can change quite dramatically. In Figure 15.3 activeness policies are given for different expiry terms. With one month left, activeness can reach close to 14%. As the expiry date approaches, there is in fact no upper limit to the activeness policy.

However, if performance is well above the high-water mark, the manager will conversely reduce activeness as he starts to protect the upside attained. Thus, for sufficiently high performance activeness always remains bounded. There is a cut-off level in the Figure, denoted X^*, below which activeness may tend to infinity, and above which activeness always tends to a finite limit as the expiry date approaches. For current parameter settings $X^* = 1.037$. A closer examination also reveals that activeness tends to zero at the lower threshold L. At this point the manager has nothing to gain from a small increase in fund value, and only stands the risk of entering restructuring if performance drops further.

Figure 15.4 looks at activeness from a different angle, giving the optimal policies as functions of time while keeping performance fixed. For performance paths less than X^*, but greater than L, activeness tends to infinity as the expiry date approaches. In

Figure 15.3 Optimal activeness level as function of performance for different terms to expiry as indicated

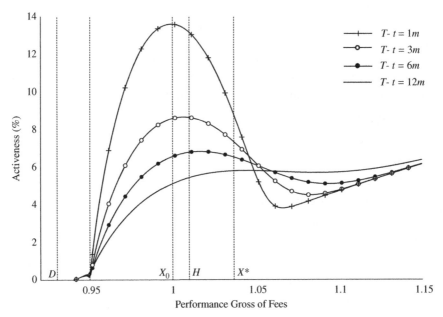

Figure 15.4 Optimal activeness as function of time keeping assets under management fixed at indicated levels

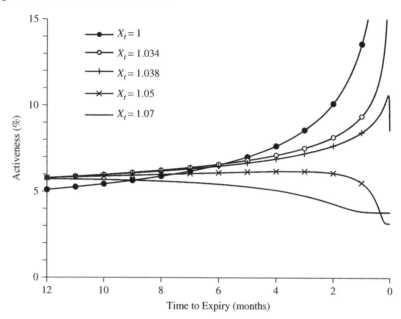

all other cases activeness tends to a finite limit. In the case $X_t = 1{:}038$ activeness is increasing up to shortly before the terminal date, after which it falls sharply. Given the optimal activeness strategy we can calculate some basic performance measures. The instantaneous return is $dX_t = X_t$, and this gives the sample mean, tracking error and information ratio, respectively, as

$$MR = \frac{1}{T}\int_0^T \frac{dX_t}{X_t},$$

$$TE = \sqrt{\frac{1}{T}\int_0^T \left(\frac{dX_t}{X_t}\right)^2},$$

$$IR = \frac{MR}{TE \times \sqrt{T}}.$$

All these quantities are stochastic, and their expected values are given in Table 15.1 gross and net of fees. (Net of fees performance is $X_t - C(X_t)$ and statistics net of fees are calculated similarly to MR, TE and IR based on $d[X_t - C(X_t)]/[X_t - C(X_t)]$. Since the starting value of the net of fees process is $(1-c) X_0$, to incorporate the fixed fee each sample mean return is further reduced by c. No further adjustment is made to the sample tracking error.)

We see that the expected sample information ratio is slightly less than the manager's internal information ratio of 1.5, even gross of fees. This follows as the dynamic adjustment

Table 15.1 Performance summary statistics

	Expected Sample MR	Expected Sample TE	Expected Sample IR
Gross of Fees	9.55%	6.88%	1.40
Net of Fees	7.24%	5.99%	1.22

of activeness acts as a separate source of variation not contributing to performance and this raises the value of the denominator when the information ratio is calculated.

Net of fees, the performance fee acts to reduce both sample mean return and tracking error. The fixed fee lowers the mean return without affecting the tracking error. The net effect is a further fall in the information ratio.

15.4 THE DISTRIBUTION OF PERFORMANCE

The optimal activeness strategy results in a probability distribution for assets under management, which is depicted in Figure 15.5. Most notably, in the region from L to X^* the probability density is zero. This corresponds to the manager's risk-taking region, where there is no upper bound to the activeness policy. Performance numbers are effectively thrown out of this region as the manager escalates activeness when the contract term approaches.

Even though activeness is unbounded, the distribution is bounded below since the manager always cuts activeness to zero before default actually occurs. In the restructuring region there is a point mass at L, reflecting the manager's resistance to enter

Figure 15.5 Probability density over performance

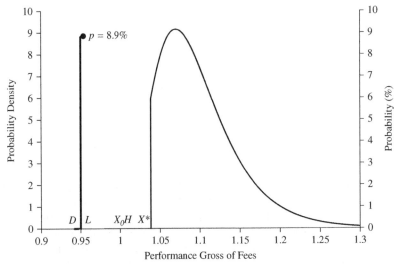

Notes: Density along the left axis. The point masses at 0.93 and 0.95 are measured on the right hand axis.

Table 15.2 Distribution summary statistics

	Mean	Standard Deviation	Distribution IR	Probability of Shortfall	Loss given Shortfall	Log-Omega
Gross of Fees	8.87%	6.40%	1.39	8.84%	5.00%	1.22
Net of Fees	6.12%	5.30%	1.16	8.84%	5.95%	1.01

Notes: Gross of fees statistics are based on $X_T - 1$, and net of fees on $X_T - C(X_T) - 1$. Distribution IR is mean divided by standard deviation. Probability of shortfall is the probability that $X_T < 1$. Log-Omega is $(2\pi)^{-1/2} \log(\Omega)$ where $\Omega = E(X_T - 1)^+ / (1 - X_T)^+$.

restructuring. Most of the probability mass is collected above X*, however, meaning that the manager most likely outperforms.

Table 15.2 gives some statistics for the distribution. A point to notice is that the log-Omega is significantly lower than the information ratio. This reflects the negative skew of the distribution.

 ## 15.5 THE IMPORTANCE OF SKILL

In general, a highly skilled manager can act with more confidence and take more risk. This is affirmed in Figure 15.6, which gives the optimal activeness policies corresponding to a series of information ratios. As long as the information ratio is positive, activeness

Figure 15.6 Optimal activeness level as function of performance for various information ratios as indicated

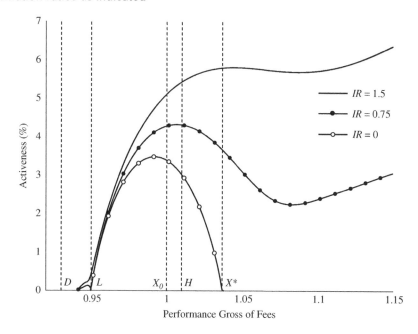

Figure 15.7 Probability density over performance for various levels of skill as indicated

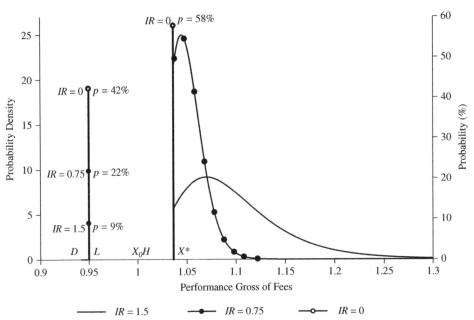

Notes: Density along the left hand axis. The point masses at 0.95 and 1.037 are measured on the right hand axis.

increases with skill. The risk of not meeting the target is successively outweighed by the higher potential upside. A point to notice is that the manager's skill has no impact on the location of X^*. This is determined by the compensation structure and the manager's risk aversion coefficient alone. For the limiting case as the information ratio approaches zero, the optimal policy is zero everywhere except in the risk-taking region, from L to X^*.

For a manager with negative skill the situation differs dramatically.[1] Outside the risk-taking region the optimal policy is zero, similarly to the case of a zero information ratio. Inside the risk-taking region, however, the optimal policy is to increase risk without bounds. This all-or-nothing strategy follows as any positive but finite level of activeness is associated with an expected fall in asset value. By increasing risk without bounds, the manager effectively takes one big bet with a binary outcome, where performance ends up either at X^* or L. Once either boundary has been reached, activeness is immediately taken down to zero. The timing of the bet is irrelevant to the manager, and can be made at any time before the terminal date. The associated probability graphs are given in Figure 15.7. These show how the distribution narrows as the information ratio falls, reflecting the manager's decrease in activeness. Moving from $\lambda = 1:5$ down to

---

[1] Ideally, when the information ratio is negative, the manager would like to short the strategy as this would reproduce a strategy with a positive information ratio of the same magnitude. It is assumed however that shorting the strategy is infeasible.

$\lambda = 0{:}75$ the distribution narrows and the point mass at L rises. As the information ratio reaches zero, the distribution collapses into two point masses, at L and X^* respectively.

For information ratios less than zero the distribution is always the same. The manager increases activeness without bounds and performance ends up either at L or at X^*. The associated probabilities are solely determined by the relative distance to the starting point, and skill (or lack thereof) has no effect on the outcome.

Performance statistics and statistics for the distribution at different levels of information ratio confirm that for positive levels of skill the expected sample information ratio is lower than the manager's internal information ratio. Gross of fees never falls below zero, however.

 ## 15.6 ACTIVENESS AND AGE

We investigate how the optimal policy depends on the manager's age. This has been taken into the model through the parameter a, which adds a linear segment to the compensation function in the underperformance region. The impact of higher age is that the manager will attribute a greater risk to underperformance. Implications for the activeness policy can be viewed in Figure 15.8. Most significantly, activeness falls with higher values of a.

Figure 15.8 Optimal activeness level at a function of performance for different age parameters as indicated. Performance fixed at $X_t = 1$

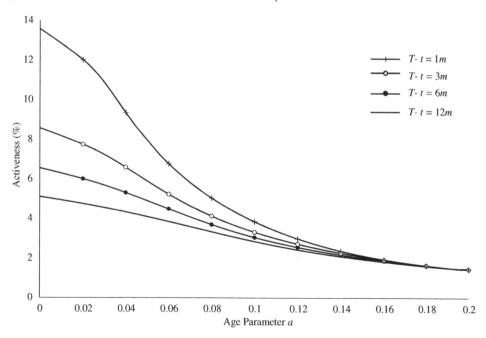

15.7 IMPLICATIONS FOR A MULTI-PERIOD SETTING

The analysis so far has considered the case with a single date for settling compensation. From the view of the asset owner it is more likely, however, that the investment horizon spans over several years, encompassing a series of compensations. The distribution of performance looking a few years ahead is often of greater interest when deciding whether and how much to allocate.

A full treatment of the multi-period case would also consider the optimal activeness policy from the view of the manager, taking contract continuance into consideration. Unfortunately, this introduces theoretical as well as numerical issues and to cut these short here we simply take the activeness policy derived in the previous sections as given. This is then iterated forward a number of times, giving an accumulated distribution over performance. The simplified route can be seen as a special case where the manager is concerned with the next period's compensation only, or equivalently as a limiting case where the manager's discount factor has approached one.

Also, this section shifts attention to performance net of fees. Because compensation is settled several times, gross of fees performance is not immediate.

15.7.1 Compensation Structure

When iterating the procedure forward we apply an updating procedure for the contract parameters. If the fund underperforms parameters remain unaltered, but if the fund outperforms parameters are updated as

$$D_n = D \times X_n,$$

$$L_n = L \times X_n,$$

$$H_n = H \times X_n.$$

Where, X_n is the value of the fund net of fees at the end of period n. Effectively, whenever the fund outperforms the compensation regions are transformed so that for the next period the structure of the original compensation contract has been restored.

15.7.2 The Distribution of Performance

Iterating the solution forward twice, the density functions for assets net of fees are as in Figure 15.9, after the first and second year, respectively. A notable difference between the distributions is the jagged shape around one in the right-hand graph. The two small humps in this region correspond to the fund underperforming once and outperforming once.

We can also record a difference in the standard deviation of the two distributions. Due to diversification over time, the 2-year distribution has a lower standard deviation on an annualized basis, 2.70% as compared to 5.30% for the 1-year distribution. The means of the two distributions are approximately equal, however, 6.12% and 5.94% for the 1- and 2-year distributions, respectively.

Figure 15.9 Probability density over performance net of fees, after one year to the left and after two years to the right

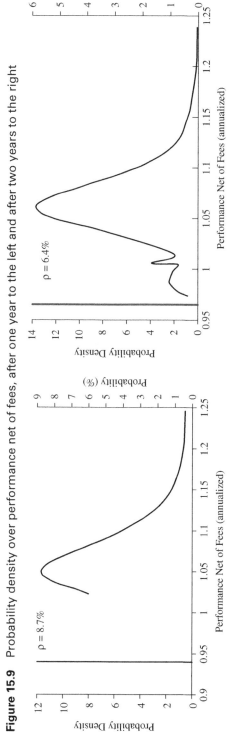

Notes: Performance is net of fees and annualized according to $X_T^{1/T}$. Density along the left hand axis. The point mass at $0.94^{1/T}$ is measured on the right hand axis.

Figure 15.10 Probability density over performance net of fees after ten years

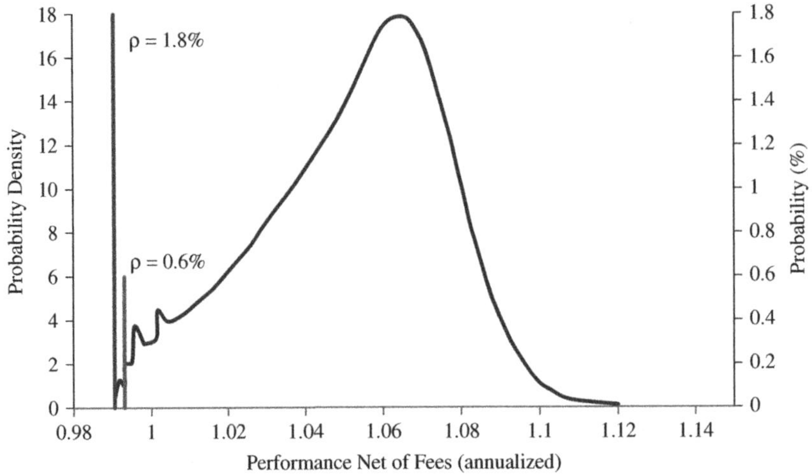

Notes: Performance is net of fees and annualized according to $X_T^{1/T}$. Density along the left hand axis. The point masses at $0.92^{1/10}$ and $0.94^{1/10}$ are measured on the right hand axis.

Figure 15.10 gives the density function after ten years. It has a clear skew to the left, which is the result of the manager's tendency to cut activeness following a year of underperformance. Cutting activeness reduces the potential of outperformance in the next year and if this fall in activeness is severe it can result in an underperformance trap, such that whenever the fund underperforms it becomes excessively difficult to recover.

15.8 EXAMPLES OF MANAGERIAL CONTRACTS

While the analysis so far has focused on the compensation structure of a typical hedge fund, the general framework allows for a range of contractual structures. Three such structures which are common in the marketplace are:

▪ A traditional asset manager
▪ A proprietary trader
▪ Guaranteed liabilities.

A traditional asset manager typically charges a fixed fee but no performance fee. In this case the model would predict a very cautious activeness policy, which appears in line with what we observe in practice as traditional managers often tend to hug the benchmark and not take any risk.

Turning to the second example, a proprietary trader can be regarded as managing his own account, which means that the manager participates in all the gains as well as the losses. This corresponds to the linear contract, in which the traditional Merton-type policy obtains. However, if there is a lower bound to the losses the manager is liable for, then again there will be a region with excessive risk-taking from the manager.

For the third and final example we have the case of guaranteeing liabilities. If a money manager is confident that he can get a positive portfolio performance, it would be in his interest to raise total assets by guaranteeing the liability to asset owners such as pension plans. In exchange for taking this risk away from the plan sponsor onto himself, it is likely that the manager has a much higher participation in the upside of the performance. This can be viewed as a case where L has been raised to the level of the high-water mark, so that the manager starts to incur costs as soon as assets drop below H. In exchange for taking this cost, the outperformance fee δ_H is increased. The structure of a typical hedge fund contract differs in several aspects from that of a manager offering a liability guarantee. Firstly, the typical hedge fund contract with a combination of a base fee and a performance fee creates a convex pay-off profile triggering a well-known incentive for excessive risk-taking in a region around the high-water mark. In the case of guaranteed liabilities this tendency is mitigated through the manager's participation in the downside, which creates a more linear pay-off profile. Of course, when underperformance is severe and the manager is close to defaulting on his guarantees, risk-shifting may again apply. But the commitment of personal funds makes it a less likely event, more resembling a regular situation of financial distress.

Secondly, hedge fund contracts are normally settled once a year. This differs from the guaranteed liabilities case in that this runs over the full period of the liability stream, which may very well span 30 years or more.

One effect of this is that it gives the guaranteed liabilities manager more flexibility in terms of performance. For a hedge fund, a year with bad performance can easily set off redemptions putting the manager out of business completely, while a manager with a longer horizon can afford a period with restructuring and recovery. There is an advantage to have the option to manage assets on a long-term basis without withdrawal risk or asset gathering risk. In favor of a manager with a hedge fund contract, however, it should be noted that the repeated convex pay-off effectively gives him an option on the maximum of the performance stream over a sequence of years. The guaranteed liabilities manager receives compensation based only on performance at the end of the horizon.

A third difference between a hedge fund and a guaranteed liabilities plan is as regards marketing costs. A hedge fund must continuously spend efforts on marketing products for the purpose of attracting new investors as well as retaining existing ones. Since investors participate directly in the ups and downs of the fund they have a natural interest in performance on a continuous basis. This contrasts the guaranteed liabilities manager who has effectively bought the rights to manage the liability stream. In this case asset owners can never expect more than their guarantee and the manager's communication to them can therefore be constrained to assuring that the present value of the liability stream is within bounds.

15.9 CONCLUSIONS

This chapter has investigated the optimal activeness policy of a manager with a compensation structure resembling that of a typical hedge fund. Looking at the optimal activeness policy we find similarly to previous studies a policy that is highly variable. The variability is such that it can in fact act to lower the sampled information ratio.

Further on the activeness policy, we document a region around the high-water mark where the manager pushes activeness to infinity as the compensation date approaches. This behavior causes the asset density to split into two parts, to the left and to the right of the high-water mark. In the region around the high-water mark the probability density is zero. This is referred to as the manager's risk-taking region.

Conversely, restructuring costs cause the manager to be extra cautious on the downside. A resistance to enter restructuring gives rise to a point mass in the distribution, just immediately before restructuring is initiated. Taken together these results support the general intuition that the asset density expands where the compensation scheme is convex, and contracts where it is concave.

In a study of managerial skill, we find that for positive levels of skill activeness is increasing in skill. In this respect the compensation structure serves a purpose of aligning the interests of the manager and the investor. For negative levels of skill, we find a quite different behavior. Optimal activeness is zero everywhere except over an infinitesimal period of time, where the optimal policy is to increase activeness without bounds. The resulting asset density in this case is two point masses located at each end of the risk-taking region.

Looking at assets under management we find that as the asset base grows, activeness falls. This is a direct consequence of the constant absolute risk aversion type of utility function. In a stylized study of manager age, we find that activeness falls with age, which is a result of the manager beginning to care not only about performance but also about the fund itself. Lastly, we look at the implications for a multi-period setting. Taking the optimal policy as given and iterating it forward we get an asset probability function some years into the future. Here, a point to notice is that if the manager underperforms one year, this significantly lowers the activeness policy the following year. This in turn makes it difficult for the manager to recover from the underperformance, and this can cause an underperformance trap where even a relatively skilled manager can find it difficult to outperform the high-water mark.

In summary we have found that nonlinear compensation structures can have significant implications for managerial behavior. The general framework we've discussed in this chapter has allowed us to address a range of issues that are of interest from the point of view of an investor. Taking managerial incentives into account can provide an investor with valuable information for the asset delegation decision.

CHAPTER SIXTEEN

From Multi-Asset Strategies to Multi-Asset Solutions

W e identify three disrupters to the conventional industry structure, which have caused a transition both in the manufacture and marketing of investment products. This structural change over the 1990s and 2000s has created a more diversified landscape of players.

1. The Fee Led Disruption

The first disruption to this structure was the advent of passive management, which challenged the efficacy of active management at a high cost. For the first time, asset managers were forced to consider the merits of active versus passive management. As passive management was a scale business, it created a couple of index management giants, while the rest of the industry clung on to revenue from active management.

2. The Return Led Disruption

The second wave of disruption came with the advent of hedge funds, which aimed to deliver the same or better excess returns than traditional active managers, but without the beta. Concurrently, they were able to transform the revenue model from a flat management fee to a performance incentive fee.

3. The Distribution Led Disruption

The third shock to the system was the concept of consumer led firms, such as retail banks, realizing that just selling the funds to their customers (no matter who manufactures them) was also a lucrative business. This specialization in marketing rather than manufacturing created an industry of specialists within the business.

Figure 16.1 depicts a map of asset management organizations with the vertical axis representing the business dimension of product management versus product marketing, and the horizontal axis representing the product dimension of absolute return versus relative return.

Traditional asset managers who have historically occupied the right half of this plot, choosing to both manage and market relative return products, are evolving to either pure marketing organizations or product managers. Product marketers in general have a greater access to asset owners and a distribution network, and generate revenue as commission income. Traditional asset managers who are choosing to have a product management arm are increasing assets and leveraging economies of scale. There are of course hybrid situations. Some who have the ability to both market products (given their brand recognition) and manage them (given their internal asset management team) continue to span the right half of the plot. Others that have the product marketing strength are choosing to invest in managing products that are non-traditional.

Hedge funds that started as product managers, claiming investment skill while continuing to occupy this space, are looking to expand into the relative return marketing space occupied by traditional asset managers, in a bid to increase assets with superior performance capability. The greater complexity and variety in availability of financial structures has also led to increased intermediation between the asset owner and asset manager. Funds of hedge funds created a space in the market, despite creating a higher cost structure and increased misalignment of interests, as they allowed "knowledgeable" access to hedge funds with operational ease. This value proposition having decayed, they are forced to represent themselves as marketing or operational-oriented, rather than skill-oriented.

Figure 16.1 The evolving asset manager market structure

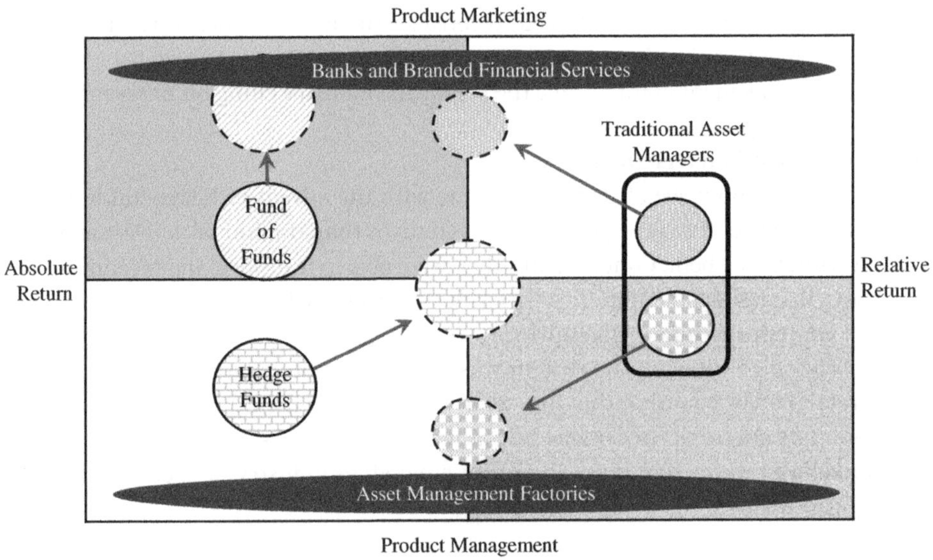

16.1 CURRENT PHASE OF INDUSTRY TRANSITION

We believe that the current transition phase will see a disruption to the current industry structure led by the allocation process. This will be driven by the realization that there is a misalignment between the asset owners' and asset managers' investment objectives and that the majority of a portfolio's total return is a function of the allocation decision, rather than the security selection decision. Currently the majority of all investment resources at investment banks, at asset owner organizations and at investment management firms are focused on the security selection decision instead. This transition will create a reallocation of resources within each market participant, and a redefinition of product segments.

▪ **Plan Sponsor**
    Most resources at plan sponsors are dedicated to the selection and redemption of external managers. The allocation decision is either done by a smaller internal team or by an external consultant. A transition to a larger multi-process allocation team and a smaller team for manager selection would be a result of this transition to come in line with what is more important for the asset owner.
▪ **Asset Manager – Index Plus**
    All index plus-type products such as enhanced indexing, fundamental indexing or various methods of non-market cap-based weighting techniques will become more prevalent and available in liquid and inexpensive form. However, unlike the current generation of index plus products which blend various exposures in an effort to beat the benchmark, the new generation will provide transparent exposure to various risk exposures in a cost-effective product, but without the promise of beating any given benchmark. They will be various forms of liquid beta, not index plus products.
▪ **Asset Manager – Long-Only Active**
    An active long-only manager will no longer have the standard market cap-weighted index as a benchmark. Instead the benchmark to outperform will be a segment of the market, such as a value biased index or a high dividend yield stock index, i.e., the benchmark is actually a combination of stocks, which collectively have a defined exposure. Hence asset owners would have the ability to allocate to various risk exposures, with or without the predisposition of active or passive management. The active manager would still have the ability to add value if he can, but over and above standard risk exposure bias.
▪ **Asset Manager – Hedge Fund**
    Hedge funds profess not to take systematic beta bets. While this may or may not be true, all hedge funds will in the future be required to detail their risk exposures with greater regularity. This will enable the asset owner to combine these exposures in their overall portfolio to arrive at the final desired allocation. Risk analysis of hedge fund portfolios thus would need to increase substantially.

▪ **Investment Bank**

While corporate analysts would still be necessary for the corporate finance business, the requirement of asset owners will shift to greater emphasis on strategy and allocation along multiple factors and dimensions. As such, allocation resources will increase at the expense of stock research resources. Further, the focus of investment banks will be to provide liquidity in products structured along beta factors for exposure. This will be the new generation of market-making activity.

▪ **Asset Manager – Investment Solution**

While the first distribution led disruption created client-focused organizations to market investment products, they were still focused on their product shelf, rather than client customization. In the second transition, the marketing organizations need to embrace client customization to provide investment solutions. The product shelf then becomes the ingredient that is used as an input, rather than the end product itself. We discuss this in detail in the next section.

16.2 MULTI-ASSET SOLUTIONS AS AN INDUSTRY FUNCTION

While we discuss the business structure of multi-asset products in Chapter 18 in detail, we discuss here the investment structure of the industry with the transition to a solution-focused environment.

Imagine that index fund providers are able to give low cost liquid funds access not just to a market cap-weighted benchmark of stocks but to stock composites which have defined risk exposures to size, value, dividend yield, GDP growth, earnings growth, volatility, low interest rates and countless other beta dimensions. Similarly, imagine investment banks were able to provide derivative instruments to give exposure to all of these dimensions as well, to take or hedge exposure if desired.

With such a market environment, long-only active managers and hedge funds would be forced to justify their value addition (and fees) by adding value over and above static bets on any of these variables. Their benchmarks would then be these new multiple beta benchmarks, and they would need to create alpha above these benchmarks for them to be deemed effective. Similarly, hedge fund managers would not only have to be neutral to market beta, as they are largely today, but also be neutral to numerous other beta factors. Their excess return would have to be garnered, with the structure of being neutral to these multiple beta variables. In addition, they would need to produce, perhaps weekly, risk reports detailing their exposure in multiple dimensions on a tactical basis.

With the availability of products providing exposure along multiple beta dimensions in a cheap liquid form and active and hedge fund investment products which produce excess return above these multiple beta factors, the plan sponsor's burden of allocation would increase. Rather than allocating simply to geographies, they would now have to allocate to multiple other variables. Only subsequent to this would they need to choose to be active or passive. The allocation process would then become more diverse and diversified than it is today and demand a greater proportion of resources compared to manager selection. Multiple horizons and multiple investment processes to perform allocation would be a natural implication.

The multi-asset solution provider then becomes the asset owner agent who would be able to provide investment solutions which help the asset owner in this new environment. These agents can be in the form of investment consultants, fund platforms such as fund of funds, or asset managers with a broad range of investment products (active, passive and alternative). Asset management marketing departments of single asset managers would also profess to provide investment solutions, although with limitations.

16.3 CHARACTERISTICS OF A MULTI-ASSET SOLUTION PROVIDER

All investment solution providers always have the dual objectives of generating revenue for their shareholders and a fiduciary duty to the asset owner, and there is a perpetual tension between the two. The requirements for all solution providers are minimal from a manufacturing standpoint, as they are client-oriented functions. The two critical aspects necessary are:

1. **Ability to Customize**

    The primary characteristic of a solution provider is his ability to customize the investment solution to the specific requirements of any client. Business profitability requirements would, however, dictate a minimum asset size for which complete customization is feasible.

2. **Access to Investment Products**

    The ability to access a variety of investment products across active, passive and alternative strategies would allow the investment solution to cater for most client requirements. However, for business reasons, asset managers will always favor their internal strategies over external ones.

16.4 CUSTOMIZATION PARAMETERS FOR AN INVESTMENT SOLUTION

The basic specifications for designing a client solution are the base currency, any regulatory constraints, asset class constraints and any negative geographic bias. A clear specification of these requirements is the starting point for the construction of a suitable client portfolio. These portfolio parameters would determine the inclusion or exclusion of specific assets. While a qualitative assessment of each parameter is mandatory, a specific numerical answer is preferred, to enable a more suitable portfolio.

Creating a specific client investment solution requires the specification of the following parameters:

■ **Return Requirement**

The return required by an asset owner for the total portfolio is generally based on liabilities, inflation or other monetary rates such as Libor. While any of these methods is acceptable, it is important to know the assumptions which have been used to arrive at the numerical required return. Assumptions can be based on aspects such as longevity, duration, mortality rates, default rates, future interest rates, commodity prices, etc. A knowledge of these parameters will help determine if the variation in the asset portfolio is related to a variation in the liability assumptions, which can then mitigate asset–liability mismatches. Ideally, the required return should be stochastic, such that asset allocation changes become a path dependent variable, and can determine portfolio risk tolerance at different levels of portfolio NAV.

▨ **Risk Tolerance**

Specification of risk is a far more difficult and complicated exercise than the specification of return. A process where the investment advisor displays various scenarios of risk is often much more helpful in the asset owner deciding what is his risk appetite, rather than the pure inquisition of a numerical risk answer. Risk needs to be specified ideally in a number of dimensions:

▨ End-of-horizon risk: The probability that the assets will not reach their target expected return at the end of the chosen investment horizon.

▨ Intra-horizon risk: The threshold at which the asset owner would become uncomfortable at any point in time within the investment horizon.

▨ Regulatory risk constraint: The gap (defined by drawdown or versus liabilities) at which the regulator imposes regulatory penalties or additional oversight to the asset owner.

▨ Any other parameter which may be pertinent to the type of plan, e.g., commodity price sensitivity (for oil plans), inflation sensitivity, etc.

▨ **Liquidity/Cash Flow Requirement**

An estimation of the frequency and amount of capital required to be withdrawn from the asset pool needs to be specified. This specification can take multiple facets, and has been done very differently in different regions. US-based structures often specify the liquidity requirement as a percentage of the assets in the plan at the end of the financial year (or the average on a rolling basis). European plans specify the liquidity requirements as a percentage of the NAV growth of the plan. The advantage of a US-based system is that it can confirm a spending level, without a reference to the variations in financial markets. This is suitable for plans that definitively require a certain liquidity, for example university endowments, where university funding is partially provided by the endowment. The advantage of the European system is that the cash flow can be varied to suit the variation in the NAV. While this leads to a variation in the cash flow itself, it allows for the principal capital of the asset pool to be more stable as cash outflow is constrained in times of financial market downfalls.

▨ **Governance Level**

The level of governance that is possible for any plan is a determinant of the types of assets that can be tolerated as part of the asset structure. The governance level, however, does not have a direct implication on complexity tolerance, for example a plan which has a long duration and in general is not able to monitor investments more than once a year could still have private equity and complex infrastructure financing strategies as part of their portfolios, as these investments are by nature illiquid and frequent governance will not change the implementation of any invest-ment decisions. The governance level does, however, determine the frequency at which the asset owner reviews performance and risk characteristics and can restrict the maximum number of external managers that are feasible in a portfolio. This frequency will directly determine the level of asset risk that is present in the portfolio.

▓ **Complexity Tolerance**

An understanding by the client of all portfolio components of a client solution is paramount for the portfolio to be appropriate. This becomes particularly important in periods of market drawdown, when a lack of understanding of the assets can lead to a break in the advisor–owner relationship. While specification of a tolerance for complexity can be very difficult to specify accurately, it is important to ascertain as a qualitative measure if the asset owner has the ability to understand the performance and risk characteristics of specific complex assets such as non-delta one strategies, illiquid investments, investments involving leverage, investments in less well-known asset classes or investments in geographies which the asset owner is not familiar with. This determination will act as a negative parameter to determine which assets can be excluded from the chosen portfolio for the client.

▓ **Cost Constraint**

The cost of management of the assets can be a significant and determining constraint for determining the chosen portfolio. The governance of the asset owner can often determine this parameter. For example, the expense ratio of government-sponsored pension plans in many countries is often benchmarked against the expense ratio of a basket of peers. The accounting methodology used will also impact the determination of the cost parameter. A plan which is able to account for management charges within the asset structure (for asset managers to deliver net of fee returns) can increase its expense ratio as it does not present a headline risk to the asset owner clients. An asset owner where the accounting methodology requires cash invoices to be paid to the asset manager, separate from the assets under management will show a propensity to minimize expenses, as they are displayed in full to all participants. The expense ratio is a significant determinant in the decision process of active versus passive management, incorporation of alternative strategies and the ability to pay for investing in fund of fund strategies.

▓ **Investment Horizon**

It is often said that a long investment horizon is an advantage for asset owners, as it allows them to ignore market noise and capitalize on inefficiencies at the long end of the horizon, which traditional investors are not able to participate in. While this is generally true, it must be emphasized that the ability to have a long invest-ment horizon must be in conjunction with the ability of the asset owner to bear intra-horizon drawdown risk. This fact is often not appreciated enough or accounted for in allocations for asset owners. As the investment horizon lengthens, end-of-horizon risk (as conventionally measured by parameters such as volatility or track-ing error) reduces. For example, an investment in equity markets is more likely to generate the expected equity risk premium if the investment is held for a long period of time, rather than a short period. This is the fact that is most often cited in support

of a long investment horizon. However, it is also a fact that lengthening of the investment horizon results in a dramatic increase in the probability of an intra-horizon
drawdown, i.e., the equity investment made above will only result in realization of
the equity risk premium, if the investor is able to sustain and hold the investments
through the cycles of market downfall. While notionally, asset owners may well
display a willingness to persevere in such drawdowns, in practice the frequency of
portfolio review, the governance by the regulator as well as the career risk aversion
of employees, often result in a capitulation at points of drawdown. This results in the
asset owner not being able to realize the risk premium, which the long investment
horizon may have afforded them. Specification of the investment horizon is therefore
in all respects as important as the specification of the risk and return requirement
itself. The implication of specifying an investment horizon is that it allows more
accurately for the calibration of risk that can be taken in the portfolio, and allows
for a greater alignment of the asset owner's "real" risk-taking ability in the portfolio.

▪ **Home Bias and Regional Bias**

It is a fact that all asset owners across the world have a noticeable home and
regional bias. In some cases, this is motivated by the structure of their liabilities
being domiciled in specific geographies and currencies. However, more often than
not, they are motivated by familiarity with the assets which are close to them geographically, and discomfort with those which are less heard about in their everyday
course of work. Asset owners from all markets, including the most sophisticated
plans from Europe and North America, suffer from this facet. While the level of
home or regional bias has continued to decrease substantially over the last decade,
as access to global financial markets has become readily available, it still stands at
about 50–60% in most markets. It is beneficial to have a numerical specification of
the client home bias, which then allows the remainder of the portfolio to be structured on a globally diversified basis. Attribution of resulting risk and performance
can then be done to account for any benefit or detraction from this bias, separately
from the performance of the actual global strategy.

The specification of client requirements across all these parameters is required irrespective of how the portfolio is actually constructed. Despite this, however, it is a fact that
even some of the most sophisticated asset owners fail to accurately specify their requirements and constraints in such a manner. The result is a mismatch between the actual
portfolio risk and the risk that the asset owners are actually capable of withstanding.

The process of creating a portfolio after specification of the client requirements can
be done in two basic ways: starting with a standardized model portfolio, and custom-
izing this based on the constraints specified by the asset owner; or creating a customized
portfolio bottom-up for each client. The advantage of the latter is that it is more likely
that the final portfolio will be completely customized to the clients' requirements, as
every single asset is handpicked and inserted into the portfolio. In practice, however, the
disadvantage of this lacking scalability means that this is reserved only for the largest
clients, and the first basic task is to create standardized scalable investment solutions,
which are applicable to the majority of the firm's clients.

16.5 REQUIREMENTS FOR A STANDARDIZED IMPLEMENTATION

A clear model portfolio is required to be maintained for each investment decision process at all times for a standardized implementation process to function. This should be done irrespective of the varieties of client demand, as it will create a base case for any client portfolio to be made on a customized basis. Clients can be of different domicile and will have their own country bias; for example, a Philippines client may want to have a local home bias and a Hong Kong client may have the same. It is necessary, therefore, that the model portfolios roll up from a minimum category to the broader allocation categories, i.e., effectively return and risk forecasts are required for each client's country, which then roll up to a regional and global risk and return forecast. This process needs to be undertaken for each asset class. It is irrelevant whether the starting point of these forecasts is from the broader category to the smaller category, or vice versa; however, it is important that there is synchronization between the various forecasts. Periodic analysis of the resulting return and risk of all investment decisions needs to be made, to ensure calibration of investment decisions for all portfolios constructed.

The parameters that need to be specified for a model portfolio include the forecast absolute return; time horizon for forecast realization; expected maximum drawdown intra-horizon; and thresholds for forecast at 95% confidence level. Assets to be forecasted for model portfolio creation include:

▓ Global and country level assets, including equity as set classes, fixed income asset classes, alternatives and foreign exchange market forecasts.
▓ Global strategic positioning using one or more allocation methodologies.
▓ Global and regional tactical positioning specifying the tactical deviations (absolute positions, positive or negative), to generate a positive return on an absolute basis on global asset classes.
▓ Expectation of alpha generation by active management in each asset category by the chosen active managers, along with other characteristics.

16.6 THE IMPORTANCE OF ATTRIBUTING PERFORMANCE

Irrespective of the approach taken to create a customized solution, it is paramount for the process to be sustainable so that the sources of risk and return be attributed back to the decisions taken to construct the portfolio. Critical among these attributions are decisions such as:

▓ The portion of the portfolio risk and return that are generated by implementing the constraints specified by the asset owner. This aspect can only be measured if the investment advisor maintains an unconstrained model portfolio, against which the client portfolio can be measured.

▪ The proportion of the risk and return generated by the strategic asset allocation decision taken by the investment advisor. This is best estimated from the return attribution of the strategy model portfolio at regular intervals.

▪ The return contribution from tactical allocation decisions. It is a popular misconception that the impact of a tactical allocation decision is a function of the choice of the strategic portfolio. Tactical allocation decisions are actually a matter of choice rather than by compulsion, and should be taken only if the advisor can demonstrate positive skill over a cash benchmark. This is irrespective of the implementation of the decision on a cash or a strategic benchmarked basis.

▪ Finally, the return contribution from active management of assets against a market relative benchmark. While this analysis would show the contribution of return from the active management perspective, it does not show the efficacy of manager selection itself, as this should be done against the pool of active managers available.

16.7 CONCLUSIONS

Clear definition of all client constraints is an essential step in the proposition of an appropriate client portfolio which is aligned with the expectations and requirements of the asset owner. Articulation of some of these parameters can prove difficult as either they are qualitative, or require careful discussion with the client to ascertain actual levels. Implementation of a standardized process has the advantage of scalability, as well as the ability to provide consistent advice to all clients; however, this needs to be carefully balanced with clients (especially large ones), where individual attention is justified either because of importance or because of the unique nature of their constraints. A detailed quantitative model portfolio is a minimum requirement to be able to create a standardized process for implementation across various clients. These model portfolios need to be made for each asset class, global and local and individually cover each domicile where clients can be expected. A process to monitor and attribute risk and performance of each investment decision is required, to enable foresight of efficacy of investment decisions advised to clients and attribute results to the source.

CHAPTER SEVENTEEN

Multi-Asset Investing for Private Wealth Assets

nstitutional investment management has evolved over the years to be a transparent product industry, where competitive pressures have led to greater efficiency in the investment processes, better risk management, lower fees and greater alignment of interest between the asset owner and the asset manager. Private wealth management on the other hand has been driven historically by the need for privacy, legal structures to protect ownership and inter-generational transfer of assets, where the client has a relationship with the individual banker rather than the banking institution. This has led to a less effective investment structure for these assets, where both the client and the banking institution did not consider management of the assets as a prime objective. With the evolution of the private wealth industry to a legal environment where privacy is no longer possible, where global legal structures are more readily available in a cost-effective manner and where strength of institutions has become a bigger factor for a banking relationship, the value of the investment solution proposition of private wealth assets has come into focus. In this chapter, we outline the changes that would be necessary in the private wealth investment process and the challenges therein, for the private banks to be able to deliver a more relevant multi-asset investment solution.

17.1 THE PRIVATE WEALTH MULTI-ASSET INVESTMENT PROBLEM

The requirements of a private client are in reality exactly the same as that of any other kind of asset owner (pension plan, SWF, endowment etc.) – to generate a defined absolute nominal or real return with a constraint on the risk taken. At first glance, therefore, it would seem that this requirement could be tackled in exactly the same way as a traditional institutional plan sponsor portfolio problem. However, there are differences, which make this investment problem more difficult to solve and implement than an institutional investment problem. These differences are elaborated below.

1. **A True Absolute Return Requirement**

Multi-asset managers managing an institutional or retail product, marketing to deliver an absolute return in a long-only environment, sidestep the issue of constant long market exposure, by creating hybrids of asset class market benchmarks as the yardstick by which they want to be evaluated, rather than a cash benchmark. This then neatly allows them to manage the assets like a relative return portfolio with a long exposure to asset classes (by underweighting or overweighting asset classes, relative to the hybrid benchmark). The mismatch between the required absolute return and the new long hybrid benchmark is left basically unmanaged.

In plan sponsor institutions, which need to deliver an absolute, inflation adjusted or liability-based total return, the same problem is sidestepped by creating a "policy portfolio" which, similar to the commercial asset management world, is used as a tool to transform the absolute return problem of the plan, to a relative return problem which is then followed by managers inside the institution. The risk of having long market exposure, against an absolute return requirement, is often put under the guise of a "long-term investment horizon" or left largely unmanaged, at the mercy of market forces. The only exception to this structure is a select group of primarily US endowments, who structurally create an absolute return portfolio for the whole plan, with no constant long market exposure, with the aim of delivering an overall absolute return.

In the private wealth world, where agency issues are of a lower priority (given that the assets belong to an individual, who would himself be the decision maker on where to bank his assets), the absolute return requirement comes to the fore. As discretionary mandates give full control of the investment process to the asset manager, the risk between long-only investments and an absolute return requirement falls within the direct responsibility of the manager and cannot be sidestepped to a policy portfolio or a hybrid benchmark. This is then a true absolute return investment problem, which in reality is more difficult than the institutional investment management problem.

2. **Customization**

Notwithstanding specific cases, institutional investments mostly follow a common framework, where assets are invested in multiple comingled fund structures – internal or external. Private wealth is, however, distinguished by the fact that every single client specifies constraints and preferences he wants incorporated into his portfolio. This takes the form of types or limits on investments, liquidity, leverage, single stock holdings, home bias, inter-generational requirements and cash flow. Given the large number of accounts in private wealth, this creates the issue of managing a large scale implementation where all accounts are different in one respect or another, and each will need a different portfolio, even though the manager may have a single market view.

3. **Account Size**

   The asset base in an institutional product evolves slowly as the product gains traction, and as such the investment process can largely be created for a single portfolio size, at any given time, be it a large or small asset base. However, in the private wealth setting, there can be dramatically different sizes of accounts which need to be managed at the same time. As such, the investment process needs to simultaneously be applicable and relevant to very large and very small account sizes.

4. **Defined Time Horizon**

   As institutions are going concerns, in general they afford a tolerance for a longer investment horizon to realize their investment objectives. While intra-horizon drawdowns can be painful, the agency structure serves to delink any emotional attachment to the assets, thus decreasing behavioral biases of the asset owner. Private wealth, especially for first generation clients, is very much an emotional attachment of the owner. As such, the tolerance for intra-horizon drawdowns is far less. Despite being financially savvy in running their own businesses, the prospect of emotionally biased decisions at points of drawdown are very real in private wealth. This has definitive impact on the possibilities of the portfolio that are feasible or optimal for private wealth clients.

5. **Limitation on Derivatives**

   The segregated legal structure of institutional assets affords their use as collateral for non-delta one derivative investments. In the private client world, while this is possible, it becomes more cumbersome to have this done for every single client account. As such, there is a limitation on the types of instruments that can be used to gain or hedge exposure in a private client portfolio.

6. **Cost of Management**

   The business model of private wealth relies on sourcing revenue from multiple points of the asset base, including flat fees for the total account, transaction fees for every trade or investment, larger bid-ask spreads and a management and performance fee for investment products. These multiple levels of fees then create a higher hurdle for private wealth assets to deliver a similar net of fees return compared to institutional assets which do not have these costs.

7. **Direct Stock Holding**

   Private clients have a bias for direct holdings of stocks, rather than investment in funds. While this is an emotional bias, it does have some rationale. It is an appropriate proposition to hold a stock directly with the objective of an absolute return, where it is acceptable to have a drawdown, rather than hold it inside a fund where the objective is market relative performance.

Given these differences, a standard institutional investment process cannot be directly ported to solve a private wealth problem. This is often under-appreciated by institutional asset managers.

17.2 BUSINESS MODEL AND ORGANIZATIONAL ISSUES

The private wealth business has always been a service-oriented model providing not only discrete banking services but also everything from legal facilitation for intergenerational wealth transfer, flexibility of multiple booking domains to villas and yachts. In order to finance these extensive services, the business model of the private banks has been to seek revenue at as many levels as possible from the private client asset base. Apart from fee structures, as discussed above, a critical component of the business model has historically been the inclusion of services from other parts of the bank into the asset structure. The most prominent of these in the investment framework has been the use of internally managed funds from their own asset management division as a compulsory feature in all assets, and the use of "favored" external managers in the asset structure, who provide a "retrocession" to the private bank.

1. **Favored Use of In-House Funds**

    In an institutional setting, it is unthinkable for an asset owner to contemplate giving more than one or two mandates to a single asset manager. Firstly because it is seldom the case that a single asset management institution has more than two best in class products, and secondly it defies fiduciary logic to have operational and counterparty risk concentrated with one institutional manager. In the private banking world however, the opposite is true. An increasingly large amount of assets of a private account are compulsorily invested in in-house funds, such that the fee revenue accrues to the same institution. This is not only a definitive conflict of interest, but also potentially detrimental to the performance on the private client assets, as in-house funds are favored over superior external funds.

2. **Favored External Funds Based on Retrocession Revenues**

    The issue of retrocession revenues in private wealth is analogous to the use of soft dollars in the institutional asset management industry, where service providers to the asset manager are given business from client assets, in return for a "kickback" paid to the asset manager. The Myner's Commission Report of 2001 led to the unbundling of broker commissions in the institutional asset management world. The Swiss Supreme Court judgment of 2012 on retrocession revenues has a similar impact on the private banking world, where retrocession revenues are deemed assets of the client and not the private bank, unless previously agreed with the client. Apart from being a drag on performance, the availability of such a structure creates a direct conflict of interest for the management of private wealth assets, when the choice is between a fund which provides greater retrocession revenue to the bank, or better performance to the client.

    The institutional world today has well-defined rules on use of soft dollars and the Financial Conduct Authority (FCA) of the UK, in its consultation paper of November 2013, proposes to make them even stricter. In private wealth, any limits on use of retrocession revenues are yet to be discussed or formalized. While private banks now need consent from clients to allow retrocession, no one governs today what retrocession revenues can be spent on by the private bank. There seems to be no reason why these should not be examined and governed in a similar manner to the institutional world.

3. **Trading Costs (Revenues)**

In an institutional setting, the trading desk is always an agent with generally no principal interest in the transactions carried out on client assets. Nor is it in the interest of the trading desk to charge higher fees, as agency traders in an asset manager are generally not profit centers, but service providers to the investment manager. In a private bank setting, however, trading desks are almost always considered as revenue generators and in some cases even profit centers. This incentivizes greater misalignment with the client's objectives, and has multiple impacts on a private wealth portfolio. First, it incentivizes the relationship manager (RM) and trading desk to churn the portfolio, a practice that is illegal by the Securities and Exchange Commission (SEC) regulations on the institutional side. Second, the private bank trading desk often charges commission to the client, over and above the commission charged by a trade executing investment bank – this is done either explicitly as a transaction fee, or worse, as an undisclosed spread on buy and sell transactions. These fees are most evident in foreign exchange transactions. These charges inevitably create a much higher hurdle for delivering performance on private wealth assets.

4. **The Relationship Manager – Investment Manager Dichotomy**

The historic service orientation of the private wealth business made the RM a focal point, acting as the point man providing client service, the investment manager of client assets, and managing the conflict between the client's return requirement and the bank's revenue requirement. In contrast, the organization structure of institutional asset managers is aligned with the objective of delivering investment performance. However, as the focus on investment performance of private wealth assets has increased, private banks now find themselves with a need to evolve their business model, in order to implement an institutional quality investment framework on private wealth assets.

Private banks choosing to identify themselves with a service and distribution business model are transferring investment decision authority from the RM to a separate investment team created from the backbone of the erstwhile institutional asset management team. Here, RMs are focused on client service, and prevented from taking investment decisions, which are either taken by the client (in an advisory structure) or by the investment team. Other banks choosing to distinguish themselves as private wealth asset managers are creating investment teams within the private bank, often at the expense of the institutional asset management business. In either model, the result is to design and implement investment processes with an institutional quality skill, while incorporating the challenging parameters and solution flexibility that private wealth requires.

Private banks attempting to run both an institutional asset management business and a private wealth business face the greatest challenge. This is especially acute in cases where the asset management business depends to a great extent in sourcing assets from the private bank for its livelihood. Such a business structure is likely to be detrimental both for private wealth clients (to get customized service from institutional asset managers) and to institutional clients (as often the majority of assets in institutional funds are actually not sourced by competitive mandate wins, but by captive private wealth asset managers, who tend to be less stringent on investment processes). Unless an asset management business can stand independently by itself, without the crutch of the private bank assets, it is likely to be a poor investment proposition for both private and institutional clients.

17.3 INCUMBENT INVESTMENT FRAMEWORKS

The standard investment solution for private wealth assets has been based on the concept of a 60/40 balanced portfolio, with some variations. Variation in the risk level of the portfolio to cater for the asset owner's risk aversion led to conservative and aggressive portfolio solutions. The need to fulfill periodic liabilities led to an income-oriented portfolio. Incorporation of the finite earning life of an individual led to the development of life cycle funds, where the proportion of equity risk taken in the portfolio is decreased as an individual becomes older. Incorporation of a retirement date for the individual or specific future liabilities led to the development of target date funds.

A dimension where investment managers have sought to differentiate themselves has been in the process followed for the equity–bond allocation decision. Similar to the debate on active versus passive management, there are institutions which believe that a static allocation structure (like the 60/40) is best, and others which advocate an active process for the allocation of assets. A third category that has been created recently is those that shun active asset allocation as a philosophy, yet use risk parity or risk factor allocation as an allocation philosophy. Idzorek and Kowara (2013), however, caution that the claims of superiority made by these managers are unwarranted, and seem more of a marketing strategy than formed by investment substance.

However, the biggest challenge faced by private banks is organizational. While the structure has facilitated client service, it has been largely poor at investment management. An improvement of investment performance requires the transfer of investment authority from the RM to specialist investment staff. Conversely, it is also true that institutional asset managers often underestimate the customization and client service element of managing private wealth assets. Hence, while private bankers are poor at managing assets, institutional asset managers are poor at customized client service and large scale customized portfolios. Herein lies the biggest structural challenge. Several implementation approaches have been tried to resolve this problem.

1. **A Core-Satellite Portfolio Structure**

    A core-satellite portfolio can be created for each client, where the RMs are instructed to invest the broad core of any account into a standard core investment product, with the remainder satellite being managed by the RM at the wishes of the client or at his discretion. The core is then managed by a professional investment team. This sidesteps the issue of asset managers being required to do extensive client servicing and yet creates investment robustness at least for the core of the portfolio.

The drawback of this approach is that a large business risk exists on the performance of the core investment product. If the core underperforms, as it surely will during a performance cycle at some point in time, all client portfolios across the bank will suffer, which presents a business risk to the firm. Further, it limits the level of customization that can be done for clients, as a standard core will present the same investment solution for all clients. Constraints such as a large home bias, or lack of certain asset classes or geographies, will be difficult to meet.

2. **Core Packaged Set of Internal Funds**

    Here, a core set of in-house investment products are bundled into a package for investing in all accounts. This is similar to the core-satellite structure, except that the core is a basket of internally managed investment products. While this facilitates better client customization, it leads to a more detrimental overall structure for the client. Every bank has a defined set of "good" outperforming products, which do not change very often. These will happen to be in specific asset classes, where the investment team of that asset class in this firm has good skill, and will vary from firm to firm. Allocation of assets to these products should first and foremost be done if the asset class is attractive in the coming period, as the private client requires an absolute return. Markets will not always favor investing in these asset classes all the time. However, if this structure was chosen for a private client, it would almost certainly force the firm to allocate to those asset classes where the firm has good products. This may lead to better alpha return, but can be much more detrimental to the overall portfolio return as the beta of those asset classes may be a poor investment.

3. **A Top-Down House View**

    A top-down house allocation view can be defined, which is then used by RMs to construct each individual portfolio. This method has high flexibility for client customization; however, as the allocation implementation process is left to the individual RM, he can choose to disregard the house view and implement his own view. This deviation cannot always be monitored or governed, and hence will create disparate client portfolios, where the house view may or may not be reflected.

17.4 A MULTI-ASSET PRIVATE WEALTH INVESTMENT PLATFORM

An investment framework for private wealth needs to cater explicitly for two facets:

a. Investment decisions made by specialized investment staff, rather than RMs; and
b. An implementation framework that can be customized to client requirements.

Consider a private wealth platform structure in a private bank, where professional money managers make available their full portfolio for investment by private clients. These "model portfolios" are replicas of the institutional fund that they would manage, and updated on a live basis like a custodial account. All investment decisions on these model portfolios are taken by investment managers. Clients have the ability to invest in the institutional fund share class of a chosen manager, or directly in the underlying assets of the fund in an unconstrained manner through the platform. The fees would be the same, so the manager and firm should be largely indifferent on the implementation choice. If the client does not specify any customization or constraints, the client portfolio would be rebalanced automatically in the same way as the institutional portfolio. If the client chooses to define constraints, then the client rebalance would be modified by these constraints. Allocation to different asset classes can be done in a similar manner. As both in-house and externally managed funds would be on the platform, the bias towards in-house funds would be reduced.

There will of course be specific products where portfolio holding replication is not feasible. For example, hedge funds and illiquid funds would be required to be held as comingled funds, and fixed income direct holdings may only be possible for sizeable accounts (as minimum ticket sizes per bond are higher). Or indeed in asset classes where the client believes he wants to "set and forget," he may prefer to have the fund holding rather than stock rebalances. However, this structure solves a number of critical issues, present in the incumbent structures:

a. It creates a fully customizable investment structure, where the client can define any constraint. This is not possible to such an extent in either the core-satellite or the in-house fund structure.
b. It facilitates direct stock holdings for the private client, which is often a requirement.
c. It retains the financial revenue base for the firm as the same fee that is charged for management of a comingled fund can be charged for the provision of the model portfolio.
d. It allows all investment decisions to be taken by professional money managers (except where the client defines preferences) which should improve the investment results. Yet it retains the implementation control to a limited extent with the RM, which should result in less disruption of incumbent organizational structures.
e. It provides a service where separate private bank teams for advisory services and discretionary services are not required. Effectively, the portfolio is the same, and the level of client decision making (advisory) is up to him.

This structure is present already as managed accounts in institutional asset management where, subject to minimum asset size, individual accounts are created, as demanded by large institutions. In the alternatives world, the platform structure has come into focus in order to provide greater transparency to the client on his portfolio, which enables better risk management. There seem to be sufficient reasons as to why this structure should also find traction in private wealth asset management.

17.5 GOALS-BASED ALLOCATION

Given the lifespan of individuals, high-net-worth individuals often have a clearer assessment of their expected liabilities due to the defined timeframe and therefore often able to structure their portfolio in a more aligned manner with their liabilities.

Rather than the traditional structure of allocation followed by security selection, an allocation structure based on investment objectives – each of which naturally has an investment horizon built in – creates a more logical portfolio. Figure 17.1 depicts such a structure.

Rather than asset class buckets, we propose performing an allocation for the assets by investment objective. A younger person may have a higher allocation to growth, whereas an older person may prefer yield. The level of liquidity required can be built in with the allocation to cash and to fixed real assets such as property. Finally, based on our exposure allocation philosophy, active allocation across any dimension and across variable investment horizons can be incorporated as an absolute return asset. Finally, if they themselves believe they can find absolute return securities in any asset class or if they want to invest with absolute return funds, they can do so in the Active Selection bucket.

This structure is an improvement over the traditional methodology as:

- Investors who can hold corporate bonds to maturity (such that there is no plausible interest rate risk) can look at these assets simply as an yield instrument, where the market value of the bond itself is immaterial. This fixed income investment is not put in the same category as those bonds which are bought specifically for price appreciation in the short or medium term.
- Equity investments are segregated by the investment objective they fulfill and the investment horizon for which they will be held. Blue chip equities, which are specifically bought as a long-term holding, and high dividend equity, which is specifically kept as a yield asset, are both kept at the long-term horizon in the growth and yield buckets respectively. Equity securities bought for price appreciation in the short and medium term are kept separate, and at a different horizon and evaluation category.

Figure 17.1   Goals-based allocation structure

		Investment Horizon				
		3m	6m	12m	36m	> 36m
Investment Objective	Liquidity	Cash, Gold, Fixed Deposits,				
	Active Allocation		Absolute return allocation-based strategies			
	Active Selection		Absolute return assets – equities, bonds, funds			
	Growth					Blue chip equities Growth equities
	Yield					Corporate bonds, Preferred shares, Hi-div equity
	Real Assets					Property

▪ Separating the Active Allocation and Active Selection categories gives the freedom
to the investor to decouple passive and active management. Passive management
by definition is an allocation decision, and would fall under the Active Allocation
bucket. Active management would fall under the Active Selection bucket, which has
great consequences for long-only active managers, which we discuss below.

17.6 IMPLICATION FOR THE LONG-ONLY ACTIVE MANAGER

Long-only managers have been blamed for a variety of ills: underperformance; benchmark hugging; buying out of benchmark stocks; portable alpha; non-performance
linked fee structures; and excessive drawdowns, to name a few. So what should be
done structurally in the long-only asset management industry to change some of these
problems?

Current positioning of long-only strategies in an asset owner's portfolio is con-
tradictory. An asset owner buys into the market of an active manager as an allocation decision that he wants to be long in that market. This decision in itself would not
cost a substantial amount of fees to implement. However, he then implements this by
investing in an active strategy in that market, where the fees are much higher, the
return impact on the overall portfolio is minimal, and worse still, the active manager
bears no responsibility if that market falls (as the active manager is measured only on
outperformance).

What if we position the long-only active manager in the Active Selection bucket of
an asset owner, where the benchmark is cash and the objective is absolute return?

It aligns the return objective of asset owner and asset manager to be above cash.
It allows the asset owner to have diversified his allocation decision, not just the alpha
decision (as he can select multiple managers in the same market). It allows the asset
manager to play traditional beta or alpha – it doesn't matter, as both are at the end of
the day return for the asset owner.

We believe this realignment of active asset management may serve to help asset
owners, and is potentially a fund category that needs some attention by asset managers. Provided the fee structure can align with the skill required here, i.e., a performance
based fee, subject to a hurdle rate and high-water mark, it may also be more rewarding
for the asset managers.

17.7 CONCLUSIONS

Private wealth is one of the largest asset bases in the world, which to date has not had a
specific focus on delivering investment returns. With the changes underway in the industry, forcing transparency of private wealth, and the realization that the services provided
by private banks are very similar to one another, greater emphasis is now underway on
the investment performance of these assets.

Investment processes followed by private wealth need to improve in order to deliver better performance and risk management, but in a manner where customization and service quality are not compromised. This requires current structures, both of institutional asset management and private wealth asset management, to evolve and embrace the specific and different requirements of this asset base.

We propose here a potential solution, which would satisfy the requirements that are normally specified by private clients for their assets, while creating a portfolio that has institutional strength investment decision making. As it has minimal organizational disruption impact, we believe this structure to be a potential option for private banks to consider, as they reorganize their structures, to deal with the new investment challenges.

CHAPTER EIGHTEEN

Structuring a Multi-Asset Investing Business

G iven that multi-asset as an investment product relates to a large number of groups within an investment organization, structuring the multi-asset business is a meaningful decision. While the actual decision is very often a function of the client opportunity set available to a given firm, and the firm's internal product strengths, it is useful to delineate a structural framework for this decision.

We discuss below the structural components that need to be analyzed in order to decide the structure of a multi-asset business. The foremost aspect of this decision is to be clear about the chosen product structure and its inherent strengths and challenges. The product decision then needs to be synchronized with the investment skills required to manufacture this product and the client segment that is likely to be the target market for the chosen multi-asset product. It is important to note here that, unlike single asset class equity or fixed income products, different multi-asset products require very different investment skills to manufacture, have different target client segments, and each has its own strengths and weaknesses.

18.1 PRODUCT STRUCTURE AND POSITIONING

The gamut of multi-asset strategies can be categorized into four basic types based on their intent, as illustrated in Figure 18.1.

1. *Product centric:* where the asset manager creates the multi-asset product by investing in a combination of internally managed single asset strategies. This approach uses the multi-asset concept to channel assets into *internal products*.

Figure 18.1   Multi-asset product design and positioning

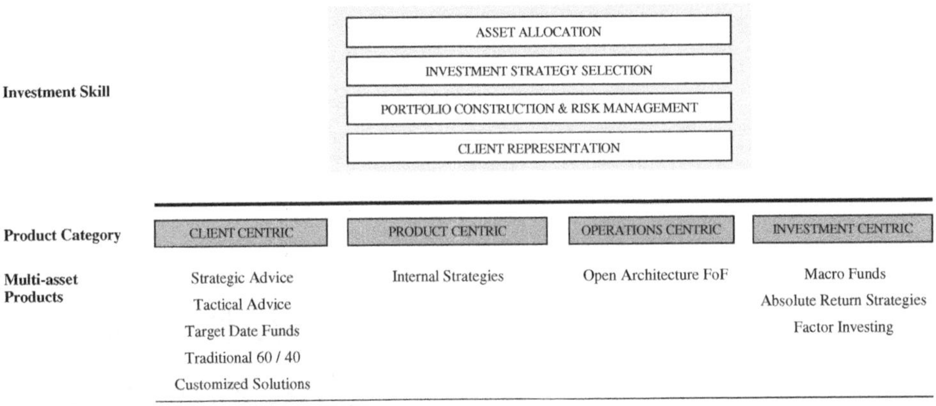

Investment Skill	ASSET ALLOCATION
	INVESTMENT STRATEGY SELECTION
	PORTFOLIO CONSTRUCTION & RISK MANAGEMENT
	CLIENT REPRESENTATION

Product Category	CLIENT CENTRIC	PRODUCT CENTRIC	OPERATIONS CENTRIC	INVESTMENT CENTRIC
Multi-asset Products	Strategic Advice	Internal Strategies	Open Architecture FoF	Macro Funds
	Tactical Advice			Absolute Return Strategies
	Target Date Funds			Factor Investing
	Traditional 60 / 40			
	Customized Solutions			

2. *Operations centric:* where the asset manager creates the multi-asset product by combining investment in externally managed strategies. This is the conventional *manager of managers* model, which can be deployed for traditional or hedge fund strategies.
3. *Investment skill centric:* A multi-asset strategy investing directly into market securities, rather than other products, which relies only on the skill of the investment manager to produce returns. *Macro hedge fund* or other *absolute return strategies,* and the newer *factor investing* strategies are examples of these investment skill-focused strategies.
4. *Client centric:* Strategies that focus on the client, instead of focusing on the investment process or products. This category comes in three forms:
   (a) Investment advice: *strategic* (long horizon) or *tactical* (short horizon) advice on asset allocation or market positioning.
   (b) Standardized solutions: products which combine multiple asset classes at different risk levels such as conservative, balanced and growth, based on a *traditional 60/40* strategy, or based on the life cycle concept such as *target date funds.*
   (c) Customized solutions: products which combine multiple asset classes *customized* to match the specific risk and return requirements of a particular client.

The core investment skills required to create any of these multi-asset products are common, namely:

a. The skill of selecting or managing individual investment strategies;
b. A skill in allocation;
c. Portfolio construction and risk management skills; and
d. Client management and product representation skills.

However, the degree to which each skill is required differs with each type of multi-asset product category.

18.2 PRODUCT ADVANTAGES AND DISADVANTAGES

The product positioning structure leads to broadly ten different multi-asset products or services, each with specific strengths and weaknesses, as depicted in Figure 18.2.

- *Strategic Advice:* The business model of most investment consultants has long been to provide strategic allocation advice to asset owners. While having the benefit of being independent advice, the creation of strategic portfolios has been challenged more recently by the fact that volatility of risk premium has increased and by clients becoming more reluctant to pay for advice.
- *Tactical Advice:* A plethora of market players including investment banks, independent strategists and asset management CIOs deliver tactical market advice to asset owners in sound bites. Given the large amount of market chatter in this area, asset owners default to believing those with whom they have a relationship. However, such advice is not accompanied by implementation which then requires performance accountability.
- *Target Date Funds:* The systematic management of the equity bond mix, based on a life cycle approach to the need for income and growth has been the most popular multi-asset product in history. The vanilla nature of this product has meant that the asset manager's brand was the most significant determinant of the product's success. While systematic reallocation has the advantage of a dispassionate approach, recent market crashes have led many to question the validity of a target date allocation structure. The large drawdowns that the investor may face intra-horizon have led to many players attempting to rethink this allocation structure.
- *Traditional 60/40:* Independent financial advisors and private banks, in advising individuals, generally structure their investment advice based on the concept of a traditional 60–40 equity-bond mix for a balanced portfolio. More than the investment advice itself, which is often challenged in poor market conditions, the brand name of the institutions becomes the determining factor in such a relationship.

Figure 18.2 Advantages and disadvantages of various multi-asset products

	Advantages		Disadvantages	
Strategic Advice	Independence		Vol of Risk Premium	Pay for Advice ?
Tactical Advice	Client Contact		No Implementation	No Performance Responsibility
Target Date Funds	Long-Term Systematic	Brand Name	Intra-horizon Drawdowns	
Traditional 60/40 Bal	Brand Name		Drawdowns	
Customized Solutions	Individually Made		Resource Intensive	
Internal Strategies FoF	Internal Capability	Risk Management	Single Vendor	Limited Range
Open Architecture FoF	Broad Product Access	Niche Strategies	Selection Skill ?	Control
Macro/Managed Futures Funds	Invesment Process	Liquidity	Leverage & Drawdown	Fees
Multi-Asset Absolute Return	Investment Process	Absolute Return Orientation	Difficult Investment Process	
Factor Investing	Quantitative Strength	Academically Robust	Difficult Investment Process	

▪ *Customized Solutions:* As customization to a particular asset owner's requirements can be resource intensive for an institution, it is often only done if there are sufficient assets or revenue to justify the expense. When provided, this creates a tailor-made investment solution for the asset owner's liabilities and particular situation.

▪ *Internal Strategies Fund of Funds:* A commercially popular route for an asset manager for the multi-asset business is to use the product to channel client assets into their existing single asset class investment products. The multi-asset product then becomes a fund of internal strategies. The commercial benefits to the asset manager are justified by the asset owner benefit of better risk management and potentially a lower cost structure. However, the drawback of having a single vendor for the full asset base is the restriction of only having access to that firm's range of strategies.

▪ *Open Architecture Fund of Funds:* Having an open architecture allows for a more unbiased best of breed structure for all strategies. However, the multi-vendor structure can lead to limitations in risk control and higher fees. It also requires the investor to have skill in manager selection.

▪ *Macro or Managed Future Hedge Fund:* A hedge fund investing in multiple asset classes is basically also a multi-asset fund. The hedge fund structure allows the strategy the additional flexibility of shorting and use of leverage across the assets.

▪ *Multi-Asset Absolute Return:* The relative return nature of market index benchmarked multi-asset funds, and the fact that investors are naturally averse to having hedge funds as a large part of their portfolio, leads to a requirement of multi-asset funds which are absolute return in nature. The absolute return orientation in a long-only structure, however, requires a much more robust investment process.

▪ *Factor Investing:* Another approach, which has recently been given much coverage, is a factor-based approach to investing. While this concept was well known as quantitative investing for decades, it has been recast in multi-asset investing as a potential solution to the issues faced in the traditional asset allocation process.

18.3 PRODUCT INVESTMENT SKILLS

Each of the multi-asset products requires a common set of investment process skills, be it strategic and tactical asset allocation, strategy selection, security selection, portfolio construction or risk management. However, the focus of investment skill required for each product is specific to each. Figure 18.3 shows the areas where enhanced investment skills are required to manage each product.

From an investment skill perspective, the most challenged products are the traditional 60/40 and customized solutions that have historically depended on a near static allocation structure which is now challenged. For these products to be viable going forward, improvement is required in tactical allocation and risk management. The products with the most stable investment processes have been the fund of funds (both internal and open architecture), and macro hedge funds. The former did not require enhanced investment process skill, and the latter were able to attract significant investment skill due to the compensation structure.

Figure 18.3 Investment skills required to manage various multi-asset products

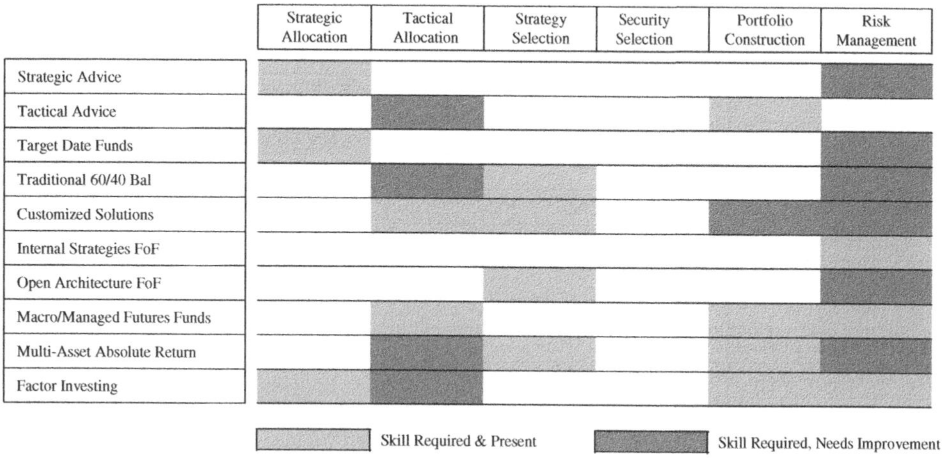

	Strategic Allocation	Tactical Allocation	Strategy Selection	Security Selection	Portfolio Construction	Risk Management
Strategic Advice						
Tactical Advice						
Target Date Funds						
Traditional 60/40 Bal						
Customized Solutions						
Internal Strategies FoF						
Open Architecture FoF						
Macro/Managed Futures Funds						
Multi-Asset Absolute Return						
Factor Investing						

Skill Required & Present   Skill Required, Needs Improvement

The new product areas in multi-asset investing which are developing as an alternative to the traditional 60/40 and target date fund structures are multi-asset absolute return and factor investing. While there is substantial debate on the merit and value addition of these products, their greatest significance is that their presence questions the investment structure of traditional multi-asset investment products, which have remained static for many decades.

18.4 TARGET CLIENT SEGMENTATION

Figure 18.4 suggests the applicability of multi-asset products to various asset owner segments.

The three product areas which present themselves as opportunities are tactical advice, multi-asset absolute return and factor investing. Strictly speaking, factor investing is an investment process category rather than a product category; however, given its rapid popularity as a concept, it is likely to have substantial impact on the broad array of multi-asset strategies and products. The increased demand for the other two categories seems to have stemmed from the need for a revision to the other traditional multi-asset categories, which we discuss in the next section.

From a client segment perspective, the institutional segment is likely to demand greater skill in the broad range of multi-asset strategies, starting with tactical asset allocation to products with an absolute return orientation. This skill will then likely spill into the individual client segment progressively, particularly in the focus area of retirement assets.

As the transition of multi-asset products happens, the major commercial multi-asset product manufacturers are taking product positioning decisions in an attempt to capitalize on the growth in demand for multi-asset solutions. While there is overlap in

Figure 18.4 Product–client positioning of various multi-asset products

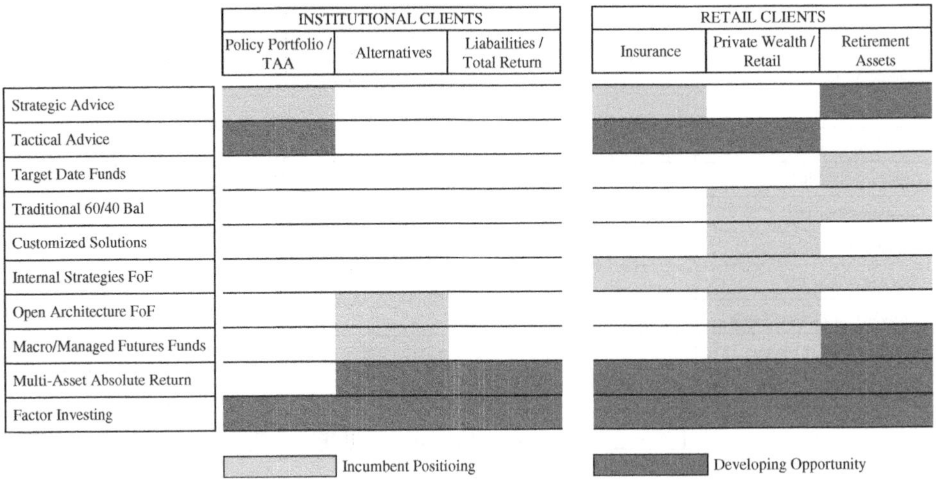

	INSTITUTIONAL CLIENTS				RETAIL CLIENTS		
	Policy Portfolio / TAA	Alternatives	Liabailities / Total Return		Insurance	Private Wealth / Retail	Retirement Assets
Strategic Advice							
Tactical Advice							
Target Date Funds							
Traditional 60/40 Bal							
Customized Solutions							
Internal Strategies FoF							
Open Architecture FoF							
Macro/Managed Futures Funds							
Multi-Asset Absolute Return							
Factor Investing							

☐ Incumbent Positioing   ■ Developing Opportunity

their positioning, each is seeking to capitalize on its strength, be it on an investment skill set or product basis, or based on the target client segment they are most familiar with.

The traditional segmentation thus far had been very clear – consultants dominated the strategic advice spectrum, private banks dominated tactical advice to individuals, and large traditional asset managers dominated the 60/40 and target date product space. This was augmented by funds of funds running open architecture fund of hedge funds and individual hedge funds running macro and managed futures funds. The client segment having been segregated, the fact that similar investment skills were required across the spectrum was not of immediate significance. This market structure has, however, begun to change rapidly for several reasons. Firstly, the increased demand for more effective allocation solutions has resulted in some client segments being dissatisfied with the incumbent investment solution being sold to them by their investment advisor. Second, the large amount of capital seeking multi-asset solutions has attracted the attention of most market players, and they have initiated processes to capitalize on this business opportunity. Finally, the grey lines that demarcated private banks from institutional managers and investment consultants have significantly ebbed, as all players increase the breadth of their products and services to capture all aspects of the needs of all asset owners. Institutional asset managers are now increasingly invading traditional private bank space and the space of fund of funds.

18.5 WHERE DID EXISTING PRODUCTS FALL SHORT?

A reason for the success of multi-asset funds in the past was that they provided an all-encompassing investment solution for client assets, without the client needing skill in asset allocation or strategy selection. The multi-asset fund was presented as a solution

Figure 18.5 Mismatch between client expectations and product reality of portfolio return

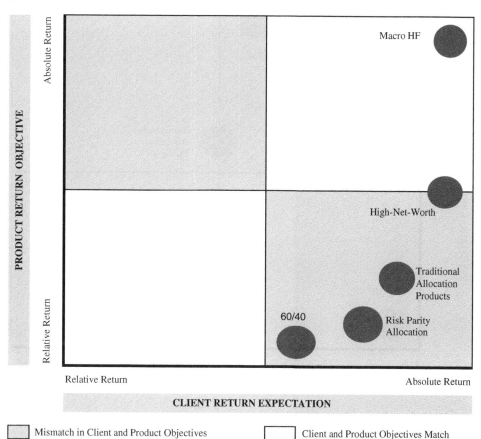

which could match and deliver the risk and return expectations of a client in a single product. However, the evolution of financial markets, as well as the recent financial crisis, has revealed a significant mismatch in many dimensions between the expectations of clients and multi-asset product structure and design. Figures 18.5 and 18.6 display a map of the client and product perspectives of risk and return.

In the return spectrum of providing (and requirement of) absolute return versus relative return (Figure 18.5), we note that while the hedge fund products match the client objective of providing absolute return, most of the other multi-asset product categories do not. All the traditional allocation products such as 60/40, risk parity and high-net-worth accounts are actually structured to provide and be measured against a relative return framework, whereas the client actually demanded (and expected) an absolute total return. When financial markets are in an uptrend this difference does not reveal itself as financial market gain reflected in the benchmark; it is credited to the skill of the investment provider. But when markets fall, the mismatch comes to the fore, and has caused substantial disillusionment for retail investors.

Figure 18.6   Mismatch between client expectations and product reality of portfolio risk

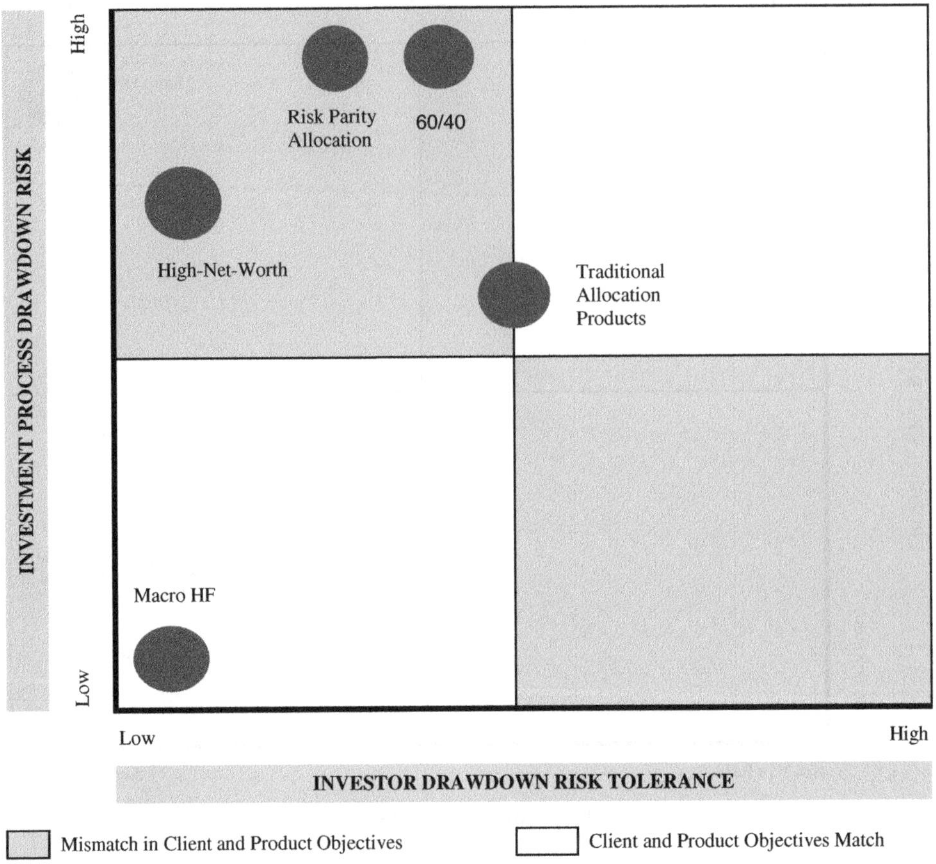

In risk space, which we specifically represent by portfolio drawdown, we note that investors overtly have a low tolerance for drawdown, which was supposedly to have been satisfied by the professed diversification in 60/40 or risk parity products. However, in reality the investment processes used in these products create substantial drawdown possibilities when financial markets fall, leading to a critical mismatch. Hedge funds have been able to match expectations as their very survival has depended on providing lower drawdown characteristics. This leads us to confirm and conclude on the necessity for an improvement in the design and process for strategic and tactical asset allocation.

Figure 18.7 displays another dimension of the mismatch between client expectations and product design – investment horizon. We have demonstrated previously the significant impact of investment horizon on portfolio drawdown. This facet manifests itself in the mismatch between product design and client expectations of drawdown in 60/40, high-net-worth and risk parity products. The investment process of these three types of multi-asset products generally has a medium- to long-term horizon. Risk parity in particular can only be verified as a successful methodology if the process is followed for a full interest rate cycle which can last for many decades, if not a century. However, when

Figure 18.7 Mismatch between client expectations and product reality of time horizon

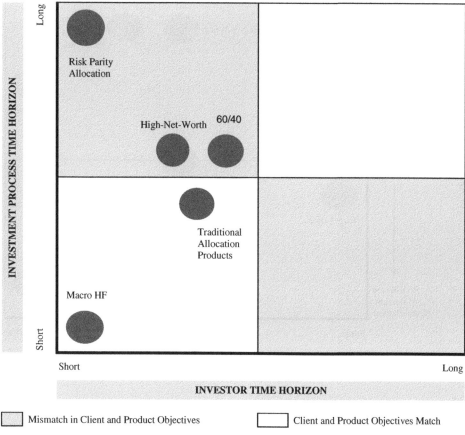

asset owners invest in such products, they seldom realize the drawdown possibilities of such allocation processes, which create a mismatch in times of financial market falls.

Traditional allocation and macro hedge funds are more aligned with respect to investment horizon when tactical decisions are employed and investment skill is present.

Figure 18.8 on the right hand side illustrates that multi-asset products vary in their allocation style as well as their implementation methodology. While the former is a result of the investment beliefs of the manager, the latter is much closer to a business and revenue decision, rather than an investment decision. Processes such as risk parity and methodologies used by CTAs are generally quantitative in nature, whereas traditional allocation methods and those used by hedge funds are fundamental view-based methodologies. In the implementation of these investment decisions, again some implement in securities, while others implement using active or passive funds. In general, products that implement in securities are stand-alone skill-based products seeking the most effective implementation, whereas products that implement in funds are seeking revenue maximization and client solution-based objectives. Target date and 60/40 and are the two methodologies with fixed weight or predetermined allocations.

Figure 18.8 Investment process positioning and differentiation of multi-asset products

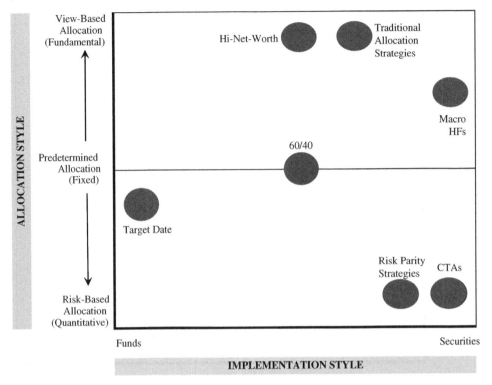

18.6 CLIENT SEGMENT – EXPECTATIONS AND EVALUATION

Just as the multi-asset product structure is varied, so is the method that is required to present it to various client segments. Figure 18.9 depicts the requirements of client-facing skills that are generally required to present multi-asset products to various client segments.

A critical point of difference is that while institutional investors focus on the investment process as a hallmark of product strength, the less sophisticated retail and high-net-worth investors give credence to the articulation of traditional market investment strategy. Given the ongoing exploration of improvement in investment processes, evidence of the manufacturer having thought leadership on any aspect of the investment process is particularly relevant for institutional investors. Meanwhile, retail investors pay attention to media presence and the ability of the representative to have broad knowledge across all products, market segments and what may be useful to fulfill their specific requirements. This varied landscape requires the asset managers to tailor their marketing and product representation to the target client segment, not to mention designing the product that they believe their target clients require.

Figure 18.9 Client-facing skills

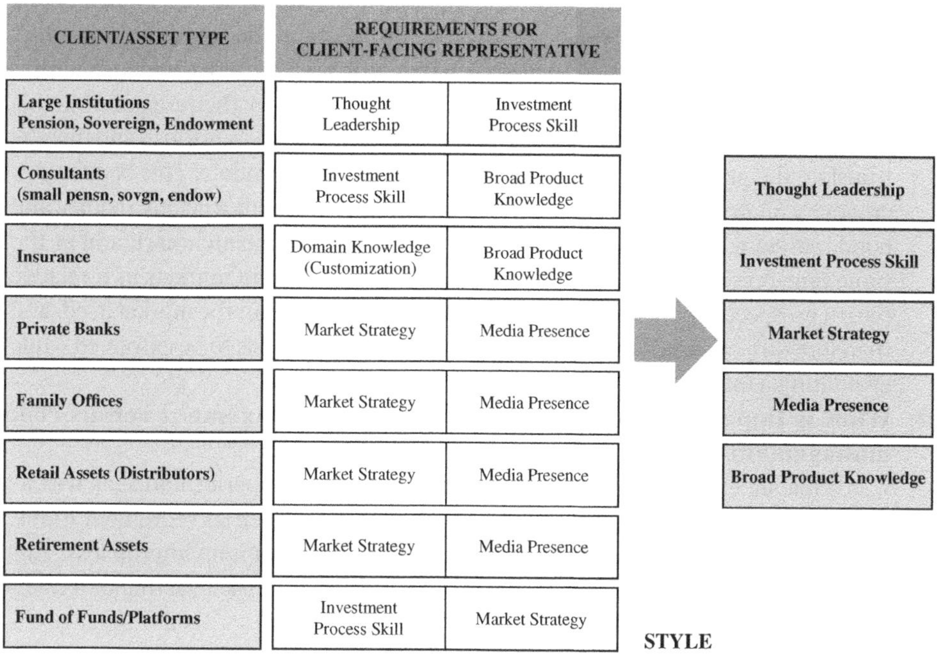

CLIENT/ASSET TYPE	REQUIREMENTS FOR CLIENT-FACING REPRESENTATIVE	
Large Institutions Pension, Sovereign, Endowment	Thought Leadership	Investment Process Skill
Consultants (small pensn, sovgn, endow)	Investment Process Skill	Broad Product Knowledge
Insurance	Domain Knowledge (Customization)	Broad Product Knowledge
Private Banks	Market Strategy	Media Presence
Family Offices	Market Strategy	Media Presence
Retail Assets (Distributors)	Market Strategy	Media Presence
Retirement Assets	Market Strategy	Media Presence
Fund of Funds/Platforms	Investment Process Skill	Market Strategy

Thought Leadership

Investment Process Skill

Market Strategy

Media Presence

Broad Product Knowledge

STYLE

Finally it is also worthwhile mentioning that evaluation of the investment skill of multi-asset products needs also to be a function of the product design, particularly when one tries to extrapolate these results to the investment skill of the manager for the future. Five specific aspects need to be taken into account while evaluating a multi-asset product:

1. **Movement of Asset Classes: Historical performance versus future performance**
   As investors are generally absolute return-oriented, it is tempting to look at a multi-asset product with a positive total return and conclude that it has positive allocation skill. However, if during the period of evaluation the equity and bond markets have had a positive return, as has recently been the case, the product return is simply a side effect of investing, rather than investing skill. As such, to estimate the forward-looking skill of the product, one must estimate the proportion of the differential return between the asset classes that the investment process has been able to capture, if at all.

2. **Source of Return: Security selection skill versus allocation skill**
   Multi-asset products are often implemented by investing in active traditional or hedge funds. This return needs to be stripped out from the total product return as the investment decisions there are not taken by the multi-asset product manager himself. Only the allocation component of the product should be attributed to its skill.

3. **Benchmark Creativity: Product performance versus investment skill**

   Asset managers, as well as private banks, in particular, create the appearance of a dual objective for a multi-asset product. On the one hand they present the product as providing a total absolute return, which is in sync with the asset owner's requirements. Concurrently, as part of their investment process they then suggest that this is achieved by a specific allocation to equities and bonds (such as 60/40), and thereby translate the product into a relative return investment mandate. This benchmark creativity allows the asset manager or private bank to present a positive equity and bond market return as their investment skill above a cash benchmark and at the same time present the negative return from equity and bond markets as a relative return prospect, where the portfolio may have fallen less than the market itself, and therefore outperformed on a relative basis. This duality needs to be extracted while evaluating a multi-asset product for skill.

4. **What is Important to Clients: Performance management versus risk management**

   While all clients at the end of the day want portfolio performance as well as risk management, it is obvious that in some structures such as retirement funds, the objective is a long run return, with a threshold for maximum interim loss. This changes the balance between a requirement of return and risk from that of a traditional investment product evaluation.

5. **What is Important to the Business: Investment skill versus client skill**

   Finally, a multi-asset product may well be a construct which is of more use to the business rather than the client. In this scenario, the asset manager may well allow the multi-asset fund to underperform, as long as business objectives are met. An example of this is the management of private wealth assets at private banks, where the banks' relationship managers are often incentivized to "churn" the client portfolio to gather more trading revenue to the detriment of portfolio performance. Similarly, internal fund of fund multi-asset products are intended to wrap internal investment products, rather than invest in the best, potentially externally managed, products.

CHAPTER NINETEEN

Competing for Better Institutional Investment Outcomes
Willis Towers Watson Investment Services

nvestors are continually competing against each other and creating a competitive advantage can help in achieving better outcomes. Greater clarity of mission, a well thought-out set of beliefs and an ability to stick to those beliefs are ways institutional investors can look to build competitive advantage. This suggests that investors should spend the majority of their time on important areas that are likely to add most value and will have the most impact on long-term results, especially the mission, investment objectives and beliefs.

While investors have typically divided their asset portfolios into equity, fixed income and alternatives, focusing instead on the underlying drivers of return is a better way to approach portfolio construction. In this chapter, this idea is illustrated with the example of an equity portfolio, which can be viewed differently based on the risk premium framework rather than the traditional asset class framework.

Investors should also consider whether their governance is aligned with the sophistication of the portfolio strategy. As compared to the average investor, a well-resourced and effective governance structure could be a competitive edge. Understanding the limitations of governance will typically lead to the conclusion that the best routes to succeed are either to simplify the investment portfolio or "raise your game."

For those who wish to "raise their game" and believe that governance can be treated as a variable rather than a constraint, there are generally two options available to add to investment governance – either build or buy, that is either building an in-house investment team led by a CIO or delegating certain portfolio construction and implementation responsibilities to a third party such as a fiduciary manager.

Within a fiduciary mandate, institutional investors have access to a wide variety of possible investment strategies and options, which can provide additional diversity and various implementation routes (from diversified pooled funds to segregated bespoke arrangements).

Delegation to a fiduciary manager can complement the strategic responsibilities of the governing function. With delegation in place, investors have more time for strategic decision making, but importantly, more time to focus on high quality oversight.

If investors were to spend more time thinking about their beliefs and ensuring that every decision they take is consistent with those beliefs and their ultimate mission, and less time on the details of implementation aspects including portfolio construction and operations, it is more likely that far better investment outcomes would be achieved.

When reviewing a portfolio's investment outcomes and investment arrangements, fund fiduciaries should not rely on short-term relative performance. Firstly, it is important to measure process as much as outcome. Secondly, the total absolute return of the portfolio is more important in monitoring than relative performance. Qualitative inputs can provide insight into a fund and its underlying managers' future performance. An annual portfolio review can help fund fiduciaries identify and prioritize areas for consideration.

This chapter suggests ways to compete for better outcomes and to free up more time for important areas that focus on strategic rather than detailed implementation aspects.

- ■ Mission and beliefs – the first and most critical step.
- ■ Frameworks: Traditional asset class versus risk premium.
- ■ Linking beliefs with return drivers and portfolio construction decisions.
- ■ Governance consideration.
- ■ Choosing an implementation route for delegation.
- ■ Monitoring.

19.1 MISSION AND BELIEFS – THE FIRST AND MOST CRITICAL STEP

When assembling an investment portfolio, there are a number of steps (see Figure 19.1) that investors should consider in order to build effective and robust portfolios and to achieve the best investment outcomes. The place to start is with a thorough assessment of the investor's mission and beliefs as shown in Figure 19.1. Yet, so often, the inclination of many investors is to hurry straight to the implementation – the third and fourth steps. Setting out beliefs and ultimate goals is frequently the part of the process that receives the least time and attention.

The portfolio construction stage is the most complex step of the entire process and therefore usually a significant amount of time is spent on it, especially the implementation aspects, often without the context of the previous steps. Once completed and the portfolio built, it is then a matter of monitoring risk positions, making adjustments and ongoing management.

Figure 19.1 Investment process – the five key steps

"Institutional investors should spend time evaluating and challenging their investment beliefs. They should ensure that every decision they take is consistent with those beliefs and their mission."

Source: Willis Towers Watson

Without dedicating sufficient time to the planning phase and moving too swiftly into the implementation, a number of key steps are likely to be missed out. This runs the risk of producing a portfolio that is not well aligned with mission and beliefs, and can undermine the diversification benefits and return potential of the portfolio.

Furthermore, it could result in a portfolio that is overly complex relative to available resources and ability to manage the investments effectively. Unintended (or unknown) risks may also result, which will likely require future attention, incurring greater cost and significant inconvenience.

It is imperative that institutional investors think carefully about the underlying beliefs that govern their portfolio construction approach.

The Investment Process at a Glance

An investment process is a continual iteration of individual steps. As shown in Figure 19.1, the example has five steps.

Step 1 is setting the mission – the ultimate goal for investors – by reference to the theory, beliefs and values of the fund. For example, this could be a funding level target or settlement for a defined benefit pension fund or target income replacement ratio for a defined contribution pension fund. This step also includes thinking about the beliefs that will be important throughout the rest of the investment process.

Steps 2 and 3 cover the framework and policy in the investment process. Step 2 is around determining the pace at which investors are planning to achieve their missions. This includes understanding which risks matter, defining the minimum-risk position if possible, understanding risk capital/buffers and limits, eventually leading to setting out the risk budget and risk management plan. At this step, reference portfolios set the accountabilities of investors for risk management and measuring value added. Step 3 is then about how to spend that risk budget. The key to this step is to balance risks across main liability risks (e.g., interest rate, inflation, currency and longevity) and asset risks (e.g., credit, equity and diversifying strategies) as outlined in Table 19.1.

Step 4 is around portfolio construction and the principle is to achieve the mission whilst maximizing total net return per unit of risk. Return can be generated from multiple sources: thematic ideas, dynamic asset allocation, best-in-class managers, sustainability issues and customized investment routes where necessary. Cost is also important and can be reduced via channels like smart beta, best-in-class implementation as well as fee negotiation. Risk mitigation comes from removing relatively unrewarded risks, increasing diversity and using multiple lenses (risk premium, themes).

The role of the last step, step 5, is to ensure that activities through steps 2 to 4 are consistent with step 1, the ultimate mission and the beliefs. Implementation of investment can be highly complex and as a result it is important to measure process as well as outcome.

TABLE 19.1 Basic drivers of portfolio returns (which are closely linked to risk factors)

Equity	Predominately driven by the equity risk premium, including traditional long-only equity, private equity and equity focused hedge funds
Credit	Mostly driven by the credit risk premium, including bonds, illiquid credit and credit focused hedge funds
Diversifying strategies	Other return drivers that include strategies not heavily correlated to credit or equities such as reinsurance, real estate and infrastructure

Source: Willis Towers Watson

19.2 FRAMEWORKS: TRADITIONAL ASSET CLASS VERSUS RISK PREMIUM

Constructing a portfolio that includes assets or strategies that have (apparently) low correlation, but still delivers their returns from similar drivers, may not provide the required level of diversification during times of stress. Investors should recognize uncertainty and understand the fundamental drivers of return, and what risks they are being rewarded for taking.

Many investors have invested in a range of mainstream asset classes or different funds (geographically or by asset class), but continue to rely heavily on the equity risk premium. An example of a seemingly diverse portfolio versus a genuinely diverse portfolio is shown in Figure 19.2.

Figure 19.2 A seemingly diverse portfolio versus a genuinely diverse portfolio

Portfolio (1): A seemingly diverse portfolio

US equities	20%
European equities	10%
Japan equities	5%
Asia-Pacific (ex Japan) equities	5%
Emerging market equities	10%
Government bonds	20%
Corporate bonds	20%
Cash	5%
Other	5%
Total	**100%**

Portfolio(2): A genuinely diverse portfolio

Developed market equities	9%
Emerging market equities	4%
Hedge funds	7%
Real estate	4%
Infrastructure	2%
Private market debt	4%
Private equity	5%
Volatility	2%
Reinsurance	2%
Commodities	2%
Emerging market debt	2%
Secured loans	1%
ABS	2%
High yield	1%
Corporate bonds	24%
Government bonds	27%
Cash	2%
Total	**100%**

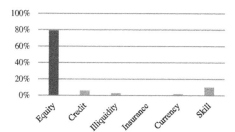

Source: Willis Towers Watson

In this example, a quick glance may indicate that Portfolio (1) is spread across a range of assets. On closer inspection, the majority of risk arises from the allocation to equities. The 50% allocation to different types of equities contributes to around 80% of the risk. Conversely, Portfolio (2) has a more balanced exposure to different risks.

Using a traditional asset class framework to build a diversified portfolio is not a complete solution to implement diversity. Investors need to identify the risk premium associated with a particular asset or strategy and generally seek exposure to a wide range of risk premium.

If investors have carried through early steps of planning in the investment process, and have an understanding of the underlying drivers of portfolio returns and the risk premium framework, then the job of portfolio construction becomes significantly easier.

"Risk premium" Framework Explained

In the simplest terms, investors expect to earn a return above a risk-free rate for taking on risk. We refer to this as a "risk premium." For example, the equity risk premium or credit risk premium compensates investors for bearing different forms of uncertainty around future cash flows. There is an illiquidity premium compensating investors for locking up their capital for longer periods of time. Also important is a "skill" premium. This is the concept that some return (positive or negative) can be driven by active manager skill. This skill should be evident above any systematic style or factor premiums that can be relatively easily captured at low cost, such as a value premium or a trend-following premium. These latter factors are often referenced as smart betas.

19.3 LINKING BELIEFS WITH RETURN DRIVERS AND PORTFOLIO CONSTRUCTION DECISIONS

Investors have typically divided their portfolios into equity, fixed income and alternatives. Let us consider the example of what an equity portfolio might look like based on the conventional asset class approach to portfolio construction.

Firstly, there may be an allocation to passive equities. Secondly, the portfolio might feature the presence of active, long-only equity mandates that run relatively low tracking errors of 3–6% per annum.

Lastly, the portfolio may include a small allocation to alternative assets. The appropriate alternative investments would normally encompass long/short equity hedge funds and/or private equity strategies. Both of these strategies can be implemented via a direct allocation to the manager, or by the indirect investment route via a fund of hedge funds/fund of private equity funds.

Figure 19.3 shows the portfolio's equity strategies that can be viewed differently in return driver terms. These drivers of return start with primarily the equity risk premium and add in a small amount of separate levels of premium for skill and illiquidity risks.

This portfolio composition begs the question about whether it merits an investor's time to appoint and dismiss active managers and tackle the additional complications of incorporating alternatives into the portfolio, if those private equity and long/short equity components do not ultimately make a significant difference to the real drivers of return.

Most institutional investors seldom discuss and challenge their investment beliefs in review or internal meetings as markets evolve.

The easiest way to tackle this issue is to tease out a set of investment beliefs that could be inferred from their equity portfolio and then challenge these beliefs.

Based on the above equity portfolio, a set of investment beliefs might conceivably be as shown in Table 19.2.

Figure 19.3 Equity portfolio in return driver terms

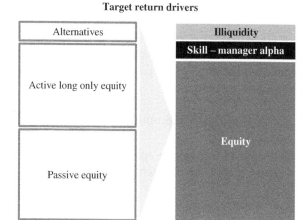

Source: Willis Towers Watson

At first glance, these seem to be reasonable beliefs. However, the resulting portfolio is dominated by equity risk premium and there is limited impact of skill and illiquidity. So the conviction behind each point needs to be challenged.

▫ Is it not possible to improve on bulk beta (market cap-weighted) with smart beta?
▫ If there is a belief in alpha, maybe alpha is easier to find and exploit in less efficient markets or with less constrained mandates.
▫ Can the portfolio still not exploit the illiquidity premium on a de-risking journey, given the likely timescale and the existence of a secondary market?
▫ Doesn't the wide range of solutions available on the market today mean governance can be treated as a variable rather than a constraint?

TABLE 19.2 Implied beliefs of an equity portfolio

Equity portfolio		Implied beliefs
Invest in long-only equity	>>>	Equity risk premium is attractive in the long term.
Use active management	>>>	Markets are not fully efficient.
Measure risk relative to the benchmark	>>>	Deviation from a benchmark index should be constrained to limit underpeformance.
Small allocation to alternatives	>>>	There is an illiquidity premium available but a limited ability to exploit.
Relatively few managers	>>>	Limited governance means that structure should be kept simple.

Source: Willis Towers Watson

19.3.1 A New Perspective

This process of challenging beliefs may lead to a chain reaction that alters the investor's perspective and approach to portfolio construction.

For example, the challenge to the belief in alpha may lead the investor to question whether or not the nature of the mandates in place is conducive to alpha generation.

To answer this question, investors with a genuine belief in (active management) skill that generates alpha should use mandates:

▪ That focus on best ideas and are significantly different from market consensus (high active share)
▪ That allow more degrees of freedom (as appropriate)
▪ Where fees are a lower proportion of potential alpha.

Each of these areas is discussed below.

▪ **Best ideas and high active share**
    Academic and practical evidence demonstrates that most long-only active equity managers add value in their largest overweight positions. If, on average, they underperform net of costs, it is because value is eroded by their lower conviction overweight positions and the numerous underweight positions that they hold which are not fully researched.
    Therefore, mandates that have preserved a concentration of risk on their highest conviction ideas have historically led to outperformance. This is exemplified by the super-concentrated portfolios of private equity and potentially those of long/short equity managers.
▪ **More degrees of freedom**
    Managers can further increase the portfolio's value if they have more freedom to improve the valuation or alter the exposure of stocks they manage. For example, long/short equity managers can vary the gross and net exposure of the portfolio over time. Private equity managers can employ activist tactics to drive changes at firms, with an aim of increasing their valuations (activist premium).
▪ **Fees as a lower proportion of alpha**
    Fees can be much higher in some of these equity mandates than in others; for example, they are usually higher when fund of funds structures are being used. It is important to measure and evaluate the attractiveness of a mandate in terms of alpha returns net of fees (or "net alpha").
    The salient issue is the level of the manager's fee as a proportion of alpha, after having stripped out both beta and leverage, rather than simply looking at the absolute dollar amount of the fee.
    If that calculation is taken into account, then the fees charged by higher performing managers in private equity and long/short equity are not as onerous as they may appear initially. In both types of mandates, the alpha can be leveraged and therefore the base fee may appear to be a small proportion of that levered alpha.

Alpha Assumptions: Which equity mandate best exploits alpha?

As measured by net information ratio (net IR), the achievable rate of return per unit of risk is expected to be much higher in private equity and long/short equity portfolios than in traditional long-only public equity mandates as shown in Figure 19.4.

Both mandates produce net IRs that are approximately 25% higher than high active share long-only and are slightly more than double the net IR from traditional long-only strategies. In terms of net alpha achievable, the differential is magnified substantially.

Figure 19.4 Expected results of different types of equity mandate

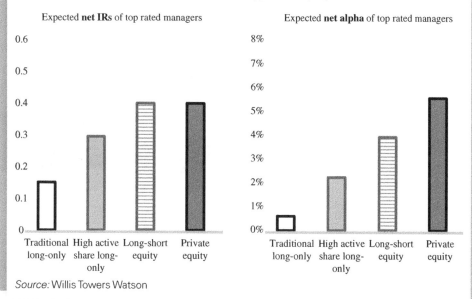

Expected **net IRs** of top rated managers   Expected **net alpha** of top rated managers

Source: Willis Towers Watson

19.3.2 A Wider Opportunity Set for Exploiting Alpha

Investors should revisit how reliant they really are on equity risk premium and consider greater diversification across the skill and illiquidity premium by taking advantage of a broader range of strategies.

When building an equity portfolio, investors can make use of the full implementation spectrum from bulk beta (traditional market cap) and smart beta through to liquid alpha and illiquid instruments as illustrated in Figure 19.5.

Within the equity space, there are multiple options for investors to exploit alpha. These include private equity, long/short equity, high active share long-only equity mandates (via concentrated portfolios), traditional long-only equity, and smart beta such as fundamental indexation or low volatility equity mandates.

Figure 19.5 The implementation spectrum for equity portfolio construction, with sample strategies

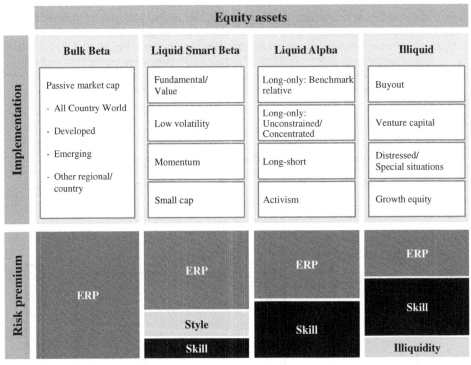

Source: Willis Towers Watson

In practice, a full portfolio construction process can include credit and other diversifying strategies that follow the same implementation spectrum as shown in the Figure 19.5.

So what does the alternative equity portfolio look like, given the challenge to the beliefs in alpha generation and those assumptions that were set out earlier?

Firstly, this suggests increasing exposure to the skill and illiquidity premium (Figure 19.6). Reshaping the portfolio in this fashion implies the allocation of as much private equity and long/short equity as circumstances permit; for example, if there are liquidity constraints stopping further allocations to private equity.

These mandates can be combined with a layer of very concentrated/high active share long-only equity, say 20–30 stock portfolios rather than the typical 50–100 stock portfolios.

The remainder of the investment program can be filled in with smart beta and some bulk beta. Smart beta exploits security weighting methods that deviate from conventional market capitalization approaches, while bulk beta can help adjust unintended positions caused by the use of concentrated portfolios (for the high active share long-only equity).

Figure 19.6 Potential change in portfolio structure (1)

Target return drivers

Illiquidity	Private equity
Skill – manager alpha	Long/Short equity
Skill – smart beta	High active share long-only
Equity	Smart beta
	Bulk beta

Source: Willis Towers Watson

The outcome that could emerge, in a best-case scenario based on all the assumptions, is an expected portfolio efficiency (return per unit of risk taken) improvement of maybe 20–40% in the equity portfolio. However, it could turn out to be a poor portfolio with different beliefs or an inability to stick to the beliefs.

The equity portfolio can be adjusted to allow any preference and constraint an investor might have for whatever reason. For example, an investor might not want to invest in any hedge funds at all, regardless of the investor's belief set. Another investor might be opposed to the concept of using private equity. Nevertheless, the resulting portfolio would still show an improvement even without private equity or hedge funds.

19.3.3 Ensuring That Everything Is Consistent with Beliefs

What if an investor believes that nobody can exploit alpha net of all fees or a fund's governance does not make this alpha-seeking possible? In that case, the next option would be in the direction of smart beta as illustrated in Figure 19.7.

Figure 19.7 Potential change in portfolio structure (2)

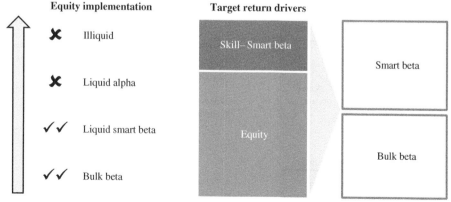

Equity implementation		Target return drivers	
✗	Illiquid	**Skill– Smart beta**	Smart beta
✗	Liquid alpha		
✓✓	Liquid smart beta	**Equity**	Bulk beta
✓✓	Bulk beta		

Source: Willis Towers Watson

If the investor is also skeptical about smart beta products then, in turn, the investor could choose to make use of 100% passive long-only public equities. Such a portfolio would be more aligned with the investor's belief set.

19.4 GOVERNANCE CONSIDERATION

Aligning desired portfolio strategies with investment governance budget is just as important as linking portfolio decisions with investment beliefs.

The "governance budget" can be expressed as a combination of time devoted to investment matters, expertise of individual(s) involved, organizational effectiveness for making and implementing decisions and the ability to monitor and manage the portfolio on an ongoing basis.

Research has demonstrated a connection between investment governance and investment success. Ambachtsheer (2006) suggests that the "good-bad" governance gap has been worth about 1% to 2% of additional return each year as depicted in Figure 19.8. It is logical, therefore, that the fund's investment governance budget should guide the investment process.

In other words, the governance budget should match the sophistication of the portfolio strategy. So it is therefore a case of "simplify your strategy or raise your game."

19.4.1 Closing the Governance Gap: Build or Buy

For those who want to "raise their game" and improve the risk–return trade-off from portfolios of equities and bonds, there are generally two options available to add to investment governance – either building an in-house team or delegating to a fiduciary manager.

Figure 19.8 Good investment governance and organizational design make a difference

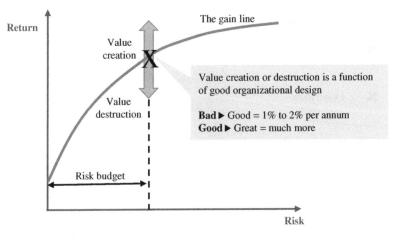

Source: Willis Towers Watson

Clark and Monk (2012) identified five key factors pushing institutional investors to move assets in-house:

- *Access:* In-source if you can get better access to asset classes or markets than widely available vehicles can offer you.
- *Alignment:* In-sourcing can be a useful means of minimizing agency problems and ensuring that your investments are structured to meet your goals and not those of an asset manager.
- *Capabilities:* Improving your internal resources can upgrade the capabilities of your organization.
- *Performance:* Maximizing net-of-fee returns.
- *Sustainability:* In-sourcing can offer the opportunity to tailor your investments to meet your needs through time, better than a combination of available mandates.

Building an internal team can offer attractive benefits. However, for many it is simply not a realistic solution as only the largest funds (perhaps US$10 billion and above) have sufficient scale to make this a genuinely viable option. This may be surprising, but the ideal environment for a sustainable in-house team includes substantial resource, collaboration and idea generation.

For funds that cannot build internally, fiduciary management is a means of addressing the gap that exists between the need for increasingly efficient investment strategies and real-time decision making, and the typically constrained governance budget of a board or investment committee.

19.4.2 The Separation of Governing and Executive Functions

Clark and Urwin (2007) identified six factors that separate great institutional investors from the rest. Of these six factors, one was identified as the single most important governance influencer – the separation of governing and executive functions. In this model, the governing function (board) sets the investment framework, focusing on high level investment strategy and management. The executive function makes decisions and implements the investment strategy within this framework.

The separation of governing and executive functions may look like this:

- The governing function involves a broad range of responsibilities, which include funding, risk appetite, adherence with applicable regulation, fund-specific legal requirements and fund or benefits administration. Some of these responsibilities, such as administration, can be delegated. Others, such as funding and risk appetite, are typically supported by advice provided by specialists. On the investment side, the governing function should set the high level investment strategy, define the fund's overall objectives and translate these into risk and return targets. In our view, these cannot be delegated.
- The executive function then puts the investment strategy decisions into action by taking the responsibility for portfolio construction and implementation. This requires

Figure 19.9 Governing and executive investment functions

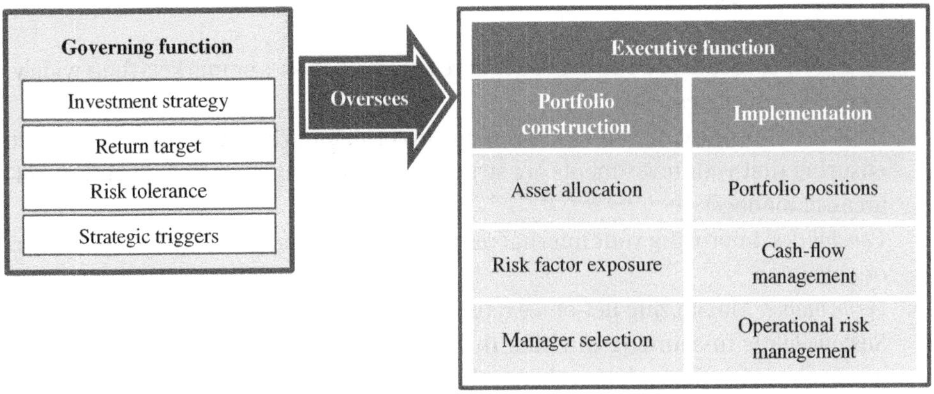

Source: Willis Towers Watson

specialist resource and expertise and is therefore managed by an internal team led by a Chief Investment Officer (CIO) or similar. For investors that do not have the scale or resources to merit the costs of an in-house CIO, they could delegate portfolio construction and implementation to a fiduciary manager who acts as a delegated CIO.

Figure 19.9 shows the range of investment decisions and activities, and which function they fall under.

The model in Figure 19.9 is no different from that of a corporate board with a management team responsible for executing the agreed strategy. For an asset pool, the board or investment committee remains in control of the high-level strategy, defining the fund's long-term objectives and determining the return requirements, while the fiduciary manager takes on the day-to-day implementation aspects, including portfolio construction and operations.

Delegation to a fiduciary manager can complement the strategic responsibilities of the governing function. With delegation in place, investors have more time for strategic decision making, but importantly, more time to focus on high quality oversight.

What Is Fiduciary Management and What Are Its Benefits?

Numerous terms such as "delegated CIO," "implemented consulting" and "delegated consulting" are used to describe fiduciary management. Fiduciary management involves the delegation of certain functions to a third party. The extent of delegation under fiduciary management can vary, but in its fullest form it is the combination of strategic advice and implementation. The ongoing management of most or all of the assets of a fund is delegated to a fiduciary manager and the fiduciary mandate is managed to an objective and within a risk level set by the board or investment committee ("fund fiduciaries").

While it may seem that fund fiduciaries who opt for fiduciary management are taking a step back, this is not the case. In fact, one of the most frequently cited benefits of fiduciary management is that fund fiduciaries have more time to focus on the key strategic issues and long-term goals for their asset pool. Accountability for the investment strategy (overall risk and return) remains with the board working with the fiduciary manager to determine key parameters such as the time horizon, return and risk. The fiduciary manager, working in partnership with the board, then implements the investment strategy within the boundaries set by the board (in keeping with the separation of the governing and executive functions advocated by Clark and Urwin).

In addition, monitoring becomes less of a burden on fund fiduciaries as the fiduciary manager relationship replaces numerous relationships with investment managers and potentially other service providers.

19.5 CHOOSING AN IMPLEMENTATION ROUTE FOR DELEGATION

Historically, fund of fund arrangements have been used to access investments in specialist mandates, particularly in hedge funds and private markets. These structures have provided a means of accessing diversified and specialized investments in niche asset classes for governance constrained investors. This implementation approach has been adapted in some fiduciary mandates where pooled fund of funds solutions can be used to implement an investment strategy.

19.5.1 Bundling Multiple Investment Strategies into Pooled Funds

The overall investment strategy would typically be constructed using a number of different asset classes and/or different investment managers. A fiduciary manager may combine some or all of these into "bundles" and create pooled funds populated with the fiduciary manager's highest conviction ideas. At one extreme, all the assets that an investor would invest in could be combined into one "bundle."

Alternatively, a number of different "bundles" could be created for sub-portfolios, for example, for each asset class. The investor would then hold units in these ranges of pooled funds managed by the fiduciary manager. It can be difficult for small, resource-constrained investors to access a diverse range of ideas; pooled funds can help such investors access these opportunities. Using a large number of pooled funds allows more flexibility in asset allocation, but can lead to a very large number of underlying investment managers being used as each fund will employ several managers to ensure it is differentiated on a stand-alone basis.

19.5.2 Fully Bespoke Implementation

The alternative to this is fully bespoke implementation (Figure 19.10). In this case the fiduciary manager enters into a separate agreement with each asset manager on the client's behalf. This allows for more tailoring of the eventual portfolio to the investor's particular needs.

There are various different issues to be aware of when deciding whether a pooled fund route or a bespoke route would be more suitable:

1. **Investment beliefs and investment restrictions**

    An investor's first task is to consider its mission and investment beliefs and to decide the amount of risk that should be taken specific to these circumstances. At the onset of a fiduciary mandate, the investor should consider any particularly strong beliefs that need to be reflected in its investment arrangements. For example, if the investor does not believe in active management in a particular asset class, then this will influence the implementation route adopted.

    If the pooled fund route is used, investors should ensure that the underlying investment funds reflect their beliefs. If the pooled funds are inconsistent with these beliefs, investors will need to consider a different or more bespoke solution.

2. **Access to opportunities**

    In theory, one should not expect any difference in the access to opportunities through either a pooled or segregated approach. However, investors should be aware of the range of different funds that are available. Some fiduciary managers already operate funds that cover the major asset classes. However, one of the benefits of a fiduciary mandate is that it should allow the investor to access new opportunities as they arise. Therefore, investors should seek to understand the flexibility that each of the funds has in investing in new opportunities.

Figure 19.10 Access to bespoke investment solutions

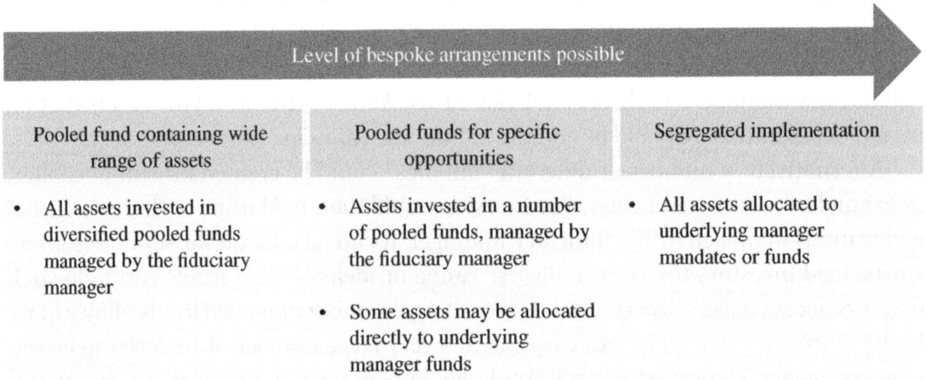

Level of bespoke arrangements possible		
Pooled fund containing wide range of assets	Pooled funds for specific opportunities	Segregated implementation
• All assets invested in diversified pooled funds managed by the fiduciary manager	• Assets invested in a number of pooled funds, managed by the fiduciary manager • Some assets may be allocated directly to underlying manager funds	• All assets allocated to underlying manager mandates or funds

Source: Willis Towers Watson

As an example, following the credit crisis, there were a number of opportunities to lend to distressed companies. If several of the pooled funds in the investor's portfolio had the discretion to allocate to sub-investment grade credit and chose to take advantage of this opportunity, this could have resulted in a higher than intended exposure to "riskier" credit at the total portfolio level.

3. Portfolio construction and management

New investment opportunities could feed into one of various different funds through the pooled fund route, whereas under a segregated approach they would be considered by the fiduciary manager at a total portfolio level.

A fiduciary manager needs to provide sufficient transparency into the portfolio so that the investor can ensure that the assets are still in line with the overall investment objectives. This involves providing clear data and understanding on risk and return, the manager's style, concentration of positions, liquidity and leverage – both at an individual manager level and at a portfolio composite level. The impact of any changes to the portfolio can then be assessed not only against risk and return objectives, but also against other risks and implementation issues (such as liquidity), and the investor's investment beliefs and/or restrictions.

The approach should broadly be the same for both implementation routes. However, in a pooled fund approach, there needs to be sufficient information flow between the managers of the funds and the fiduciary manager. The fiduciary manager not only needs to ensure that each fund is in line with the client's needs, but also that underlying managers are appropriate for each client. The risk of an allocation to an investment via a fund needs to be managed effectively without compromising the impact on other investors in the funds.

4. Costs

Fees and costs can influence a portfolio's outcome materially. The level of fees will vary depending on the implementation route chosen. On the one hand, a pooled fund may have additional administration costs for the vehicle, in addition to the underlying manager fees. On the other hand, the large size of a pooled fund may allow a fiduciary manager to negotiate more favorable fees for investors, bringing the costs down. Regardless of the level of fees, it is important for investors to get full visibility on all fees and costs, particularly investment and fiduciary manager fees and expenses embedded in any pooled vehicles – both the fiduciary manager's pooled funds as well as the underlying investment managers' pooled funds.

5. Liquidity

Liquidity refers to both the cost and ease of being able to sell an asset. While the liquidity of underlying fund managers is largely dependent on the asset managers, the structure of the fiduciary offering can also impact liquidity.

In a fund of funds approach, there is an additional layer of liquidity considerations dependent on the terms of the fiduciary manager or the funds used. Where a portfolio already has some assets that it does not want to sell, moving to a fiduciary mandate via a fund of funds route could result in a forced sale if these assets cannot be transferred to the pooled fund. Similarly, if the investors were to change fiduciary manager at any time in the future, then a new fiduciary manager is unlikely to hold investments in a competitor's fund – this could result in the requirement to disinvest the entire portfolio, and incur the commensurate costs of doing so.

There are a large number of fiduciary management options available to investors. The benefits of a bespoke approach and the simplicity offered by a fund's route should both be explored. Of course, with some fiduciary managers, it may also be possible to combine investment in some funds with a bespoke mandate in other areas to harness the benefits of both.

19.6 MONITORING

As briefly described at the beginning of this chapter, the last step in the investment process is "monitoring." The role of the last step is to ensure that activities through steps 2 to 4 are consistent with step 1, the ultimate mission and the beliefs. Implementation of investment can be highly complex and as a result it is important to measure process as well as outcome.

Are fund fiduciaries monitoring the right things? Below are some suggestions for investors to consider when reviewing their investment outcomes and investment arrangements

Fund fiduciaries should be focusing on the *total return of the portfolio* (relative to liabilities, where appropriate) rather than relative (to index) returns of the portfolio's underlying managers. Typically fund fiduciaries monitor each of the underlying investment managers against an appropriate benchmark.

While performance measurement can determine whether the underlying managers are achieving their targets, fund fiduciaries need to understand that even skillful managers can be unlucky (just as unskillful managers can be lucky). Looking at relative performance alone can give a misleading perspective of investment skill as typical approaches to benchmarking active managers do not consider the market environment.

Measuring *longer term results* is also important, as some asset managers appear to rely on the randomness of returns in markets to produce a positive short-term track record, which is then used to market products to advisors and clients who are attracted by short-term performance.

Fund fiduciaries need to *continually assess the risk* associated with delivering that performance, where the biggest risks are and the expected fall in assets due to a bad outcome.

Therefore, appropriate assessment of the success of an investment program needs to involve a combination of metrics and *qualitative inputs* that provide insight into a fund and its underlying manager's future performance.

On an ad hoc or annual basis, *a high-level review of the entire portfolio*, checking various areas of a portfolio against "best practice" in terms of investment efficiency (return per unit of risk taken), can help fund fiduciaries identify and prioritize areas for consideration in future investment meetings. This may include, for example:

- Is the fund exposed to a variety of return drivers?
- Has the fund diversified its active management risk?

- Is the fund paying a reasonable amount for active management?
- Is there a regular check that the portfolio remains consistent with the mission and beliefs?

 19.7 CONCLUSIONS

Ultimately investment is a competition. It is absolutely essential that institutional investors identify what their competitive edge is or where it comes from. For example, a well thought-out set of beliefs or a well-resourced and effective governance structure as compared to the average investor could be a competitive edge.

What should investors do in order to gain a competitive edge and compete for better outcomes? To sum up, investors should:

- Spend more time on important areas, in particular their "mission and beliefs" which focus on strategic aspects rather than on detailed implementation.
- Look at a portfolio through multiple lenses, for example, via drivers of return (or risk premia). The exception being the use of a traditional asset class framework, under which one or two risks may dominate.
- Ensure that every decision they make is consistent with their beliefs and mission.
- Consider whether their governance is aligned with the sophistication of the portfolio strategy – therefore, it is often a case of "simplify your strategy or raise your game."
- Explore the options available which add to investment governance, that is either building an in-house investment team led by a CIO or delegating certain portfolio construction and implementation responsibilities to a third party such as a fiduciary manager.

Delegation can complement the strategic responsibilities of the governing function and thus free up more time for investors to develop areas that will have the most impact.

Assessment of progress towards mission success or failure should focus on process as well as outcome. An investment process for institutional investors is briefly described in this chapter. "Monitor" is the final step of an investment process, to ensure that all activities throughout the entire process are consistent with the ultimate mission and the beliefs, which should be clearly defined in the first step.

A high-level review of the entire portfolio on an ad hoc or annual basis, checking various areas of a portfolio against "best practice," can help fund fiduciaries identify and prioritize areas that require more attention.

About Willis Towers Watson Investment Services

Willis Towers Watson is a leading global advisory, broking and solutions company that helps clients around the world turn risk into a path for growth. With roots dating back to 1828, Willis Towers Watson has 39,000 employees in more than 120 countries.

Willis Towers Watson has a flexible range of research-driven investment services to meet the specific needs of local institutional investors, ranging from providing investment tools to offering advisory and cost-effective solutions.

Globally, Willis Tower Watson serves sovereign wealth funds, pension funds, reserve funds and other institutional asset pools as clients. Willis Towers Watson's clients include some of the world's largest and most sophisticated asset owners.

Learn more at willistowerswatson.com or email to wwic.hk@willistowerswatson.com.

Bibliography and References

Ambachtsheer, K. (2006) "How Much is Good Governance Worth?" The Ambachtsheer Letter 245, KPA Advisory Services Ltd, June 2006.

Asness, C.S., Frazzini, A. and Pedersen, L.H. (2012) "Leverage Aversion and Risk Parity," *Financial Analysts Journal*, January/February 2012, 68:1.

Avramov, D. and Zhou, G. (2010) "Bayesian portfolio analysis," *Annual Review of Financial Economics* 2010:2, 25–47.

Bank for International Settlements (2001) "A Survey of Stress Tests and Current Practice at Major Financial Institutions," Global Financial Systems Committee.

Basak, S. and Shapiro, A. (2001) "Value-at-Risk based risk management: Optimal policies and asset prices," *Review of Financial Studies* 14, 371–405.

Bawa, V.S. (1975) "Optimal rules for ordering uncertain prospects," *Journal of Financial Economics* 2, 95–121.

Bernanke, B.S. (2010) Monetary Policy and the Housing Bubble, Speech at the Annual Meeting of the American Economic Association, Atlanta, Georgia, January 3, 2010.

Black, F. and Litterman, R. (1992) "Global portfolio optimization," *Financial Analysts Journal*, September/October 1992, 48:5, 28–43.

Brinson, G.P., Randolph Hood, L. and Beebower, G.L. (1986) "Determinants of portfolio performance," *Financial Analysts Journal*, July/August, 42:4, 39–44.

Brooks, C. and Kat, H. M. (2002) "The Statistical Properties of Hedge Fund Index Returns and their Implications for Investors," *Journal of Alternative Investments* 5:2, 26–44.

Carpenter, J. (2000) "Does option compensation increase managerial appetite?" *Journal of Finance* 55, 2311–2332.

Chen, N.-F., Roll, R. and Ross, S.A. (1986) "Economic forces and the stock market," *Journal of Business*, 383–404.

Chevalier, J. and Ellison, G. (1997) "Risk taking by mutual funds as a response to incentives," *Journal of Political Economy*, 106:6, 1167–1200.

Clarida, R., Gali, J. and Gertler, M. (1999) "The Science of Monetary Policy: A New Keynesian Perspective," *Journal of Economic Literature*, XXXVII (December), 1661–1707.

Clark, G.L. and Monk, A.H.B. (2012) "Principals and policies for in-house asset management." December 2012. Available at http://ssrn.com/abstract = 2189650.

Clark, G.L. and Urwin, R. (2007) "Best-practice investment management: lessons for asset owners." Oxford-Watson Wyatt project on governance. September 2007.

Cremers, J.-H. Kritzman, M. and Page, S. (2005) "Optimal hedge fund allocations: Do higher moments matter?" *Journal of Portfolio Management* Spring 2005, 31:3, 70–81.

Deutsche Bank (2008) *100 Years of Corporate Bond Returns Revisited.*

Elton, E.J., Gruber, M.J. and Blake, C.R. (2003) "Incentive fees and mutual funds," *Journal of Finance,* 58, 779–804.

Fama, E.F. and French, K.R. (1992) "The cross-section of expected stock returns," *Journal of Finance,* June 1992, 427–465.

Financial Conduct Authority (2014) "CP 13/17–Use of Dealing Commissions," FCA Consultation Paper, November 2013.

Fishburn, P.C. (1977) "Mean-risk analysis with risk associated with below target returns," *American Economic Review,* 67, 116–26.

Fraser-Jenkins, I., Stancikas, R., Diver, M., Guerrini, G.A., Katiyar, S. and Thombre R. (2012) "Multi-Asset: A bright spot in fund management," Nomura Equity Research, October 24, 2012.

Goetzmann, W.N., Ingersoll Jr, J. and Ross, S.A. (2001) "High-water marks and hedge fund management contracts," *Journal of Finance* 58, 1685–1718.

Gordon, M.J. and Shapiro, E. (1956) "Capital Equipment Analysis: The Required Rate of Profit," *Management Science,* October 3:1, 102–110.

Grinold, R.C. and Kahn, R.N. (1993) *Active Portfolio Management.* New York: McGraw Hill.

Grinold, R.C. and Kahn, R.N. (1999), *Active Portfolio Management: A Quantitative Approach for Producing Superior Returns and Controlling Risk,* 2nd edn. New York: McGraw-Hill.

Grossman, S. and Zhou, Z. (1993) "Optimal investment strategies for controlling drawdowns," *Mathematical Finance,* 3:3, 241–276.

Gupta, P. (2014) "Specifying and managing tail risk in multi-asset portfolios – A summary," CFA Institute Research Foundation Year in Review 2013, March 2014, pp. 55–59.

Gupta, P. and Straatman, J. (2006) "Skill based investment management," *Journal of Investment Management,* 4:1, 1–18.

Hanoch, G. and Levy, H. (1969) "The efficiency analysis of choices involving risk," *Rev. Econ. Stud.,* 36, 335–46.

Harlow, W.V. (1991) "Asset allocation in a downside-risk framework," *Financial Analysts Journal,* September–October, 5, 28–40.

Hodder, J.E. and Jackwerth, J.C. (2003) "Incentive Contracts and Hedge Fund Management: A Numerical Evaluation Procedure," Working Paper.

Idzorek, T.M. and Kowara, M. (2013) "Factor-based asset allocation vs. asset class-based asset allocation," *Financial Analysts Journal,* May/June 69:3, 19–29.

Ilmanen, A. (2012) "Do financial markets reward buying or selling insurance and lottery tickets?" *Financial Analysts Journal,* September/October, 68:5, 26–36.

Kaminski, K.M. and Lo, A.W. (2007) "When do stop-loss rules stop losses?" EFA 2007 Ljubljana Meetings Paper, available at SSRN: http://ssrn.com/abstract=968338.

Kaplan, P.D. and Knowles, J.A. (2004) "Kappa: A generalized downside risk-adjusted performance measure," *Journal of Performance Measurement,* 8:3.

Keating, C. and Shadwick, W.F. (2002) "An Introduction to Omega," The Finance Development Centre, London.

Kunno, H. (1988) "Portfolio optimization using L1 risk function," IHSS Report 88–9, Institute of Human and Social Sciences, Tokyo Institute of Technology.

Li, Y. and Kazemi, H. (2007) "Conditional properties of hedge funds: evidence from daily returns," Working Paper.

Litterman, B. (2004) "The active risk puzzle: implications for the asset management industry," March 2004, Goldman Sachs Perspectives.

Magdon-Ismail, M. and Atiya, A.F (2004) "Maximum drawdown," *Risk*, October.

Magdon-Ismail, M., Atiya, A.F., Pratap, A. and Mostafa, Y.S.A. (2004) "On the maximum drawdown of a Brownian motion," *Journal of Applied Probability* 41, 147–161.

Markowitz, H. (1952) "Portfolio selection," *Journal of Finance*, March 1952, 77–91.

McFall, L.R. (2003) "Asymmetric returns and optimal hedge fund portfolios," *Journal of Alternative Investments* 6, Fall, 9.21.

Merton, R.C. (1969) "Lifetime portfolio selection under uncertainty: the continuous-time case," *Review of Economics and Statistics* 51, 247–257.

Merton, R.C. (1971) "Optimum consumption and portfolio rules in a continuous-time model," *Journal of Economic Theory* 51, 373–413.

Myners, P. (2001) *Institutional Investment in the United Kingdom-A Review*, HM Treasury.

Pástor, Ĺ. and Stambaugh, R.F. (2012) "Are stocks really less volatile in the long run?" *The Journal of Finance*, Vol 67:2, April, 431–478.

Pástor, Ĺ. and Veronesi, P. (2003), "Stock valuation and learning about profitability," *The Journal of Finance*, October, 58:5, 1749–1789.

Ross, S.A. (1976) "The arbitrage theory of capital asset pricing," *Journal of Economic Theory*, December 1976, 341–360.

Sharpe, W.F. (1964) "Capital asset prices: a theory of market equilibrium under conditions of risk," *Journal of Finance*, September 1964, 425–442.

Shiller, R.J. (2000) *Irrational Exuberance*. New Jersey: Princeton University Press.

Siegel, L.B., Ibbotson, R.G. and Riepe, M.W. (1988) *Asset Allocation: A Handbook of Portfolio Policies, Strategies and Tactics*. Chicago: Probus Publishing.

Svensson, L.E.O. (1997) "Optimal inflation targets, 'conservative' central banks, and linear inflation contracts," *American Economic Review*, March, 87:1, 98–114.

Swiss Federal Supreme Court Judgment (2012) Ruling no. 4A_127/2012 and 4A_141/2012.

Taylor, J.B. (1993) "Discretion versus policy rules in practice," Carnegie-Rochester Conference Series on Public Policy 39, 195–214.

Wise, M.B., Schwarzkopf, Y. and Bhansali, V. (2011) "Fat tails and stop-losses in portable alpha," *Journal of Investment Management*, Third Quarter.

Ye, J. (2008) "How variation in signal quality affects performance," *Financial Analysts Journal*, 64:4, 48–61.

Zellner, A. and Chetty, V.K. (1965) "Prediction and decision problems in regression models from the Bayesian point of view," *Journal of the American Statistical Association*, 60, 608–616.

INDEX

Compiled by INDEXING SPECIALISTS (UK) Ltd., Indexing House, 306A Portland Road, Hove, East Sussex BN3 5LP United Kingdom.

Printed and bound by CPI Group (UK) Ltd, Croydon, CR0 4YY

23/04/2025

14660948-0001